Hungry
Heart
Roaming

First published in 2021
by the Black Spring Press Group
Suite 333, 19-21 Crawford Street
London, W1H 1PJ
United Kingdom

Graphic design and typeset by Edwin Smet
Author and cover photograph by Rosanna Moseley Gore
Cover photo of the author's shadow on a cobbled street in Berlin
Printed in England by TJ Books Ltd, Padstow, Cornwall

Set in Bembo 13 / 16 pt
ISBN 978-1-913606-05-3

WWW.EYEWEARPUBLISHING.COM

Hungry Heart Roaming

An Odyssey Of Sorts

Charles Moseley

 **EYEWEAR** PUBLISHING

Thoroughly unprepared, we take
the step into the afternoon of
life. Worse still, we take this step
with the false presupposition
that our truths and our ideals
will serve us as hitherto. But we
cannot live the afternoon of life
according to the programme
of life's morning, for what was
great in the morning will be
little at evening and what in the
morning was true, at evening
will have become a lie.

Carl Jung,
Modern Man in Search of a Soul
(1933)

Rosannae meae Petrae

Thanks, too brief

First, to those who regularly put up with me when I am in the throes of writing, 'byting my trewand pen, beating my selfe for spite': friends neglected, neighbours ignored, and above all Rosanna Petra, who had to endure my silences and my not listening, distrait, to what she was saying. Which was, more or less, 'Foole, said my [wyf] to mee, looke in thy heart and write.'

Next, to all those who read one of the many drafts of this book: Morag, Jenny's sister, a warm and appreciative guinea pig, and Rosanna, my dearest and most perceptive critic. But I also owe so much to the support, suggestions and encouragement of Nicholas Boyle, Helen Cooper, Eamon Duffy, James Humphreys, Jean Lambert, Piers Plowright, John Raffan, Dame Fiona Reynolds and Bishop Rowan Williams. My agent Bill Hamilton, whose business is words and who does not mince them, has exemplary patience. He rightly told me that the first two drafts were unpublishable, but at the same time encouraged me to keep on cutting and re-shaping and generally to get used to murdering my children. Many did get chopped; may they rest in peace – until perhaps I resurrect them in another book, and bother Bill with that.

Especial thanks are due to my meticulous, tactful and charitable editor, Cate Myddleton-Evans, who spotted many infelicities and errors in what I had thought a clean MS. Edwin Smet, intrepid and artful, a thank you for his typesetting and design. I also owe many sincere thanks to Eyewear's director, Dr Todd Swift, who believed in the book from the start, and, in what must have been the worst of years for a publisher, stayed with it and despite all the vicissitudes of this Coronavirus year, brought it to birth, to begin 2021.

Many people walked with me on the journeys that made this book. Some are mentioned by name, more are not. To all of them I owe debts, and love, beyond words. But two have to be singled out: Jenny, my first wife, my Penelope, whose loom could weave many stories that will now never be told this side of eternity; and Rosanna Petra, my rock, who met me when we were both wandering among the shades, and joined her steps to mine for the rest of the journey.

And Hector the Labrador, my comfort and conscience – 'I must take the dog out' – during the long, long years when the house was silent.

CWRDM, Reach, Lent 2020

Contents

Overture

Late afternoon, and time to leave the desk where I write this and take Hector the Labrador out. He is meithering, as we used to say in Lancashire, but in the nicest possible way: a black nose pushed under my elbow to disrupt my typing, a big sigh as he resignedly sits down again, with a thump of his tail. He hates me writing. Sometimes he leans against my chair so that it slides on its casters away from the desk even as I type.

So after a minute or two I give in. I usually do. We set out. The wind that kept stirring the ivy today has dropped, and the sky is quite clear, and the blank afterglow of the sunset just five minutes ago flares in the west. Low in the western sky the new moon is thin as a nail paring. There will be a frost. Then: across the level vastness of the Fen, against that bright sky, sudden, first one black speck, then another, then a whole cloud, like crowding thoughts, swirls and swoops, swift, now dense black, now open, now quite invisible, now as billowing as a thundercloud. It towers into a cumulus – but no cumulus moved like this – and flattens into a stratus. It is thousands upon thousands of starlings, spaced as evenly and with the individual and unique response to the force as iron filings polarised by a magnet. They appear, come from nowhere, and disappear like thoughts, like memories... make sense, and none, and then another sense. Again, a towering climb, like surf shooting up against a rock in a gale, and as quick a fall back into another pattern, another meaning. They gather again, and swoop and swirl, and gyre into what seem solid shapes, and then evaporate into a cloud of tiny specks like blown smoke, and then again a hard line like a galaxy seen end on across its disc, and, then – how fast are they flying? – a great billowing storm of murmuring birds rushes over me with the wind in their wings, and suddenly, in a tightening vortex like a reverse of those little tornadoes a hot summer afternoon brings to the black soil of this flat land, they spiral down into the shrubs and reeds to roost. They chunter and squabble and seem to come together in a sort of meaning, but it is not stable, till all is still and night falls. A small miracle. Was it joy, exhilaration? Could we ever know? But to perform that great aerial ballet every bird had to fly ever so slightly different a course to its neighbours, as if they were all cells of one great individual being. Yet they are separate, autonomous. Hector looks at me as if puzzled: he is used to me stopping to talk when I meet someone, but now there is nobody but myself, and can I not realise that there are some very interesting smells demanding his attention over there? And he is not interested in starlings, only in pheasants.

David, who stopped his car and got out a few minutes ago, has been leaning on the fence a hundred yards – a happy typo made that 'years' before I corrected it – away. He walks over. 'It makes you think there must be something else.' I think I know what he means, but I do not understand any more than he does. The single starling never sees the dance of the murmuration. Just so, I, like a starling, know there is a dance out there but can only know the steps I myself take. So let me tell my story, my memory, which is also a part of the long story of my flock, before I am once more whirled back into the shifting shape on the changing sky against the setting sun. To another meaning.

★

Apologia

How do you start to tell, to put into the finality of words, that which has no clear beginning and no end? This book asked to be written, nudging my mind in idle moments, just as Hector used to nudge my elbow to remind me it was time to take him for his walk. It started as simply a series of sketches, memoirs, of journeys, some now long ago, and of more recent ones seen with older, different, but perhaps no more perceptive eyes. But almost immediately the problem presented itself of how do – *can* – you remember and convey what it was like to see with those young eyes when you had got neither the language nor the mental baggage of accumulated years. How do you remove the sepia filters of memory and hindsight to see what you saw – and did not see? So what was true – and what does that word mean? And who might listen, anyway?

Writing, in the early stages, was rather like a stream which chatters shallowly and carelessly along in its self-centred youth, then, as it gets older and into less headlong country divides into many braided channels, like parentheses, which then recombine, and then do it again, and again. (There is nothing wrong with, and much pleasure in, serendipitous meandering, like good conversation.) But all the time, as the stream gets fuller and deeper-voiced, as its water get more and more darkened with what it has seen and picked up, with the unexpected tributaries that join it from God knows where, it is making its progress to the limitless sea where it gives up its charge. The young stream never knows where its waters go, or what they might do or mean. No more does the mature river, swelling with the confidence of many other waters.

The journeys I recall were made – somewhat to my romantic shame – in an unglamorous security of person and ease of body of which a traveller could only have dreamed even a century and a half ago, in the last afternoon of civil Europe before the long storm broke in 1914. Nothing heroic, remarkable or unusual there. But more and more the journey that mattered has been – in fits and unexpected starts – to the interior, to the heartland where what one thought was known and familiar came to be the most disorientating and disturbing of all. Writing took me in many unexpected directions, but all leading to the same inconclusive end: the impenetrable puzzle of our nature and existence, of how the same species can compass Bach and Belsen, the longing and striving for the light and what seems like the ingrained bias to the darkness. In each of us. As Jung pointed out, to know your own darkness is the best way of dealing with the darknesses of others. Inextricably mixed with that mental clouding is the memory of place – in both senses, for there are places on this earth which resonate with half-heard echoes of what happened there, people who lived there. I am convinced places have memory – not, obviously, in our sense, but rather as clothes keep the odour of someone who wore them, or the handle of a tool remembers the smoothing of the palms that held it. (That is one of the reasons why I love working with old tools, like old Seth's hammers and chisels or my father's spade.) Places hold more than fossils. Dimly, they hold feelings and passions. The sense that something irreparable once happened *here* I have had too often to dismiss it as mere fancy. It shadows some places, pretty tourist places, almost to cloud the sunlight: Prague, Munich, Berlin. The Swedish poet Tomas Tranströmer put his finger on it for me: 'Time is not a straight line, it's a labyrinth. Press your ear up against the wall at the right place, and you can hear footsteps, voices, even yourself moving about on the other side.'

Well, why the title I gave to this book? (Many were tried, from *A Time to Come Clean* to *Murmurations*. I did quite like that one.) A title is supposed to be both informative and intriguing enough to make you pick up the book – it did! – and publishers like that. (It is also a good idea not to have a title which will have too many look-alikes on search engines.) I ended up, as I usually do, with Greek myth. That is never a bad idea, for stories are how we structure our understanding of the world we live in, and you might as well go back to the stories the Ancients – our own ancestors, not that distant – told, and why not Odysseus if you are writing about travel? For myth – the Biblical Creation stories, the fall of Prometheus, Ragnarøk – need not be literally true richly to express Truth: myth is *trans*rational rather than *ir*rational, its stories are deep, paradigmatic insights into the puzzle of what the world means for us. This matters: it can be forcefully argued that the loss of mythic consciousness since the Baconian, Cartesian, materialist – call it what you will – revolution of the seventeenth century has led to the dire growth of rigid fundamentalisms: there is not much to choose between the consequences of that perverse certainty of exclusive and excluding rightness in radical Evangelicalism, in Islamic fundamentalism, and in Fascism or Communism – the very thing that the great religions through their use of infinitely polysemous stories of Truth refuse.

The *Odyssey* begins with the word ἄνδρα: 'Man.' By searching for his father, Odysseus' son Telemachos has to find what it is to be 'a man'. Only then can he stand beside his father to fight the band of suitors who have eaten up Odysseus' kingdom and laid siege to Penelope's fidelity. In turn Odysseus, πολύτροπον, 'tricksy', or 'resourceful', (the first, deeply ambivalent, qualifier of that word 'Man'), has to undergo many trials and many journeys before he can find his way home to Ithaca, to his fullness of return. But no sooner has he done that then it is clear that is not enough. For there is no rest yet: he has to abandon all he has won, his newly recovered kingdom, wife and son, all his reputation as a hero of the Trojan War, all his knowledge, and set off into the unknown lands far from the very idea of the sea, carrying only an oar on his shoulder, until he encounters a wayfarer who will think he is carrying a winnowing shovel. Then he will know his journey is over, for he is at last himself, unknown, without reputation, power or possessions, just fully a Man: ἄνδρας. Only then will his peace be made with Poseidon the sea god whose son Polyphemus he blinded, and only then will Athene give him the wisdom finally to reign in his kingdom Ithaca. To leave the place where you are comfortable to take a chance on the unknown was the challenge to Abraham, to Mohammed, to Siddhartha, to the great saints. I think it is something we all have to do, in our measure. Odysseus had to go on that further journey to know what he was seeking in his first. It is no simple extension of the trip already made, but a change in key, and what was key in your first journey, though it went into the making of you, may be useless in that further journey. You don't use your skis to cross the desert.

So increasingly the describing of earlier journeys became itself a journey, into other territory and strange seas of thought: what we inherit from, how options are closed by, the entail of the past. Here again Greek myth was a catalyst of what crystallised. Zeus, they say, got around quite a bit in various disguises, and the ladies who found themselves the objects of his desire often came to unusual ends. Leda, for example, after that business with the Swan – well, one of her children caused the Trojan War where traditionally European history used to start, another took an axe to her husband in his bath – a sort of justice – when he came back from it, and her two boys became stars by which mariners sailed and gave their name to the grain ship on which St Paul sailed for Rome and a very different world. In the Swan's white rush, which she could hardly refuse, did any of that destiny slip into Leda's mind, the aw(e)ful importance of her inescapable conceiving?

> ... A shudder in the loins engenders there
> The broken wall, the burning roof and tower
> And Agamemnon dead...

Or again, Europa: carried off in all innocence from the eastern shores of the Great Sea, by a sportive, courteous and very masculine white bull, to Crete, one of the nodes of the ancient world, and as it happens one of the first places in which I began my own journeying – avoiding the livestock, of course. There she gave birth to Sarpedon, who fell in the Ur-war at Troy, to

Rhadamanthus, lawgiver and judge of the ever-growing community of the dead, and to Minos lord of Crete. Minos' wife Pasiphae, they say, after having several children perfectly normally, had an affair with another white bull (this one sent by Poseidon), perhaps hoping to emulate Minos' mother Europa and be seduced by a god. But she bore instead the hideous creature in whom the bestial and the human held uneasy truce demanding of regular sacrifice, and Minos had Daedalus build the labyrinth for it. Be careful of what lurks at the centre, at the heart... Europa's name marks the little sub-continent, at the margin of Eurasia, which is our home; her story shadows the incalculable consequences of attraction and desire. Another title I nearly gave this book was *Europa's Brood*: for it is very much about how we are members one of another, descendants of the six women who entered Europe with their hunting and gathering families, and of one who came millennia later with the first farmers. We are children of a common culture that seeded where Leda embraced the Swan and Europa the Bull. Our mythic history starts with the Fall of Troy, when the world changed. The world changed again with the Fall of Berlin in 1945. Things were let loose in what I call the Long War of 1914-45 which will never go away. That war not only killed unimaginable numbers of people but also ground to bits the norms and conventions of a culture that reached back to Rome, Greece and Palestine. We live with, still take our bearings from, the ghosts of that Europe of the past, we meticulously reconstruct bomb-obliterated cities 'just as they were', but we have seen deep into the darkness and the knowledge will not go away. New maps were made of Hell.

In the end, mere journeys became a pilgrimage, and a pilgrimage of any kind is a search for something you know you need, do not understand, have not yet found; and one pilgrimage only leads to another, another gyre in the dance, in the endless spiral round the Centre, seeking understanding. For we can never return from travel: to come home is to come to a place no longer the same, a strange familiar land from which the next journey must start. That is why this book has the associative structure it does. For so many things that come to be important to us were/are first seen, so to speak, out of the tail of the eye when looking elsewhere. What matters is the search, not the knowing, the things seen and felt on the way, not the destination you wrongly thought you had. The destinations we give ourselves are mirages. So my story journeys through time – bluntly, to the point where I know I have not many years left – as well as space. But that also implies a growing polyphonic apprehension – *not* knowledge – of other times orchestrated into some sort of meaning by others' lives. Each one of us is restlessly swirled into the great dance of being, like the starlings in those shape-swift-shifting clouds that darken the sunset on a clear winter evening. I have always loved starlings and their incessant chatter and quotation of what they hear. (Just like the don I have been all my adult life...)

Sometimes our individual stories seem to come together into a sort of sense, but it may be a nonce-sense, and then disappear again to reform otherwise, changing as we change, before the final quiet.

Words have been the business of my life, but most by far of those I have uttered have been about other people's books, and ideas, and history (reliable or not), and as the shadows lengthen in my own Autumn I now feel I must put down my lecture notes and come out from behind the desk to write – well, a sort of testament: which, etymologically, is a word connected with an act of witness. An earlier book of mine was called *Coming to Terms*. This one too is a coming to terms, but I have no idea whether these are the final ones. If there are any.

★

A (Brief) Warning

Once a lecturer always a lecturer. It is not easy to relinquish, avoid, abandon – what you will – the hugely enjoyable habit of being informative whether or not your victims want you to be. It is as difficult for me to avoid parentheses, or digressions, on paper as it is in conversation. Indeed, this whole book is virtually one long parenthesis in my journey – it ought to be in brackets entirely. So, for those of you who, like me, have a propensity to enjoy tedious detail, I have put excursus on things I find interesting in a section at the back: when one is on offer there is a note in the text – rather like those asterisks in his guidebooks for places Herr Baedeker found more interesting than most. But you don't have to follow it.

★

I

UNCHARTED

Casting Off

When do I begin?
Once...

A small boy is walking, then running, in stops and starts, over the low flat field, past the wind-laid hedges that line the ditches, towards the sea. He is in his own world, his own time, which is simply a now. He has short trousers, a grey jumper and, though it is warm, he has a dark blue gabardine mac. His long grey socks, held up by elastic garters, end in the cheap brown leather sandals children wore then. (After all, they would all too soon grow out of them and anything more expensive was waste of scarce money.) He changes his pace: now the stiff legged iambic rhythm with which he imitates a horse's canter, now what he imagines is a slow and stately stride, now a furious gallop. His mac, without his arms in it, is buttoned only at the neck, so that when he runs he is a cloaked highwayman, or a traveller galloping through the night from Ghent to Aix with the good news – or, as the mood changes, he wears the mantle that draped the shoulders of one of Arthur's folk. All are now. But as he breasts the last rise before the beach, up to the sea wall, his world changes. Now he is standing still, looking west under his levelled hand out across the ocean, his left knee flexed as he puts his foot on a stone, silent, upon a peak in Darien. (He has not read Keats yet, nor *Swallows and Amazons*. He will.) His grandmother is waiting, sitting on one of the Council benches along what They call the Promenade. 'Where have you been?' 'With Walter Raleigh, and I have been to America.' 'Were there any Indians, dear?' 'Oh, lots, Nana, and we traded with them and I got tobacco. Look!' He pulls out a scrap of dried bladder wrack from his trouser pocket (that hard seaweed also tells him when it is going to rain.) The other pocket has useful shells, a bit of string, and a dog biscuit. But the dog is at home. Never mind. The boy quite likes dog biscuits. 'Tomorrow, Nana, I am going to build a boat and sail with Drummond to where the sun goes down.' (Drummond is the dog.) 'That's a good idea. You will come back safe?' 'Of *course*, Nana. I'll be back for tea.' And he runs off along the concrete path to where, last week, looking inland, he saw two hares boxing. At least, that is what he said they were doing. He is now a big game hunter.

The Promenade runs along the top of an old floodbank – needed, for the sea has an uneasy truce with the land in these parts, north of the low boulder clay cliffs of Bispham. It eats away, it gives back. The boy is ignorant of that, yet. But long ago the sea washed away, with other houses and farms, the hall where in 1532 another wanderer, William Allen, third son of John Allen of Southwark, was born. Where he learned his horn book and did his crisscross row is now a flat beach scoured by the erasing tides. He left aged fifteen for Oriel College, Oxford, and a Fellowship, and eventually, in the agony of the later Reformation, for Douai, and the cardinal's hat for which Philip II recommended him. Douai he intended as a Catholic Oxford or Cambridge: for Catholics were debarred from the two universities. ('Platforming' in institutions supposedly of learning is nothing new.) In later years he set up the English College in Rome: John Milton, fierce polemicist (when needed) against the Romish church, stayed there in 1638. He went a long way for a local lad and never came back. He too must have run about his father's windy fields like this lad centuries later, his head also full of dreams and causes that would be lost. He too must have heard the ancestors of now's winter geese as they flew in to feed, a flock shepherded and guarded so they may safely graze by one wise goose, alert, neck straight. Perhaps the place remembers this other childhood, for places do not forget. For him too Rossall was a place of departure, of becoming, an in-between place, a place too of un-forgetting.

The boy does not know any of that. (He will, one day, and may be tediously informative about it.) But he does know that a little further along the shore is a steep bank and a rifle range, and if you go there (when the red flag is not flying) and crawl under the barbed wire fence you can find bullets in the sand rampart behind the targets. He has quite a collection: he loves the sleek shape of the copper-covered lead, and he sometimes polishes them on his woolly dressing gown when he is supposed to be going to sleep so they gleam in the sun on his attic window ledge. Sometimes they become spaceships, and he is Dan Dare from the *Eagle* comic. Further along the shore still is an old single-decker bus, abandoned, where he has been forbidden to go because the big boys go there. He did once, daringly, but did not like the smell. And then there is a big bleak building unsheltered from any winds of the world where he knows old folk go. ('Will you go there one day, Nana?' he had asked. 'No dear, I used to live there before Mummy and Daddy came here.') He does not yet know about death. But he does know about wrecks, for one, its ribs fuzzy and greenly frothy with weed, is on the beach. He walked out to it as the tide receded one day. It happened – well, it was a long time ago, and to him it is just there. Like the old people washed up on a last shore in the big grim building next to where he finds the bullets never fired in anger.

Even further along the shore, where he rarely but daringly goes, the sand a strong fierce wind blows off the beach at low tide forms dunes that almost overtop the sea wall. The sand, dry and sharp, annoyingly gets in through the cutwork in the toes of the boy's sandals when he runs down the slopes of the dunes, which he has been told not to do. And so he does. Sparse tussocks of the deep rooted marram grass colonise, grasping the blowing sand into drifts, which become mounds, which become dunes, and then in a big winter gale are sometimes blown away to coat the streets of the town on the estuary behind them with drifts of pale sand. Dig deep in that fine sand and you feel the cool damp round the long white rhizomes of the marram, and a salty smell rises from what one day, with luck, will be soil. The sharp points of the hard-edged blue green leaves prick knees in short trousers. Where the leaves bend to touch the dry sand, the breeze's constant stirring of them has made them scribe little arcs. In the summer season, the tassels of the seed heads are the colour of ripe barley: their cousin. Here and there, sea holly spreads its fleshy arms, and in season its blue flowers startle. (It is not a holly at all, but a sort of thistle.) Where there is a bit more moisture, sea cabbage luxuriates. It too is a bluey green: the whole landscape, sand, plants, immense sky, is a watercolour landscape, washed in soft Corot colours, and over all the ever changing light.

On the storm beach of big stones the high tide leaves a mark of dried seaweed – where the boy got his bladder wrack – and bits of wood, the occasional dead gull. (Drummond loves to roll and wriggle on his back on those, his four feet stiffly in the air). There are bits of net, very occasionally the green glass floats off fishing nets, and, as the sun warms the tidemark, sandhoppers and flies make it a happy hunting ground and the sweet iodine smell which the boy loves scents the wind. He likes to loiter along that line, for once he found a treasure: a tiny little boat carved from cork and weighted with a lead pin so it floated the right way up.

Burnet moths live among the sand dunes and do not bother about people, boys or not. So do rabbits, and behind the dunes, on the better, richer, grass, hares, and there, in those fields plotted out by those hawthorn hedges bending under the weight of the wind, graze the big black and white, deep-uddered cows from the cob-built whitewashed farm at the end of the road where he lives. They look at him with their big wet noses and their big soft eyes, with the eyelashes of film stars, and he is not afraid of them. Not really. He just walks that little bit faster when they stop their grazing and begin to gather round him, munching slowly, thoughtfully (perhaps), drooling slow strings of saliva. Far away, the sound of the sea on the beach, and on the distant horizon, far beyond imagining, hills: he had asked to be told their names, for he knew they must have them: Black Combe, Bleasdale, Fair Snape, Parlick. Naming and knowing is almost as good as having.

The time will come when he can say, 'I will arise and go now', and will silently add, 'and not come back'. But not for years yet.

It is odd to see what has now become bungaloid and concreted desert as one of the in-between places of this world, but it remains so, as it was when the boy ran about its summer fields. (For some, those brash bungalows will indeed be the ultimate point of departure.) It always was a place where the restlessness of the sea is always questioning the temporariness, picking away at the hardness, of the concreted land where people have invested their certainties. It is still somewhere, as it was for generation upon generation, where sea marks wink in the dark, reminding that out there, beyond the yellow street lights, beyond the flickering light of TV screens in thousands of ready-meal-smelling-after-work-uncurtained living room windows that nearly but don't quite overlook the sea but near enough the estate agents said – that out there is the way to the uttermost parts of the earth. Here is no abiding place, this spit of temporary land, which once sheltered the boats that came home from far faring and, like gulls coming home to their nests, gratefully folded their wings in its lee, as the tidal mud of the river dried out and they took the ground.

Change. Always. Yet nothing is erased: the place holds it in a never-ending palimpsest of what was. Where the big *knarrar* of the Norsemen, where the hulks and single-sailed cogs – the workhorses of the middle ages – took the ground, where the barques and schooners of a later age furled their salt, damp canvas, has become a marina where the expensive steel rigging of pleasure boats taps against the mast in the wind, with a note always slightly flat. The Ship Hole, the Norsemen called it. Once, one summer afternoon, when he was very small, his mother and father took the boy there on the Ribble bus. He loved it, he loved the sharp smell of the saltings, and it was then a quiet place, with hulks beached in little creeks off the channel, a couple of fishing boats, a broken backed wreck. Not like this smart marina. Yet the saltings still smell as they did when the boy was young, and the smooth brown of the muddy banks of the creek still sweats shinily as the tide drops. Opposite, on the farther shore, in another creek, they once built schooners of 400 or so tons and then released them to the wind that would take them... wherever. There, on that farther wilder shore, the much older boy – he never grew up, though he thought, once, he did – could sit very still with a gun in the mud in a creek at the edge of the marsh saltings, waiting for the geese to come of a winter dawn – they were hatched once upon a time (for they can live a long time) in Greenland or Iceland... a skein of greylags honks past along the other shore. His dog is tense, ears cocked, shoulder muscles quivering with every sound he hears above the little wind. In the half light a busyness of redshanks chutters past, almost at his feet, feeding on the creatures of the mud with their long beaks. They are predators too, these visitors, birds of passage. Moments can be trapped in memory as sharp as insects in amber.

A black-backed gull, standing alert on the parapet of the Promenade, near her seat, took off as the old lady stood up. 'Come home now, dear. They will be waiting for us at home.' His grandmother gathers up her things, and shivers lightly, for the wind blows cold when you reach September, and she is getting a little chilly. I once knew that boy, and that youth. It was a long time ago, a long way away.

From an Antique Land

... Salad days, / When I was green in judgment, cold in blood...
Shakespeare, *Antony and Cleopatra*

Once... not quite so long ago. Waking up.

We turned to leave the church. Jenny stood in the porch doorway against the strong Greek sunlight, her slim thighs showing as dark shadow through the fall of her light skirt. I loved her, heart-stoppingly. Behind us the great mosaic Pantocrator on the vault raised his hand in blessing. For it is not good for man to be alone.

The world was all before us. We went out into that hot light. The sun was near its zenith: little shade. After the dim interior and the soft glow of the ikonostasis reflecting the outside light from the door, our eyes were dazzled. *Tsitsikoi* stridulated, or whatever it is they do – their name in onomatopoeia enough. The grass was sunburnt gold on the darker brown of the limy soil. Chips of marble reminded of what might have been here, once. A little wind off the sea soughed in the almost black needles of the pines. A lizard was basking on the wall by the door: sudden alarm, a scutter and it was gone.

I wanted some lunch, so holding each other's packs we eased each other's hot shoulders into the straps. The road was quiet, a black, hot, smelly river of tarmac between the deserted fields, running down the hill towards the sea. Sparse pines along it gave some shade. Everyone sensible was inside, at this time of siesta – the old canonical hour of Sext, when the Rule of wise St Benedict says that you can rest on your bed. High up on Monte Cassino, he understood this Mediterranean midday. A good mile we walked, and as we turned a corner we spotted, way across a field of ripe sunflowers, a hut by the sea. It had an awning, and seemed to have tables. A notice crudely painted in black on a board by the road said 'καφενείο', which suggested a café, and an arrow below it pointed across the field. So we made for it through the sunflowers, hoping at least for a drink of water. But luck was in: it was a little taverna, and just by it a man was fishing from the shore. Gratefully we dropped our packs, and sat down on the metal chairs under the vine-draped trellis. The padrone, without our asking, plonked down a yellow metal carafe of retsina and two large glasses of water. We could smell the pine cone of Dionysus in the wine. No sign of a menu. (Did we seriously expect one?) So, in my halting Greek, I said, 'Οπου μπορούμε να φάμε ?' 'Where can we eat?' Big smile, expansive gesture across his swelling singlet: 'Εδώ.' Here. I said, tentatively, 'ιχθοι?' Big smile again, and a gesture to the man fishing – for he was just bringing in a nice bream. The padrone took the fish from him, gave it a bash on the head, and took it straight inside. Soon we could hear sizzling, and then the lady of the house, all in black, appeared with a plate of tomato salad, with garlic and peppers, and bread. 'Ευχαριστώ,' I said, as politely as I could, suddenly my mind flicking back to another broiled fish eaten by the shore of a sea. A Eucharist, a thanksgiving indeed. It was one of the simplest, yet most memorable of meals: bread, fish, fruit, oil, wine. A moment out of time.

But the sun was westering, and the temperature easing, and we had (we hoped) miles to go before we slept. We paid what we owed, shook hands all round, not forgetting the fisherman who had not yet caught another fish, and set off back to the road through the dry sunflowers. As luck would have it, almost as soon as we got on the road and started walking, a van spotted the Union Jacks on our rucksacks, stopped, we piled into the front bench seat, and we had our lift to Corinth.

Conversation was limited, in a mixture of broken Greek, broken English and Italian, but goodwill filled in the gaps. For at that time simply to be known to be English opened many doors in rural Greece: memories, traditions, of the War were still sharp. Later, in Crete, in the hills, we found many who remembered the legendary Paddy Leigh Fermor – or said, plausibly, that they did. But, gradually, the social effort in the cab, hot despite the open windows, grew too much for the driver and for us, and we drove on in cheerful silence, Jenny's head drowsing onto my shoulder despite the jolting of the road, and me trying to avoid getting in the way of the gear stick as Konstantinos crashed through the gate on each of the sharp bends in the road. We crossed the Canal – we sailed through it later, on a ferry to Brindisi which almost touched the limestone sides of the steep cutting – which had at last been achieved in the nineteenth century long after Nero had his first go at one to replace the portage across the isthmus. (Nero's workers, 6000 Jewish prisoners of war, got about 700 yards on the same line as the modern canal. A contemporary relief of Hercules can be seen in the canal cutting today. We did not know that then... there was so much we did not know!) Konstantinos dropped us in the middle of Corinth, with expressions on both sides of goodwill and friendship.

But... *this* was Corinth? This huddle of mean, low, grey buildings, wires drooping from poles, dusty trees, and dogs lying in the shade scratching at their fleas? Where was the city we had read about, the city of ancient luxury and wealth, the city of one of the most famous courtesans of antiquity, Laïs, the city that gave its name to good fellowship and high living? (And the city to whose Christian community St Paul had to write two stern reminders.) And there seemed to be nowhere where we could sleep. Then Jenny spotted a sign at a road junction, pointing left: 'Archaio Korintho' – Old Corinth. We looked up, and there, high on the hill, was the fortress built by the Byzantines and enlarged by the

Villehardouins, Princes of Achaea after the disgraceful Fourth Crusade had put a Latin Emperor on the throne of Constantinople. We could see a little village on the slopes below it. Old Corinth: where the town was in Antiquity, safe on a defensible hillock, commanding both the road across the Isthmus and the portage route from the Saronic Gulf to the Corinthian. This was the town where St Paul earned his keep as a tentmaker – a tough trade, for that harsh goat's wool plays the devil with your fingers. At least if we got up there we should find somewhere to unroll our sleeping bags among the olives that dotted the slope in their regular quincunx. So we set off. A stiff climb, and the sun on our backs reminded us that evening was near.

The village was not much: a few houses, a little square, a small terrace with tables in front of a taverna, the shade of plane trees, and the inevitable, invasive eucalyptus. Food, anyway. But beyond the little village were all sorts of interesting mounds, and it was very clear that this was indeed the Corinth of Antiquity. Seven columns remained of the great Temple of Apollo. Somewhere in someone's field lie the ruins of the house where St Paul lived with Aquila and Priscilla. The ground plan of the basilica, or judgement hall, had been excavated: that was where the proconsul, 'sweet Gallio', had held court. Gallio was Governor of the Roman Province of Achaia, cousin of the poet Lucan and brother of Seneca the philosopher: it was before him St Paul was questioned

when the local Jews made a fuss about his preaching...
I had 'done' the Journeys of St Paul at School – almost
the only detailed knowledge I had about this country –
and I could be loquaciously tedious about it. High above,
where the walls of the old fortress now crowned the
hill, was clearly the ancient Acropolis: Akrokorintho.
Thence, perhaps, Medea took off in her chariot drawn
by dragons after exacting her terrible revenge on Jason.
Perhaps. But that sort of exploration would have to wait
– in some instances, long into the hindsight of the future.
Meanwhile, food and somewhere to lay our heads. The
taverna came up with a very decent moussaka and retsina
and cool water, and when I asked the owner where we
might camp he simply shrugged and said, 'Why? Sleep on
the roof here.' Ideal: so we had an ouzo in the soft warm
darkness, while people loitered in the square talking, and
the radio played the latest *bouzoukoi* hits – one very catchy
one by Mikis Theodorakis I still remember.

When you are sleeping *à la belle étoile* you wake early,
with the dawn's first rosy fingers drawing aside the curtain of the night. You might turn over and try to sleep
a bit more, but the sun's touch on your face soon gets
you up. This early waking became very much a routine.
For most of the time on that trip we were sleeping in the
open – on beaches, in olive groves, on people's roofs. It
was no real hardship, for the early morning is a delectable time, and if you are going to go clambering up hills
and exploring Greek remains the sooner you start the less

exhausted by the midday heat you will be. And you will hear the sound of sheep bells in the morning quiet, and the cicadas will still be quiet. On the other hand, there can be unexpected complications. At Olympia we found a nice level spot among the olives above the ruins that the Germans had excavated with what some would call pedantic precision: they left the drums of the massive columns of the Temple of Zeus exactly as they found them, fallen in rows like so many child's building bricks. But all was well, that evening: the stars were bright above, the moon rose about 11pm, we heard the odd owl, and in the distance a dog barked. Peace. But at first light came a sudden abrupt waking. A drove of pigs, no respecters of persons, came charging across us, only just avoiding stepping on us, and one bolder than the rest paused and sniffed at my rucksack which pillowed my head, smelling perhaps the bread that was in there. Behind them, whistling, came the swineherd. He did not bat an eyelid at these two bebagged people: 'Καλημέρα'; 'Good morning,' he said, and I said 'Καλημέρα' back, adding boldly 'είναι ωραίος' – 'it is beautiful', (meaning the morning, of course), just to show that such a wakening as this was quite normal, no problem at all, for me.

I suppose we did the usual tourist route – but it wasn't then, really. Mass tourism had not really got going. We knew very little: we went equipped with no guide books, and indeed, *Lonely Planet* and *Rough Guide*, telling you what the traveller 'ought' to look at and saving you the bother of finding it out for yourself, were yet to be invented. In our naïve pilgrimage to the relics of a distant past which we both somehow knew – we had had, after all, some smattering of education – was the foundation of the glories and horrors of what our Europe was. We had a Penguin copy of Sophocles and Aeschylus and unjustified confidence. Our heads held a good deal of Greek mythology, but it was mainly filtered through Roman writers, especially Virgil and the notes to the *Aeneid* in the red Oxford editions. We knew we 'ought'/ wanted to see Athens, Corinth, Argos, Delphi, Sparta, Mycenae... these names were resonant. I remember as if it were yesterday – clichés sometimes hit the spot – seeing Mycenae's low brown hill rising out of the summer olives. The limestone bulk of the big hill – I don't know its name – behind it dwarfed its little majesty. Cities and Thrones and Powers... From the top of the big hill the Church of the Prophet Elias looks down on the ruins of time, and was built when men had forgotten the Lion Gate and thoughts of Agamemnon entering for that last fatal time under its massive lintel, and those two lionesses ramping on the tympanum were covered by centuries of accumulated soil. People had forgotten the shaft graves where Schliemann found so much treasure and had said, when he found the gold mask, that he had had 'looked on the face of Agamemnon'. The mound concealing the Treasury of Atreus was just a mound, where the sheep and goats browsed and the lizards flickered among the stones. I tried to peel back the centuries to when lions roamed here and men fought them with spear and shield, as on the dagger from Shaft Grave IV- about 1600 BC – that had so recently caught my imagination in that glass case in Athens. To no avail: in the here and now, a bee settled busily on the thyme, rifling its treasure, and its minute weight bowed down the tiny spray. The cool darkness of the Treasury's open mouth said nothing. But it is neither treasury nor Atreus', but a huge stone-corbelled beehive tomb.

I remember reading about Schliemann when I was very young. My parents used to be given copies of the *Readers' Digest* when our neighbour had finished with them, and I was of an age when anything in the house new in print, good or bad, indifferent, edifying or rubbish, was devoured. (I even read, time and time again, the label on the HP sauce bottle.) One of those *Readers' Digest* articles was on Schliemann, by his daughter Andromache. I was impressed by, dazzled by, envious of, this man who had so many languages which he learned so quickly, awed by his standing for hours working at his tall clerk's desk, thrilled that he had discovered (as I read) the site of windy Troy by pacing out the ground with the *Iliad* in his hand, recalling that on the night operation Ulysses hears the cry of a marsh bird. I was already as a mere boy in love with the past, hopelessly, romantically, ignorantly. In a small way, I suppose that *Readers' Digest* piece fed an already nascent interest in the Classical world, which grew and grew so that though I was at a Greekless school I became a decent Latinist and came to know the ancient epics behind Virgil pretty thoroughly in translation. So when we did make it to Greece, for me it was to a country as much of the mind as of actuality, and the journey was indeed a sort of pilgrimage. (We even did the Temple Sleep of Antiquity, but of that more later.) And I was not going to let Jenny get away with not hearing the stories I wanted to tell her...

We had flown in to what was then the only airport. Built in 1938, by the sea, four miles south of Athens, the Nazis took Ellinikon over for a Luftwaffe base from 1941. Now it sits abandoned. Weeds grow through the cracks in the concrete. No sign of redevelopment. Greece is now broke. But then... we arrived late one night, and were disgorged from the BEA Comet into the heat of an August night. We walked across the tarmac, and Jenny said, 'Where are we going to sleep?' I shrugged as nonchalantly as I could. 'They say the beach at Phaleron is nice.' 'No,' she said firmly. 'We find a hotel.' Well, in the end, in a side street near Syntagma Square, in the small hours, we did, of sorts. I am not sure what the other guests were doing, as there was a lot of tramping up and down the stairs all night, and we did not ask. But the management spoke English, a bit, and the knowing leer that had appeared when I said I wanted a room for myself and my wife disappeared when Jenny came through the door, hot and bothered, with her rucksack on. It was cheap enough – it had to be: but hot, hot, and noisy, for the window gave onto a sort of light well and across it was a very busy garment factory where the sewing machines went on all night and the workers talked loudly over them. Jenny was not impressed with her first taste of Greece or Greeks.

That first night made us pretty determined to get out into the countryside as soon as we could. But, being young and aware of a) how lucky we were to be there and b) how ignorant we were, we had first to 'do' the museums and sites of our cultural memory – such as ours was. So we looked for somewhere else in Athens. We found, for the next few nights, a sort of student hostel where we could sleep on the flat roof under an awning, with a cold water tap in the corner. The noise of the traffic came up from the street, deadened somewhat by the height. We felt on our faces the night breeze, which brought scents of thyme from Hymettos, and it flapped the awning, and above, unseen (but they were there, I thought) wheeled the stars the Argonauts steered by.

A sense of the past is an odd thing. Some never have one: it was just 'then', in 'the old days'. My father, like so many then and now, had little sense of a past behind his own and his parents' generation, a past which extends through the long arches of the years like a perspective into worlds circling different suns. What mattered was the Now time, the *jetztzeit*. What happened during the Civil War, say, could have happened yesterday. In Talke, the village where my father was born, they told me, an earnest lad in short trousers, that the next village, Red Street, was called that because the street ran with blood after 'The Battle': their parents had told them, and it might have been yesterday rather than three centuries back. To see otherwise, to see the past as a perspective has to be learned, and when I was about nine I certainly had not even begun to develop that. Mum revered the memory of her adored father, often talked about him, and quietly hoped, I am sure, I would be a scholar and parson like him. She once said to me, thoughtfully, 'He was a saint, you know'. And I knew his name was Charles, and I could not fit him into the Twelve, so I assumed he must have had another name (like Peter), and said, 'Which one?'

Now, though, I look at a site, or a town, and see a pa-limpsest, generation after generation writing its name and telling its story to itself, that story half effaced by the next, and that one's by the next, and all one long and complex multivoiced story. The last strand in that tapestry is one's own knowing about it, and one's own memories of it. That comes with age. But then, a confusion of centuries as I looked at Athens, the first really ancient place apart from Hadrian's Wall this lad from Blackpool had ever visited, and I saw the past all round me, but undifferentiated, as if the ancient world of Athens between the downfall of the Peisistratids in 510BC and St Paul's visit at the height of Roman power – six turbulent centuries! – were collapsed into a span. Yet all those buildings I knew from black and white photographs had stories attached to them, and as we laboured up the steps of the Propylaea in the hot morning I saw before us in my mind's eye not the Parthenon ravaged by time, and half destroyed in 1687 by the explosion of the gunpowder the Turks stored in it during one of their periodic scraps with the Venetians, but the glory I knew it had once had, with bright colour and gold plastered all over the Pentelic marble and, inside, the great gold and ivory clad wooden statue of Athene, the warrior virgin, her sandals on the level with a man's eyes, whose gift of the olive won her the loyalty of the people of Athens. Outside had stood Pheidias' huge bronze statue of Athene Promachos, helmet 30 feet above sandals, her gilded spear slashing the sunlight. Anciently, seamen used to look out for the sun on that spear as the first sign of Athens as they rounded Cape Sounion and made up the coast to Piraeus. Alaric the Goth saw it four centuries after Christ, after the Parthenon had become a church dedicated to another Virgin, and turned tail with his ships and fled. The Maiden defended her city still, long after its glory had departed. The ruins were the keys to memories of books read and stories told, and clothed themselves once more in their ancient glories.

There was nobody about: it was still early, and, then, you could wander in and out at will. Jenny posed by the Erechtheum as a Caryatid: not very convincingly, for in the breeze her red dress refused to drape itself in the dignified folds of the sculpted maidens. We found an olive tree growing in the thin soil, a small miracle feeding, it seemed, on sunlight and the almost bare limestone... Athena and Poseidon both claimed to be the god of Athens, and to end the dispute held a contest in which both would display their powers. Poseidon struck the grounds with his trident and sea water flowed out, as you would expect: he was after all god of the sea. Athene then struck the ground with her spear. But now the result was the first olive tree, the wealth of Attica: so Athene won, and was thereafter revered by the Athenians. I did not know then to tell Jenny that the olive we were looking at was planted there by no goddess but by Sophia of Prussia, granddaughter of Queen Victoria, in honour of the Athenians. She was Kaiser Bill's sister, and the queen of Constantine I, King of the Hellenes.

If only those Hohenzollerns had stuck to planting trees...

★

I first noticed her while Jenny was on the other side of the massive columns of the Temple of Olympian Zeus. I don't know where she came from. Svelte, dark brown hair, the lustrous dark eyes of all her race, she moved beautifully. She came towards me, her eyes fixed on mine, and it was difficult not to see her gaze as a sort of adoration. We had no common language. She came and stood next to me, and leaned against me: she lifted her head to me. She was not begging. I was uncertain what to do... I know I would have taken her home with me had we been in England... and then Jenny, seeing what was happening, came back, and we set off across the wide hot space towards the Arch of Hadrian – that Philhellene emperor completed the huge temple 638 years after work had originally started. I turned and glanced back. She was following. She caught us up as we paused briefly before crossing the big road and came and stood slinkily next to me. Nothing was said. We drew a bit ahead, and I said to Jenny, 'I am so worried about her: we have got to lose her somehow' – knowing full well that was the last thing I really wanted. We quickened our steps: ten paces behind, she did too. We turned sharply right off odos Lykistratous down odos Galanou, then left into Gkoura, then right again into Aphrodite Street... left, and then Jenny hastily put on a headscarf and covered her arms, and said, 'Quick, in here' and we dived into the church of St Catherine. She was just behind us. As the door closed, the look of pain and rejection in her eyes almost, as the cliché goes, broke my heart.

We sat in the church for about half an hour. I was worried about her: she had come far, and where had she come from? What was her story? Who was – or had been – her man? She was clearly not destitute: she was well groomed, not thin. In the end, not knowing what I was letting myself in for, I stood up. 'Better see', I said to Jenny. We went to the door, cautiously opened it. She had gone. She had gone out of our lives for ever, yet that encounter neither of us was ever able to forget.

She was a beautiful bitch and I wish we could have taken her home. It is strange how dogs can affect you: a bond of love and across the species – in the strict sense of the word – sympathy. The Greeks had a word for it.

★

Modern Athens – well, it was modern then – was a terrible disappointment of our hopes of a place where the myth of the glory that was Greece would become real. The main streets were a noisy, smelly place of undistinguished architecture and cars that used horns as punctuation for the irritation of driving. It has got much worse since. True, it was – is – lively enough: men talking, loudly, passionately, big gestures, drivers in drab singlets leaning out of their truck windows and gesturing with their brown arms at people they think have got in their way, who hoot in return; men sitting at pavement tables with little cups of sweet thick Greek coffee and glasses of water, reading the endless newspapers – *Ta Nea, To Bhma* and all the host of others – and quarrelling with the news when not disagreeing with their companions. Those gestures: hands, bodies and faces are rarely still, and sometimes you think you get the gist of a conversation by watching from yards away. The palm upturned, the fingers together and the rapid, repeated downwards motion of the whole arm, as if milking a goat, to stress *polykala* – 'very good'; we soon got used to the slow down movement of the head to one side, slightly closing the eyes, as the head is lowered that meant 'ne' – 'yes.' 'No': the entire head moves back, the tongue is clicked. Sometimes these movements are too subtle and quick, and you can't be too sure that he/she's answered at all. You can repeat the question again and again, and find he's been saying 'No' from the start. But off the main streets, into the rather down at heel areas where 'real' – that bit of argot was still in the future – people lived, we felt more comfortable. Serendipitous wandering turned up minor delights. There were little tavernas which made us welcome, and the news of these two English went round the room and everyone wanted to drink with us. Little shops which sold bread, and a riot of fruit, and cheese – just the right sort of lunch to eat in the shade as the sun became blinding on the pale marble of the ruins. Through the odd open gate one looked down a narrow passage to a little courtyard where a lemon tree luxuriated in the sunlight. As we got to know our way better through the Plaka, clustered around the northern and eastern slopes of the Acropolis, we came to love its labyrinth of narrow streets of humble white houses, some grubby, punctuated by the odd tired neoclassical façade. Metres deep under it (for the detritus of centuries has made the ground higher, as in all ancient towns), lie the residential areas of really ancient Athens. In 1884 a useful fire burned down much of the Plaka neighbourhood, a calamity which gave people the chance to excavate in the Roman Market and Hadrian's Library. (The homeless were perhaps not so enthusiastic.) When we first went, the edges of the Plaka were being nibbled by opportunist archaeologists, for there is tourist money in antiquities. Our money too; for the museum in the (reconstructed) Stoa of Attalus in the Agora delighted both of us with the intimacy of the lives glimpsed: a child's potty; the indispensable pots; a quern; a child's toy.

Under the centuries of Turkish rule after Byzantium fell in 1453, Plaka was the Turkish quarter, and the seat of the Turkish Voevod (Governor). The Turks did nothing very much, and did it very well. They did not build a lot, but neither did they pull down very much. True, they might burn the occasional marble statue for quick lime, or build its bulk into a new wall round a garden or field, but wholesale destruction was just too much bother. They turned the Church of the Blessed Virgin Theotokos which had been the Parthenon into a mosque and added a discordant minaret to its lovely proportions. Later, they put that gunpowder in it. But the wholesale vandalism of their modern co-religionists in the Taliban and Islamic State would have been unimaginable. Indeed, such a nihilistic ideology was unimaginable to us and to anyone else at that time when we had so much to learn, and feel.

The place, Turkish, Roman, Hellenistic, Attic, Archaic – it was all so overwhelmingly, seductively, *old*. Our vision of it was still planar, though: stereoscopy (if it ever fully comes) was years away. But we felt people: as we walked on the shady side of the little street, past a high windowless wall, inside the house we heard a child being scolded when it should have been taking its siesta. Jenny said to me, 'A child cried like that here 25 centuries ago.' We both thought of the ancient clay potty we had seen that morning in the museum, and the clay horse toy, and hoped that that modern child had toys too.

Evening, in the theatre of Dionysus. The sun was westering, low over Piraeus. Soon the sun was below the horizon and the shadows were rising The sky was still bright. Hesperus shone gladly alone in the bright western sunset sky. *Kalispera...* The stones felt hot to the touch, pleasant in the cooling evening. Columnar cypresses on the slope behind were black in the failing light. The cicadas were deafening. Yet sometimes suddenly all together they come to a moment's stop, and the silence is painful with expectation. Then first one, then all resume. I imagined naively the marble seats with the names of the archons carved in them went back to the time of Sophocles – whom I already loved with an uncritical and un-nuanced delight – and that what I was seeing had somehow leapfrogged the Roman centuries. To be sure, they probably did not change its layout that much, and on this spot indeed the play contests had been held during the great festivals – the Greater Dionysia in March, the Panathenaea in June, the Lenaea, Dionysus' lesser festival, in January. But it is now known that the earliest theatres were wooden, even temporary, that they lasted into the third century and that, far from *le tout* Athens sitting on pale marble in the clear Attic sunlight of democratic courtesy listening to Sophocles and Euripides, Aeschylus and Aristophanes, the audience was restricted and perhaps even quite small. But it pleased me then to imagine the gods coming and sitting in the front row in effigy; incense was burned before them; the stories of the doings of men and gods by the miracle of narrative addressed the eternal issues of justice, and law, and duty, and honour, and love that humans always face, and also – just as Elizabethan and Jacobean history plays did – the pressing political and moral controversies of the moment. I think I knew even then, as I sat where the archon sat, that Sophocles' *Antigone* of 428BC was highly topical, given that the Assembly had just forbidden the giving of decent burial to those who had fought against the state. If I did not, I did soon after – it is so difficult to remember old ignorance. It was all rather like being slowly woken up, like something thawing.

★

The Lykabettos hill is a lump of Cretaceous limestone which Athene is supposed to have dropped as she was bringing stone from Pallene for the construction of the Acropolis. She was furious after the box holding the infant Erichthonius was opened; goddesses don't stamp their feet, but do more significant things. On the top is the modern St George's Chapel. I like St George: the Crusaders brought back his cult to England, and made him the patron saint in succession to St Edmund King and Martyr. He does a good line in defeating dragons and rescuing helpless maidens, which is what Romance heroes ought to do. But his legend is extraordinarily like the story of Perseus and Andromeda: one of those story templates that seem to underlie stories across the world.

It had been a hot day, again, and we had climbed up in the later afternoon. Jenny was wearing a skirt as we knew that it was good manners in Greece to do so if you were going into a church, but she had bare arms and her copious hair needed no hat. As we made to go into the chapel, an arm stopped her: she had to cover up or not enter. Of course the verger or whatever was only doing what was expected, but it brought us up with a jolt to realise that what was tolerable in England might be impolite or worse in a country we thought we understood. Disconsolately, neither of us went in. At least there was the view. I tried to tell Jenny the story of St George as I remembered it from *The Golden Legend,* and having got that one over, was just starting on Athene and her outbreak of temper, when she turned to me and said, 'Don't you ever stop talking? Just look.' I think she must have been upset about the verger. But she was right: it was a good place to follow the brightening path to the sunset on the distant sea.

★

I always found it hard to realise that when St Paul came to Athens, the time of Pericles and Aspasia, Themistocles and Aristides, the time of Plato and Aristotle, the disasters of the Peloponnesian War – the tragedy of the Syracuse expedition, the muffed chance of peace after Sphacteria – were as distant from men and their lips as are from us the Wars of the Roses and what Tennyson called 'the spacious times of great Elizabeth': and perhaps as mythologised. The last sparks of Greek independence had been snuffed out by Rome's legions under the praetor Lucius Mummius at Corinth in 146 BC. It was not pretty. He slaughtered all the men of Corinth, sold the women and children into slavery, and shipped all the statues, paintings and works of art in that rich and beautiful city to Rome. Corinth was burned.[1] Mummius' cruelty, by no means characteristic of him, Theodor Mommsen suggested, was instigated by the Roman Senate, prompted by a mercantile party eager to destroy a serious commercial rival at one of the nodal points of trade. (Just so, the War of Troy may have been as much about trade and control of routes as it was about a flighty Spartan lady. Cygnificantly, neither daughter of Leda came to much good.)

Romanised and Roman gentlemen of good birth, or means, or both, finished their education in Athens, in a town that once held the gorgeous East in fee, and was now politically nothing: as Cicero did. (I suppose our visit was a wraith of the same impulse for 'improvement', for drinking at ancient wells.) Some say Virgil travelled there about 19 BC to revise the *Aeneid* – the beginning of his last journey, for he died of fever on the way home. Julius Caesar began the new Agora, Augustus completed it. Nero, a cultured enough monarch and a great if somewhat pyromaniac builder, was benevolent; Hadrian gave a fine library. Horace remarked *'Graecia capta ferum victorem cepit'* – as Alexander Pope rendered it after the Peace of Utrecht in 1713, in one of his witty *Imitations of Horace*, 'We conquer'd France, but felt our Captive's charms;/ Her Arts victorious triumph'd o'er our Arms'.

St Paul, Roman citizen born himself, would have admired, and walked in, the Roman Agora. Like us, he would have walked past the elegant octagonal horologion, the Tower of the Winds, built by Andronicus of Cyrrhus in 50 BC. Its elegant beauty drew us both, and to our credit we did find out about it the next day by borrowing (politely) a guidebook we saw someone was reading at the next table in the taverna. Inside it had a clepsydra or water clock, fed by water from the Acropolis: St Paul, unlike us in our ignorance, would have known instantly what it was and was for. (Unlike us, as an educated man he would have spoken the Greek that was the *lingua franca* of the whole Mediterranean world: he seems to know his Euripides, if 1. *Corinthians* 15. 33 is anything to go by, and he can hardly have escaped Homer.) Then the Tower of the Winds became the bell tower of an Orthodox church, which then, under the Turks, was used by the Mevlevi Dervishes. I like to think of that strange history, of the dervishes in their whirling, trance-inducing dance imitating the motions of the stars beneath a tower that measured the span of man's days. And even then, in my salad days, I liked to think that my eyes had looked at what Paul saw: I do not know why.

Paul's Athens was not even capital of the senatorial province of Achaia. The port of Piraeus had silted up; trade was centred on Patras, or Corinth (the capital), or Nicopolis. Athens had to be content with being the intellectual centre by virtue of her past. Athene Promachos still towered over the city, but there was neither state nor commerce to defend. The city gave herself the airs of greatness, but no longer created anything: she merely criticised. She no longer did anything, but read her own history instead. Her academies and streets buzzed with rich youths discussing just about every General Theory of Everything that was on offer. They visited and took part in the multiplying festivals, and commemorations of battles like Marathon or Salamis, and anniversaries of famous men like Socrates and Plato. And doubtless the common folk just went on living and partly living, providing the food and services tourists need, acting as guides to the monuments, on which the visitors scratched their names for us to read twenty centuries later. To judge from Philostratus' life of the neo-Pythagorean philosopher Apollonius of Tyana, a near contemporary of St Paul, the city was full of fast living, frivolous dissipation and intellectual excitement: any religion or philosophy, or none, was on offer.

It is most unlikely that a cultured man like St Paul did not do the tourist thing in this famous city. *Acts* certainly says he went daily to the markets, and disputed in the Jewish synagogues and with the Epicurean philosophers and the Stoics – then the two most fashionable philosophies. He seems actually to have been invited (*Acts* 17.19) to speak in the Court of Areopagus. Noting the significance of the Athenian altar 'To the Unknown God,' standing in the midst of the Areopagus, he opened splendidly: 'Men of Athens, I perceive that in every way you are very religious. For as I passed along and observed the objects of your worship, I found also an altar with this inscription, "To the unknown god." What therefore you worship as unknown, this I proclaim to you...' He plays it very well, with his keen sense of his audience, making no mystifying reference to the Scriptures of those strange people, the Jews, and all goes well until he comes to the idea of the Resurrection and the Last Judgement. He is then interrupted – and what one would give to know exactly what was meant when someone said, 'We will hear thee again on this matter.' Serious – they mean it? Courteous dismissal of a crank? Amused tolerance?[2] Sitting there, on the bare limestone Hill of Ares, god of War, where there is so little now to take you back to that hill's history, we were not, yet, thinking of St Paul. Both of us knew he had been there: but the outline was not yet coloured in, and our imaginations were full of meze, tomato salad, *dolmades* (perhaps), with retsina, and ouzo to follow. And getting out of Athens to the places of the nymphs and satyrs. If they were still there...

★

We were given a lift from the outskirts of Athens by a very courteous, educated, sophisticated businessman with impeccable English. Conversation was of this and that, as it is among people who are well disposed to, but hardly know, each other. In time it turned to myth, as it would with someone as obsessed as I with things ancient. He – I wish I could remember his name – told me that in parts of rural Greece, despite television and relatives in America, people throw corn out three times a years to placate 'the monster. I have been told he has cloven feet. They call him Pan.' Encouraged, I mentioned the old stories of the oreads and dryads and naiads, the spirits of hill and wood and water. I made the facile link to animism – I had just read Frazer's *Golden Bough*, not knowing how dated it already was, and thought I understood all mysteries. Our driver said nothing. I carried on, blundering, and finally asked a direct question. 'Do people still believe in the nymphs – I mean in the country, of course?' He seemed uneasy. 'Some do.' 'What do *you* think?' 'I don't know... once, late evening, in the woods in Sparta...I saw something strange moving in the olives... I don't know, I can't be sure.'

There was a silence, except for the car engine, and a gear change.

★

We found our way to Nauplion: someone said it was worth it, and we wanted to go eventually to Epidauros, so it seemed a sensible idea. It was dark when we were decanted from the back of the friendly lorry into the main street. We ate, somewhere, but were too tired to do more than think about a place, any place, to unroll our sleeping bags. There seemed to be a dark area, and trees, just a little steeply uphill from the street, and we thought, well, it's dark, nobody will see us, so we scrambled about thirty yards up into the little wood, found a more or less level bit of ground, and unrolled out bags. We were asleep almost immediately. I woke once when something ran across my face, to see the bright stars burning above the filigree of branches. And went to sleep again.

But we had not gone far enough. People get up early to avoid the heat of the day, as they always did in the South. At pretty soon after first light I woke to the noise of many voices, and realised that we had collected a sizeable group of curious spectators who had gathered on the street below us. I sat up, and said, politely, 'Kalimera'. 'Kalimera', came back the chorused reply, which stirred the other sleeping bag into life. With as much dignity as we could muster, we got out of our bags – fortunately we had not undressed – and made our way down to the throng. On the whole it was well disposed: we were bought thick sweet coffee. A few older women, in black, with their heads bound in those black kerchiefs that seemed so much a part of middle-aged femininity in the South, pursed their lips and shook their heads. One crossed herself in what we had realised already was the Greek way – right to left, not the Latin way. The embarrassment passed.

Nauplion ought to have been interesting enough: after all, it was the first capital of Greece after the War of Independence. Even we, uncouth and uncultured as I now see we were, could see that it had had some style. For it had been a favourite haunt of nineteenth century fashionable Greek society. But I suppose with the sort of tunnel vision to which the half educated young can so easily fall prey, anything that was not 'Classical' was therefore uninteresting and not worth notice.[3] Yet we ought to have at least looked at the spectacular Venetian fortress of Palamidi crowning the hill. But that was way out of our ken then, and we would have found it as boring as I do when I set down bald facts in the note you have just passed. It would have been all 'too modern' anyway. But what you come to know later does affect your memory of the earlier, like reading a book again which you thought you knew... coming to a place you knew, and knowing it for the first time.

We stayed only a couple of nights. We did not again make the same mistake as on the first night, but by day found our way over the ridge to a beach on the other side, and memorised the way so we could do it in near dark. We did. Deserted, level, with the sea gently breaking in the moonlight a few yards away. Bliss. But next morning we were woken by voices... this time it was women, black clad, black stockinged, black head-scarved, who averted their gaze as they passed us, and then walked straight into the sea, standing there up to their ample breasts in the wavelets. It was an unexpected way of having a bath, but that is what I think they were doing. And as Jenny said, 'When the sun gets up they will soon dry off.'

A bus would take us to Epidauros. To see that theatre was one of the reasons why we had come to this part of Greece. Looking back, I suppose that what we were doing was constructing our own Greece: putting flesh on the bones of our (too sketchy but passionately lapped up) education, which told us what was 'important' to see, and blinded us to the actuality of the present. For there was much to see in Nauplion, and elsewhere, that our callowness simply ignored because it was not old enough.

There is an enormous and attentive, remembered, emptiness of a Greek theatre in the early morning, before anyone is about and the sun has still to warm the stones. The only chorus is the frogs in the nearby marsh. They synchronise: they start, first one, who must be the protagonist, then all together, arrhythmic, cretic, and the slightest noise from other new actors on their stage stops them in their start. Βρεκεκεκὲξ κοὰξ κοάξ, Brek kek... So we duly tried the theatre's acoustics — marvellous, and a constant reminder to my sourer, older, self of how much architects have forgotten.

★

You can't get the stories out of your head. Both of us had been to primary and grammar schools where the Greek Myths and the Greek Heroes had been part of the diet. Jenny had a School Prize ('for Progress') of Grueber's *Myths of Greece and Rome*; both us had recently read Graves' *The Greek Myths* and *The White Goddess* (as a bedside book!) with much enthusiasm and little critical sense. Neither did us much harm, and we were consciously and subconsciously throughout our journey matching place to story and myth and *vice versa*. Our present was coloured by stories of long ago in someone else's words.

The Argolid, the plains where Homer's horse-taming Argives grazed their sheep and built their citadel... A bronze helmet in the Argos museum had, I thought, a crest of a horseshoe. (In fact, it is the clamp that would have held the sort of nodding plume that terrified little Astyanax as Hector his father bent over to kiss him... 'He stretched his arms towards his child, but the boy cried, and shrank into his nurse's bosom, scared at the sight of his father's armour, and at the horse-hair plume that nodded fiercely from his helmet. His father and mother laughed to see him, but Hector took the helmet from his head and laid it all gleaming upon the ground...') Here, perhaps, the House of Atreus honoured its entail of hatred and crime begun by Tantalus; here, perhaps Thyestes ate all his children, whom brother Atreus had served up to him as a stew... save the one who avenged him and gave another twist to the spiral of horror. Here, perhaps, Helen... but her name means simply 'the Greek woman', so perhaps she never existed, but – as some dour scholars argue – symbolises Greek trade with the Black Sea which Troy commandeered. Perhaps. (Yet Hector of the shining helmet and Andromache of the white arms and their little Astyanax live in my memory.) But that story of the bitter seed of Pelops, of revenge plucking on revenge, in an endless progress of terrible justice, is just too like what humans do, still do, and always have done to each other to dismiss as simply euhemerist. No wonder it was one of the cores of the heritage of story that was played out years on years in the theatres of Athens. Justice is one of the things humans rightly desire, demand: but it leaves no room for mercy, forgiveness, reconciliation. An endless exchange of eyes and teeth, stretching to the end of time, each exchange making the next the more inevitable. Mix male honour in for a truly hellish brew.

But Athene's wisdom found a way of quieting the chthonic spirits of hearth and home, of blood and *oikos*, of giving them their due but making them know their place in a polity where the greater good of the greater number might demand the sacrifice of the personal debt. But do they go quiet for ever? Is Clytemnestra never to be revenged, the matricide never to be punished? We shall find out.

★

I don't think I can recall much of those days of crossing the quiet miles between Argos, and Tripolis – I know we must have gone there, but I remember nothing about it – and Sparta. Somewhere on that road I shared a piece of bread with a friendly brown dog. Somewhere else by a cold and busy stream there were lemons growing, golden, luminous in the thick dark foliage. Yet somewhere else I lay full length in the shade and watched a grasshopper at the edge of the sunlight, rubbing his gantry legs against his wing cases. When Jenny sat up and spoke he (she?) released his springs and left us. The road was quiet, and the tarmac hot to our feet.

But one thing I do remember: and I did not a minute ago. (What else might come back if I let it?) It was in Tripolis. We were standing by a petrol pump. A Citroën 2CV was being filled up – not that those cars took very much. Quite suddenly I felt almost sick, dizzy. Then I saw that the car was bouncing up and down on that famed Citroën suspension. '*Seismos*!' the driver said, patently alarmed, and it needed no translator to tell us that word meant 'earthquake'. The earth was moving, as we could feel: the water in a nearby bucket was sloshing about. It was curiously interesting. The tremor passed, and did not return. The driver finished filling his now quiet car, and put the pump nozzle back in its holster. He shrugged. 'It happens. We get them from time to time.' Too well I knew that, having seen so many of the earthquake-tumbled columns of temples already. What none of us there, then, could know was that that twitch of the earth's skin, like the twitch of a horse's withers when a fly settles on it, miles away was much more serious, a paroxysm of faults and planes being rearranged, and devil take anyone or any city that was about when Gaia did a real shudder. In Asia Minor the death toll was large. And the two plates – but nobody knew about tectonic plates then, for Wegener was quite discredited – found a new equilibrium. A temporary one.

We got a lift, I now remember, in that little grey 2CV, with its black canvas roof rolled back. Our rucksacks were on our knees, and the car leaned to one side, and the driver asked me by gesture to sit in the excruciating middle of the two back canvas sling seats to balance it. I had always wanted a 2CV ever since, a few years earlier, François and André and Nicole and I had crossed the Pyrenees in one. And this one took us to Sparta, in appropriate discomfort.

The Eurotas, the river of Sparta, flowed swift and cold from the high hills. Even though the summer was getting late, there was still plenty of water, and in deep winter the stream would be dark and turbulent. Until we damp northerners see the summer aridity of the South, I don't think we realise how sacred water was to the ancients, how the spring welling up from the rock was clearly holy. Of course the nymphs should be honoured, propitiated even, for without their miracle of water the land dies.

Sparta: the street names showed a certain civic pride.
They led into an ever more complicated story. There was
a Helen Street, of course, and a Menelaus street. (One
goes roughly north-south, the other east-west: quite
appropriate, really.) Helen's patron, Aphrodite, who
used her to bribe Paris to give her the Golden Apple
of Discord, has a mention. (And so the Trojan War
started.) There is a street named after Helen's brothers,
the Dioscuri twins Castor and Pollux, masters of horses
and boxing and whose names the ship bore that took St
Paul on his journey to Rome. There is an Iliad Street.
Of course there had to be a Thermopylae Street, and a
Leonidas Street. There is a broad thoroughfare named
after Lycurgus the lawgiver, and another after Heracles.
But nothing in this rather dull huddle of low buildings
suggested the famed hardness of the Spartan culture,
the subjugation of the Helots, the city that had sent its
best men to fight the Persians – 'Come home with your
shield, or on it,' Spartan mothers said to their sons as they
sent them to battle – at the Pass of the Hot Springs north
of Thebes. The 300 had been outflanked. In his Book 7,
Herodotus, the 'father of history', says that Dienekes the
Spartan, the bravest of the brave, 'as men report, uttered
this saying before they engaged battle with the Medes:
being informed by one of the men of Trachis that when
the Barbarians fired their arrows they darkened the light
of the sun, so great was the number of their host, he was
not dismayed by this, but making but small account of
the number of the Medes, he said that their guest from

Trachis brought them very good news, for if the Medes obscured the light of the sun, the battle against them would be in the shade and not in the sun.' (At school a gifted Latin master had had me translate an account of the battle of Thermopylae from English into Latin 'in the style of Livy, by Monday, please.')

I know now we did not 'do' Sparta properly, and even then we sensed that there was something missing as we turned our backs on fast flowing Eurotas and set our faces to Mistras. A man we met in Athens said it was worth it – he spoke rapid French, '*Il vous faut absolument que vous y alliez, le berceau de la Grèce libre*' – and he seemed to know what he was talking about, but did not say why, and we did not know enough to ask.

So, being obedient by nature, off we went, trudging with our rucksacks along the hot road to the hills. We found a small hotel that gave us a room overlooking a little square with a big plane tree. Odd how you remember things, what you remember... sunlight streaming through the slatted shutters the next morning, a praying mantis motionless on the wall. (I told Jenny that ideas like that insect seemed to be meditating did not become her.) Breakfast outside the hotel in the sunlight, getting strong now. We sat on iron chairs with slatted wooden seats, at a table with a slatted wooden top. Breakfast was cold clear water – they seemed proud of their water, '*kali nero*' – and thick sweet coffee from a copper pan, and black bread and a dish of honey flooding over slices of sweet white butter. I can taste it now. It was good, and old women in black bowed and said '*kalimera*' as they went past. So we had another coffee, then reluctantly packed our bags, paid the small sum we owed, and set off to the nearest church in the ruined town. It had been deserted by those inhabitants who had survived Ibrahim Pasha's terrible revenge on the insurgents in 1825. That man who sent us there had told us that, but we only had a vague idea who Ibrahim Pasha was: we knew he must be something to do with the attempt to suppress the Greek War of Independence, but then we were both a bit hazy on that too, apart from knowing that Byron died at Missolonghi. We had met, after all, several men named after him.

The ruins smelt hot – and the heat of the day was not yet at its fiercest – and the grasshoppers were fiddling away, ignoring an anthill at the side of the road where exemplary diligence was obvious. I called Jenny over to watch one ant taking a minute piece of leaf into the hill, kindly pointing out that the load to body weight ratio was far worse for the ant than for us with our rucksacks. That fell on deaf ears.

Mistra had some seven churches (as many as Asia in *Revelations,* I thought: my grandfather's research had been on them, but he died before completing it. I never knew him.) The dedications – Holy Wisdom, St Demetrius, Holy Spirit, Blessed Mary Leader of the Way, and so on –

we only found out later. We did not explore them all, and we had no idea of their chronology. We did know that the town was not older than the 1200s, though, that the Franks had built it, and that then the Byzantines had made it the capital of the Despotate of the Morea – funny how words like 'tyrant' and 'despot' in Greek carry no bad sense – and that the oldest church, Agios Dimitrios, was about 1270. Our informative and eager acquaintance had told us. The one we loved on sight was Panagia Perivleptos, almost hanging from the rocks amid thick trees. Even we could see that the (14th century) monastery had some spectacular frescoes. Just uphill was Panagia Pantanassa, a hotchpotch of various styles but again with excellent frescoes. The great Mary Theotokos in the Pantanassa, holding Her Son and gazing out from the apsidal vault on those who came to her church, drew us into silence. And everywhere that remarkable architectural synthesis of circular drum and dome supported on squinches over the square or Greek cross of the ground plan – I had done my homework about that! – called one into that harmony of shape and proportion where awe, a silence of the mind, is the only response. If you will be still and not talk too much...

We passed on. It had been a beautiful place, but we had not been fully awake enough to realise what we were seeing: reading the iconography of even the Western tradition with any confidence was years in the future. Years, many years, later, as I had come to know about the Council of

Florence in the 1430s which so nearly healed the breach
between the Latin and Greek Churches, I sat for hours
in the chapel of the Palazzo Medici-Riccardi in Florence
gazing at Benozzo Gozzoli's Fresco of the Coming
of the Magi. The Kings and the train have the faces of
real people, of the Greek Emperor John Palaeologos, of
assorted Medicis (including the young Lorenzo before he
became, some said, Magnificent), of the painter himself,
of Holy Roman Emperor Sigismund – who betrayed the
trust of John Huss – and I was able by then to wonder
which was Bessarion, which was the Neoplatonist Giorgos
Gemistos Plethon, who had seen the swallows flickering
over the domes of Mistra for so many years. Plethon and
others who worked here, one of the great centres of late
Byzantine scholarship and power, had no little effect
on what we have come to call the Italian Renaissance –
indeed, it was Plethon who introduced Plato's thought
to Florentine scholars he met at the Council, and the
result was the founding of the Platonic Academy and the
changing of European thought. They would have prayed
and contemplated under those frescos, have known the
church named of the Holy Wisdom who, according to
the *Wisdom of Solomon*, 'ordered all things by number,
proportion and weight.' With that idea ingrained in
their very soul they would have seen shape and form and
proportion – in building, in art, in music, in poetry –
quite differently to us. A world of transcendence. The
big stern eyes of the Byzantine style, so ancient and
tenacious a tradition, looked down on many lives of

learned and holy men as well as of many average sinners. In the winter they would have warmed their cells with little braziers of olive stones, which slowly turned into grey ash with not a spot of red seen, and would have been glad of the rough black wool of their habits. They would have chanted their offices in that ancient music that still frames the Greek services even far from Greece in space and them in time: and which one day I would hear in far away Bucharest. Now – or rather when we went – the place is silent, save for the *tsitsikoi*, and over roofless halls the swallows describe their rapid gyres in the summer sky and the geckos, their forefeet spread, tails braced against the stone of the walls, contemplate whatever it is geckos contemplate.

And the Turks... Mehmet II took Mistra in 1460, seven years after he took Constantinople. The Venetians had it from 1687 to 1715, the Russians – trying to liberate Greece from the Turks – took it over in 1770, but the Turks soon had it back. Ibrahim Pasha razed it in 1825. The old olives have seen much. And while the great ones quarrel and kill, poor folk try to tend their sheep and goats and dress their vines and gather their olives, Athene's gift. But nobody listens to their voices.

★

At Pylos, once, old Nestor lived. Or so Homer says, and the Greeks always believed him, or said they did. But what

now goes by the name of Pylos is not where Homer's
Gerenian horseman had his *megaron* and welcomed
Telemachos son of tricksy – how else do you translate
polytropon? – Odysseus. It has an interesting enough
history, being at the entrance to the superb natural
harbour of the bay closed by the long island of Sphacteria.
There the Athenians won the upper hand in 425 over
Sparta, and could have made peace with magnanimity.
But did not, like so many before and since, and were in
the end destroyed by their own pride. The Venetians, of
course, held it for a time, and called it Navarino. In 1827
the windows of the little whitewashed town watched
the Ottoman armada sent to squash the Greek rebellion
humbled by the combined forces of Britain, France and
Russia. Those few with glass shook with the shock of
the broadsides reflected off the hills, and Ibrahim Pasha
was forced to withdraw from the whole Peloponnese. It
is a more peaceable place now, and keeps its memories
of Cities and Thrones and Powers to itself. Summer
yachts with no apparent evil intent crowd the harbour.
As they always have done, the migrating birds in their
thousands touch down gratefully on the lagoons of the
Gialova wetland, their last stop before Africa. It is some
miles away where Nestor (perhaps) was, a knoll on that
harsh, hot, reddish soil, where the absence of trees is ill
compensated by a profusion of sage, broom, cistus, and
other shrubs which start from the innumerable cavities of
the limestone. In the ruins of a great – well, is it a palace,
or an administrative centre like the Council Offices, or

what we would call a church, or all three and more? – were found the tablets with the Linear B writing. They record not great poetry, but the things that daily matter like laundry lists and tax returns and tributes owed: and those dull details may be why writing needed to be invented.

Her father had taken her there. She was young, but not too young to know her Homer and to be half in love with wise Nestor. Across strange seas and centuries her ancestry had brought her to this spot: Sephardim fleeing Spain; prosperous German Jewish intellectuals; a boy just in his teens on the *Kindertransport* saying goodbye to his schoolfriend who could not leave Hitler's Germany because his family knew nobody in the West; a Russian engineer building a railway across the steppes of Asia, trapped with his family in the utter East by Revolution and civil war; a grandmother, graduate in Materials Science of Moscow University under the Czars – imagine that in England in the 1890s! – escaping across the frozen Amur. And here she is: her parents, both academics, have brought their children back to Greece, to the ancient wellsprings of that intellectual life they lead, which is their prop and stay making sense of the turbulence their families have suffered, to stand on this sunny hillside scattered with small stones and loaded with memories for the few who care. Voices of memory in the wind. A destination; also a point of departure, an in-between place. She bends down, and in the dazzling light picks up a shell (she thinks) from the ground where her Nestor (perhaps) trod. But did not Homer call Pylos 'sandy', and was it not by the sea? But she can see the sea is miles away. She looks at what she holds: she sees it is not a shell, but a fossil shellfish that once lived its slow life in lime-rich waters of a forgotten time. She lifts her eyes to the deep blue of the now distant sea, silent, time stands still. Or she stands outside it for an instant. This is her Darwin moment, before she knew about Darwin and his marine fossil found high in the Andes. She closes her hand on the precious fossil: that stone will never leave her until she gives it to her husband.

Hanc petram... That was my Rosanna Petra, Heaven's last best gift to my old age. That is her memory, and my memory of Pylos can never be the same again for me.

★

I met a man from Crete, who told me all Cretans were liars. That sort of logical Möbius band always amuses me. The mainland was hot. 'Go to an island,' they said. Crete was an island. So we went. (Why Crete? it was the first ferry we came to in Piraeus. Vaguely I remembered that Zeus carried off Europa to Crete, and had his way with her.) But a hot wind from Africa made Crete very hot. 'Go to the mainland', they said. So we stayed put, and panted in the shade in the heat of the day.

The boat came in at Souda. An American warship was in town, and the cafés were full of sailors in white ducks being loud and good tempered in lilting accents from south of the Mason-Dixon line. I love that sound. A couple of officers bought us a couple of coffees with the usual glass of cold water, before draining their own coffees and standing up. A big white Dodge pickup stood nearby. 'We're going back to the ship in that old cotton-pickin' truck, get some real coffee. See y'all.' And they were off. So were we. We walked miles along the coast, the road quiet save for the odd three-wheeled Piaggio Ape struggling noisily with the inclines. As it neared noon, the sun got hotter, the reflection off the sea to our left yet more dazzling. We could see a clump of big trees ahead. 'We stop there,' I said. 'Lunch.' (We had bread and cheese.) But as we reached the trees, we realised the expected idyll of a *déjeuner sur l'herbe* was off: they shaded a farm, and a family party was going on. Children in various stages of dirt, a teenage girl with flashing black eyes, a goat, a couple of sheep, a bored dog scratching and then sighing deeply when he realised we were not very exciting, grandmother (all in black), mutton chop whiskered grandfather in those baggy black Cretan trousers and high boots that then were still common garb, and father and mother. And Uncle, in rope sandals and trousers and grubby singlet over his large belly, who called out to us in English, with a strong American accent, 'You English! Come! Drink with us! Eat with me! I have come home, after many years, to the house where I was born! I was New York taxi driver! I shall never go away again!'

So we did, under the palmate leaves of the planes kneading the sunlight into shifting patterns on the dry brown ground. We sat, and tried to talk in Greek, and later went down to the shore and swam with our new friends, (grandmother just walking in as she was), and as the sun was westering began to make moves to leave: miles to go before we slept. I stood up, picked up my rucksack, and held Jenny's for her to slip her shoulders into. 'No!' said Odysseus the returned traveller, determined and imperative as ever. 'NO walking! She is tired! There is a bus! I make it stop here!' And he did. He heard it chugging up the hill, and went and stood in the middle of the road. He knew the driver. Thirty years earlier they had been neighbours. 'They go to Georgioupolis! You take them! You do not charge them!'

He had his way. We could not argue. We had no idea why he was sending us to Georgioupolis. We had never heard of the place. (Nor had anyone else, then.) We inserted ourselves into the hot rummage of bags and people, found a couple of seats, and waved goodbye. Bless them, they had kept up, with a vengeance, the ancient tradition of welcoming the traveller, no questions asked. That was Platanoi, the place of the plane trees. A place in-between, a stage on a journey. A golden memory, ever blessed.

★

As afternoon deepened the golden of the light, the bus arrived in a dusty square in a huddle of a few houses. 'Georgioupolis', the driver said. So we got off; a woman got on with a couple of brown hens held upside down by their tied feet. Their wings hung open: it must be tiring to keep your wings by your sides when all your muscles are working in the wrong direction. They craned their necks to try to see things the right way up. The bus engine roared (if that is not flattering it), and off it went, leaving a smell of diesel briefly on the wind off the sea. Nobody seemed to be about. We looked at each other. Between two houses we could see the sea and a little white church at the end of a mole. So there must be a beach, and we could sleep on the beach. But what about food and drink? There was clearly no shop of any kind.

We wandered down towards the church, and realised that the mole ran alongside a sweet river on one side and on the other gave onto a vast expanse of beach, stretching as far as the eye could see. Quite, quite empty. A little further, and round a corner we heard a radio playing: it was the summer of Mikis Theodorakis' *'Ta Paideia tou Piraea'*, *aka* 'Never on Sunday', and Merlina Mercouri's dark red velvet voice tempted us into a little *kapheneion*. Two men stopped playing cards as we entered. *'Kalispera'*, I ventured. Silence. We dropped our packs, and sought a couple of chairs. The men's eyes followed us. Then one caught sight of the Union Flag sewn onto mine, and immediately smiles broke out. 'Not German! English!

Welcome! Drink with us!' And one clapped his hands and called, 'Phoebe! *Xenoi*! Guests!' A curtain parted, and out came Phoebe, old and bent, her hair bound in a black kerchief. I stood up and offered her a hand. She took it, and attempted what might have been a curtsey. Jenny shook hands too: all was smiles.

We found they could give us a room, two iron bedsteads on a red-tiled floor, giving onto the flat roof, in sight and sound of the wind scuffling the eucalyptus trees bordering the river. (That Antipodean species makes a very useful windbreak if you can put up with a permanent smell of cough sweets.) They could offer food: bread, wine, water, and, since the hens were laying, an omelette, and tomato salad. Giorgios was going fishing in the morning: there might be fish tomorrow. We ate: a full moon rose, shining straight into our uncurtained room. Phoebe had blessed us and we slept a long and dreamless sleep.

Morning broke. We had hardly needed our sleeping bags, and now the sun was seeking us out as Helios, so Homer says, had sought out Ares and Aphrodite. People were already astir. Round the corner someone was hammering. Hens were clucking and scratching in the dust. A boat engine started up. And then, across the river, some goats – perhaps half a dozen. Now, I have a soft spot for goats, and they can be delicious too. But my friendliness to individuals is moderated by what I know the species did to the landscape of the Mediterranean. And we were about to get a startling example of that. For there was a youthful eucalyptus growing just over the river, abut ten or twelve feet high. The leader of the goats came to it, and after a nuzzling sniff or two stood on his hind legs and tore off a mouthful of leaves, and stood there chomping them with as much delight as a goat chewing eucalyptus might be expected to show. (The combination of smells must be interesting.) The others gathered round, and one grabbed a leaf that stuck out of the side of Goat No 1's mouth. Terrible manners... and this was the cue for them all to get stuck in. They were all on their hind legs, then they started chewing off the bark, then the wood itself, until in half an hour the tree was barkless, and about three ragged feet high. The goats moved on. Imagine that across the hills and valleys, each small tree of what could have been the forest of the future, where might roam the descendants of the Calydonian Boar or the Nemean Lion, masticated into goat dung. And the soil, no longer held by the networks of roots, washes away in the storms of winter.

Giorgios was lucky: there were fish. That night we had bread and retsina and fish stew, a massive fish stew, the only dish on offer, which others in the little village came to enjoy too. Nothing was wasted: the heads and livers went in too. Jenny took a spoonful — it was substantial, and indeed delicious — and then paused. For, white and round as dried peas, on her spoon, the cooked eyes challenged her.

In an older time, the challenge might have been greater. For the innards would have been fermented into *garum,* a condiment used all over the ancient world. It was exported in amphorae as far as Britannia and the lands beyond the north wind. Sometimes the amphorae were stamped, saying this was the real thing from the right place, and Beware Of Imitations.

The curve of the beach extended for miles. Nobody. Not even a hut in sight. Further along, another little river, falling from the high hills that lay to the south, hurried across the strand to join its fresh water to the salt, and where it stalled in the pool before the little bar, a stand of rushes grew. We swam, and lazed, and swam again. I came out of the sea, tired at last, just where the river released its sweet water into the salt, my legs astride the thermocline. An ideal place, in ancient times, to do the washing. But there was no Nausicaa to take me home to her father. Jenny and I lay on the hot sand, our feet tickled by the coolness of the larger wavelets that reached us. The sun was drying the salt Mediterranean into crystals on our bodies. Her lips were salt. Impatiently, she squirmed off her bikini and raised her knees. The oleanders at the edge of the sand tossed their heads in the breeze off the sea. The reeds whispered to each other their ancient secret. An age of gold.

'Come back one day,' said slow Phoebe – for her slowness, between ourselves we nicknamed her Lightning. Fish-smelling Giorgios wiped his hand on his singlet before he embraced Jenny. We left on the odorous bus to Rethymnon. We did, indeed, go back. But that is another story.

★

They did not like Germans then in Crete. Some of the men in their forties and fifties had fought with the partisans; the women remembered the privations of war, the civilian suffering of what we have come comfortingly to call, as if it did not mean blood and death and destruction of man and innocent beast, 'collateral damage'. (So that's all right, then.) We were often mistaken for German, and only when we spoke did the deep freeze thaw.

When we hitchhiked, I carried a piece of cardboard with 'ΑΓΓΛΟΙ' – English – on it, and made sure, if we were walking, that I was on the outside so my Union Flag could be seen by motorists. It worked, more or less. We got a lift with a couple of friendly farmers, brothers, in their lorry. They had been to Souda, and were going back over the mountains, by one of the high passes, to their farm, near Timbaki in the south. We had not intended to go that way, but it seemed too good a chance to miss, so we piled in to the empty back.

Soon, as the lorry climbed up from the sea and the road got steeper, the tarmac ran out. It was now a limestone track, and dust rose in a great plume behind us with the wind of our passing. As the lorry slowed to take a sharp bend, the plume was no longer a plume but a cloud, and soon our packs and ourselves were covered in a fine white dust. Hairpin after hairpin, and we were going very slowly now, high above the valley. But occasionally the road turned into a street, where a quiet little village clung to the slope of the hills along the road. Sometimes people waved, for they recognised the brothers. Meanwhile, we sat in the back, occasionally bracing ourselves against the sides as the road got rougher, and glad of the water we had brought with us, for the sun was hot.

After an hour or two, the lorry slowed, and we turned a corner, and began to descend. The watershed. Downhill now, eventually to the coast facing Africa, into the hot breeze. After an hour of more hairpins pinning back the fall of the hills, the lorry came to an easier gradient, and speeded up. Soon we turned off, down a track, apparently miles from anywhere. But all around were the signs of a well cultivated farm: vines on well-maintained wires shaded the ground so you could walk in shade underneath their pendant fruit, there was a field where corn had been recently reaped, a plot of rich, luscious tomatoes, onions pulled and laid to brown their tops in the sun, and orchard. Good land. This was the brothers' farm, and as the engine died their mother came out of the white house with a white apron and floury hands. We could smell the bread that she had baking. 'Guests, mother', one of the brothers said, and then went into Greek so rapid I had no idea what he said. His English was sketchy and optimistic, but hers was better. She turned to us, with a warm smile: one gold tooth and several black ones. 'You are welcome. We have seen no English since the war. Stay with us.' Who could refuse? Bread, cheese, honey, wine, water appeared, and the dusk drew in. We ate together, she waiting on her sons. Conversation was difficult but cheerful, and as the light faded we asked where we could camp – or to be more accurate, unroll our bags. 'Here,' she said, pointing to the little loggia under yet another laden vine. We shooed the last hens away, and spread the bags, and were soon asleep, early as it was.

We woke as the sun rose above the mountains and touched our sleeping faces. It was very early, but the household was already abroad. A donkey brayed its heartbroken lament a couple of fields away. A cock was challenging the morning, and was answered by another a few hundred yards off. The *tsitsikoi* churred. A bee, intent on plunder, buzzed past. These sounds must have been heard on mornings like this in this place millennia ago. We smelt cooking. The cold pump did for a shower, and we dashed the water from our faces and rolled up our bags. Mother came out carrying a dish with a mountain of chips cooked in olive oil, and some raw garlic, and bread, and five little glasses. She went back inside, and returned with a tray with five glasses of water and a bottle of some strong dark sweet wine, with which she filled the little glasses. 'Come and eat with us,' she said, 'the day will get hot.'

Clearly, there was much work to be done as the brothers had been away, and despite their offer we made them understand that we would walk into Timbaki if they would show us the right direction. 'Two hours,' mother said, 'once you get back to the road.' So once more we shouldered the packs, and set off, embraces all round, and promising to return.

★

The walk was certainly a good two hours, and plenty more, into the sun, across the plain. The road was packed limestone, raised on a causeway as the river could readily flood in Autumn rains – due, as it happened, before very long. Timbaki is now, as I write this, a rich town which sends its produce from its fertile ground all over Europe. The wide flat cardboard boxes in which I store my Cox's Orange Pippin and Egremont Russet apples each Autumn have 'G. Giannankakis S.A., Timbaki' on their sides. But that development was then all in the future, Timbaki was a place you could walk into and out of in fifteen minutes, and even now it is not exactly a metropolis. It is near enough to the sea and a beach on which you can fry to have attracted a certain type of tourist, and does a decent trade.

'Mother' had been right: by mid morning the day was impossibly hot. Our sweat dried off instantly, leaving white tidemarks of salt on the creases of our shirts. We came into the near noon quiet of the square of Timbaki. A dog was lying in the shade, and wagged its tail as I passed, but hardly looked up. In a *kapheneion*, men in faded work clothes and old-fashioned flat caps sat at a few little tables under a trellis with a vine. They had tiny cups of coffee and glasses of water. Heads turned as we walked in and sat down at one of the tables outside the café, which was also a small hotel – the only one then, I think. Nobody greeted us, and conversation stopped. We were too hot and tired to bother, and I asked the silent waiter for water and coffee. He went off without a word.

We got our coffee and water, silently, and in the grateful shade I closed my eyes. Then a chair scraped on the ground next to me. A large perspiring policeman was bowing, and asking, in German, if he might sit down. 'Ich spreche ganz wenig Deutsch, aber ich kan ein wenig verstanden,' I replied, gesturing towards the chair, to indicate, 'Please join us.' A broad smile split his face and he turned to the silent onlookers: *'einai Angloi* – they are English.' And suddenly men were saying 'Καλώς Ορισες', 'Welcome' and smiles were everywhere. One old man came up and bowed and shook my hand and bowed to Jenny. A curious moment of a welcome and gratitude we had not ourselves deserved.

The policeman's English was quite good – his cousin had a restaurant in Soho, he told us – and, as ever in Greece, conversation got round to politics. He was increasingly loquacious, passionate, and we knew only enough to nod occasionally. He told us of increasing strains: the division between Left and Right was bitter and only a few years before had been unforgottenly murderous. The economy was shaky and memories long and detailed. The Left seemed to be gaining ground electorally, and that was making our policeman and the Americans nervous, for in American eyes Greece was a vital link in the NATO chain. The King's role was ambiguous. 'The King, well, he is a good young man, but he is young, and he does not learn fast,' said our policeman, making a deprecatory gesture. 'I think he will have to choose soon.' There was little we could say in our ignorance. But a few years later, English newspapers were full of the King's choice, his failure, and the Colonels' takeover. We had heard, had we known it then, the first whispers of the gathering storm.

It was too hot to move. After bread and a salad swimming in olive oil, and yet more garlic, we thought about a siesta. The hotel had a room, and we looked at it. Two grubby looking beds. The door opening – no door – was due south, and gave onto the flat roof, and dead opposite was the toilet. No door, and what was then the common enough squat Continental model which puts great strain, I find, on the quadriceps. Flushing was with a bucket of water from the tap, and paper went into a bucket with a lid. Fair enough, and the heat dried everything up quickly enough. But we looked at each other doubtfully. And went down and had another coffee.

We had a map with us, not a good one, but we needed to get some idea of where else we might go as the day cooled. Clearly we could not camp hereabouts, and after so much sleeping in the open neither of us fancied the room. 'Phaistos,' Jenny said, pointing at the map. 'It's close and I heard someone in that place in Athens say it was beautiful and we should go there.' That was a decision. But how? Our friendly policeman was appealed to. He pursed his lips, and shook his head from side to side. 'A long way to walk, a big hill. You take a taxi? My friend has a taxi.' The heat swung it. Jenny, sweating, spoke before I could look across at her. 'Yes, we will take your friend's taxi.' Our friend got up and walked over to another of the tables, and found his friend who was playing cards. He nodded in our direction. And off he went and ten minutes later came back driving an old black Ford. We loaded the packs and got in. Somehow, nobody had told him we spoke little Greek and he kept up a continuous cheerful monologue over the noise of the engine all the way to Phaistos. The tyres squealed a low note on the hot tarmac as the curves of the road tightened.

It cost very little. He dropped us outside the café building at the top of the hill by the ruins. The view over towards the sea was spectacular, and that wind from Africa even felt cool. From the terrace we could look over the ruins. They have been much more fully explored and much better interpreted since then, of course, but your first Bronze Age palace is bound to be a pretty impressive experience. (Actually, why do we always use that word 'Palace'? It begs so many questions, about hierarchy, authority, economics, religion, etc., etc., about which we can only make guesses.) We read up what we could (not much) in the café before going into the ruins, and little stuck. But the intricacy of the stone work, the precision with which huge blocks had been cut and fitted together – as at Tyrins, near Nauplion, a site of similar date – demanded a sort of awe, and is certainly one of the earliest stimuli that prodded me out of a complacent chronological snobbery that is the default position of the young and made me increasingly aware of how dangerous it is to underestimate the ancestors and how provisional our narratives are. (I could not have thought that then, much less expressed it, but Phaistos is where the journey, I think, began.) And after Timbaki, perhaps our minds were running a bit on toilets, for both of us recognised with delight a beautifully excavated and preserved latrine, which looked as if it would work without any trouble. I still have, somewhere, the black and white photograph I took with our cheap box camera, with Jenny beside it for scale.

Where could we sleep, we asked the girl at the café. She looks surprised. '*Edo, exoterike* – Here, outside,' she said, gesturing to the terrace as if it was the most natural thing in the world. There were mattresses aplenty. We slept a luxurious, not esoteric, sleep, the wind on our faces and the *tsitsikoi* in the pines keeping up their tireless conversation.

One other memory of Phaistos, sharp as a pin. The plain below is very fertile and we could see it plotted and pieced into garden and orchard. So we walked down the hill, and met a man hoeing between his melons. He was naked to the waist, and I wondered if he took old Hesiod's advice millenia ago, 'Plough naked.' Hesiod would have recognised this scene, many of these plants. He paused, and bowed to us, and then took out a pocket knife and cut a melon off. He split it and gave us a half each, and as the luscious juice ran down our chins he held out some apricots and figs. 'For you. Come back to my garden soon and taste my new wine.' Bees bumbled in the late flowers. The swallows flickered past, intent on insects.

★

We did not then know much about Arthur Evans and his fondness for concrete and his own myths and prejudices. We did not know then about how so much excavated evidence was simply not recognised as important, to put it kindly. Nor did we know – I only read Dilys Powell's fine book years later – about Evans' Villa Ariadne – it had to be called that! – about 25 miles east of Chania. The villa had been the residence of General Kreipe, the German commander during the Occupation. Despite frequent bloody reprisals, there was dogged resistance to the Germans by Greek partisans and some British officers, including Patrick Leigh Fermor. Their most spectacular coup was to kidnap the German commander.

On the run with him, three Cretans and two disguised British officers spent an uncomfortable night on the slopes of Mount Ida. It is one of the places where they say Zeus the Thunderer was born. Ida holds its snow till late. I myself have seen it with a thatch of snow quite late in the year. As dawn broke, and lit the high snows, Leigh Fermor heard the General muttering to himself the first line of Horace's Soracte ode, *Carmina* 1.9, *Vides ut alta stet nive candidum / Soracte*: Horace wrote the poem when he was an old man, looking over to the mountain from the little Sabine estate Augustus' minister Maecenas gave him:

> *Vides ut alta stet nive candidum*
> *Soracte, nec iam sustineant onus*
> *silvae laborantes, geluque*
> *flumina constiterint acuto.*
>
> *Dissolve frigus ligna super foco*
> *large reponens atque benignius*
> *deprome quadrimum Sabina,*
> *o Thaliarche, merum diota.*
>
> *Permitte divis cetera, qui simul*
> *stravere ventos aequore fervido*
> *deproeliantes, nec cupressi*
> *nec veteres agitantur orni.*

Quid sit futurum cras fuge quaerere, et
quem Fors dierum cumque dabit lucro
  appone, nec dulcis amores
      sperne puer neque tu choreas,

donec virenti canities abest
morosa. Nunc et campus et areae
  lenesque sub noctem susurri
      composita repetantur hora,

nunc et latentis proditor intimo
gratus puellae risus ab angulo
  pignusque dereptum lacertis
      aut digito male pertinaci.

Which, the untranslatable being translated, goes:

Do you see how white is Soracte in deep snow? See how
the old branches sink under their burden, how streams
stand silent, ice-gripped. Come, friend, turn from this cold
outside, break out the wine, put more wood on the fire.
Leave everything else to the gods, who have stilled the winds
raging over the heaving sea: the cypress and the old ash trees
are still at last. Cease wondering what tomorrow or next
year will bring, count each day Fortune gives you as a gain;
and as for you, you lads and lasses, don't spurn the sweetness
of love, nor the dances, while your green youth is not yet
frosted with sober white hair. Seek out now the quiet courts,
and the riverbank in the cool of the evening, listen for those

low whispers at nightfall as a tryst is kept, and the sudden ray of a girl's laughter piercing the summer dark.

Leigh Fermor recognised the line, and quoted the rest of the poem. As he later said, '...for a long moment, the war had ceased to exist. We had both drunk at the same fountains long before; and things were different between us for the rest of our time together.' This moment of ancient, shared civility overcoming a terrible present is a little miracle. It is commoner that one might think, looking into the eyes of one whom you thought an enemy and finding a man just like you, with his memory of old love and youth and their inexpressibility. But it is not just sharing the poem, but sharing what the poem explores, the common mystery of aging, of the youth that still inhabits the frame that bends under the weight of memory, and the mystery of the loss that is also gain. These things outlast, transcend, ideologies and customs and polities. I know that, writing these words by a winter fire when age has snowed white hairs on me, and the memory of summer dusks tempers the growing chill.

That poem's perfection now always seduces me, but I did not know Horace well then. Nor did we know much more than stories about the bull dancing of ancient Crete – which, it has been argued, was Evans' invention – or the myth of the Minotaur, the Labyrinth, and the story of Theseus. (Whom I always consider rather a cad, if a brave one.) I had read Frazer's *Golden Bough*, and was prepared to sound confident and authoritative, even tedious if given a chance, on matrilinear societies, 'The King Must Die' pattern of succession (connecting it to the Oedipus story), and the catastrophic demise of the Minoan Bronze Age culture. But it was all very superficial stuff, and I am now a bit ashamed of my old confidence. And when we came to Knossos, it added colour and depth, and zest, to what we saw, and what we imagined in what we saw, and the interest it gave did lead to other, more nuanced, ways of seeing the past. But then... well, we found a café that served good *dolmades* and moussaka opposite the excavations, where we could sleep on the roof, and we settled in for a couple of days. We just enjoyed the ruins by day, and climbed into them by night – Jenny hitched her red dress up nearly to her waist to straddle the wall – to have them to ourselves and the ghosts we imagined. We were well met by moonlight in the gatehouse where the frescoed bull charged, forever in motion, forever still. The *tsitsikoi* sang an epithalamion, of sorts. Horace would have understood.

Day brought busloads of tourists from nearby Heraklion, many of them American, from cruises I suppose. They wandered through the puzzling interlocking rooms, they sat (as I did) on the stone throne in the throne room, they took pictures (as we did) of each other standing against the huge *pithoi* or storage jars, and wives took pictures (as we did not) of smiling husband framed by the huge stone – or more often concrete – horns that were so much a feature of the site. But how were those rooms used? How did the whole place fit together? Why were there no defences? *Were* there no defences? And what great shuddering of Gaia as she stirred in her sleep had bent those courses of stone and toppled this complex edifice? The site was making us begin slowly to frame those questions, but each time they pressed one came up against one's own ignorance. (And one still does.)

The museum had beautiful things. But one exhibit stuck in the memory. There was a small painted clay figurine about six inches high, a wasp-waisted woman, in a full skirt, holding two snakes at arms' length, spectacularly bare breasted, and the caption – I swear it! – read, 'Goddess of Fertitity'. (A caption to be treasured almost as much as one I saw in a tired museum in Punta Arenas, Chile which told everyone who did not understand the Latin name of the threadbare stuffed bird in the case that it was 'Some Kind of Bird.')

★

Somehow, days later, we found ourselves in a large American car with a lonely man. He was not young. He spoke good English, knew England well, and knew his history. He was clearly well off. His name was 'Vyron' – 'Byron'. And he had read the poet in some depth. He loved *Don Juan*. He insisted on buying us a long lunch. We were, I remember, in Aegion, and were going to take the afternoon ferry across to Itea, sleep on the beach there, and then take the bus up to Delphi. He had, he said, a friend in Delphi: be sure to call on him. The afternoon wore on. He bought coffee and honey cakes, and insisted on having the honey cakes parcelled up for us for the journey. (Honey cakes, I thought, what you feed to Cerberus, drugged or not.) And as we parted, he said something I shall never forget: 'Go home and make many babies and send one to me, for I am childless.' Poor Byron. I lost his address.

To Delphi then, the navel of the world. The bus screwed its way round the bends up from the coast, each one graced with a little shrine. Like so many arrivals, that at Delphi was anticlimactic. Save the name and its memories, nothing remarkable. Below the main road to Athens the olive groves fell steeply to the valley bottom – little in the way of ruins there was then exposed – and much of the ancient site was covered in aromatic scrub. Delighted, we found the theatre, where dutifully, slightly self-consciously/ironically, we recited a chorus on the nobility of man from Vellacott's translation of Sophocles. Then up to the Temple of Apollo, where the Pythian priestess, possibly high on nitrous oxide or other gases from the volcanic fissure, gave her ambiguous pronouncements; to the remains of the delicate tholos, already familiar from countless photographs, almost a symbol of Summer Holiday In Greece. I ran round the stadium in the evening cool because it seemed to be what one ought to do. And we went, of course, to the small museum. On the steps some men were trying to lift a large slab of carved marble from a trolley, get it up the steps, and into the building. They had clearly disagreed. For the slab was half on, half off the trolley, resting one (uncarved) side on the second step. Nobody was touching it. The three men were arguing furiously. First one would point to the stone and then to the doorway and make an exasperated gesture and turn away in clear disgust. The youngest sat down on a higher step, but did not stop arguing. After a minute or two the third sat on the stone with his arms folded and his back to the others. It was clear that eloquence was their strong suit and if the stone, which seemed to be addressed with some frequency, had been sentient it would have walked itself up the steps. The gestures got more and more passionate. In actual fact, with a lever or two there would not have been much problem getting it up the steps: a five minute job at best. But clearly the argument had gone on some time, and looked good for a bit longer...

I had seen photos of the Charioteer – indeed, that bronze was one of the reasons for coming here – one 'ought to see' that, they had said back home. But nothing had prepared me for the calm, tall majesty of the figure, the delicacy of the bronze folds of his garment, the grace of his hands, or the challenge of the unseeing eyes which gazed into a world I could never know. Who were you? – for it was clearly a portrait. At what Olympiad did you triumph, your team rounding the meta with the ironbound wheel hub of the chariot almost grazing the stone? For the first time, a work of art had me in tears. I do not know why.

Everything after that was anticlimax. The Omphalos, the navel of the world – well, seen one omphalos, seen 'em all. The *kouroi* – yes, graceful enough. The Sphinx did stir our questions, and Jenny said, 'I wonder if there is any link with those Assyrian sculptures in the British Museum?' – having lived in London she had seen them: I had not. But there was nobody to ask.

We came out, blinking, into the light blazing reflected from the hot marble. Two men were now sitting on the stone. One of the seated men had his head in his hands. The other was in exactly the attitude, even to the turn of the head, of that Hellenistic statue of the Seated Boxer. (Our man had more clothes on.) The third was clearly angry, and kept pointing down the hill. The Boxer was smoking one of those sweet-scented, oval-sectioned Greek cigarettes, looking across the valley. We had no idea what it was all about.

We had that sort of introduction from Vyron to his friend, who kept the souvenir shop in the then small village. 'You go and see Kostas and he will look after you.' Not knowing quite what 'look after' might mean, in we went, into grateful shade, and shyly said, 'We bring greetings from your friend Vyron whom we met in Aegion.'

Kostas got up. 'My friend's friends are my friends! I shut my shop! We drink some wine!' And his wife ran up to place chairs for us, and brought water, and glasses, and white wine, and a little dish of white cheese and black and green olives. 'Olives from my trees! Wine from my vines!' Kostas spoke good if heavily accented English, very loudly, and we got on well, and toasted each other, and we toasted Kostas' smiling but silent wife, and then his absent children, and then Vyron, and then the young King of Greece, and then Her Majesty, and then Greece and Britain, and then...

By this time it was growing late, and we had to find somewhere to sleep. We had food – bread and sausage – in our packs. So we got up, a mite unsteadily, to leave. Kostas enveloped Jenny in a bear hug; I could not quite do the same for portly Mrs Kostas, but tried. 'You come back! We drink again together! Where you sleep?' 'We camp.' 'You go out of village towards Athens, you go into trees below road by big Temple, you find lots of places to sleep! Come back tomorrow!' Handshakes and hugs again, and we leave, into the aromatic darkness, the stars bright above Parnassus. We cross the spill of light from the open door and set off down the road.

I become benevolently talkative under the influence of wine. I have always thought it one of my more attractive characteristics. Jenny remembered me talking that night, for some reason, at some length about the missionary journeys of St Paul, which, as I said earlier, I had 'done' at school, and about the urgency of the letters he had written to the little communities he had founded on his travels. (How did I dare! In my chatter I had not even begun to grasp the majesty and subtlety and wisdom of that mind!) She bore it in silence, most of it. Patience was her long suit. And then we came to the tricky bit: getting down a pretty steep slope in the dark, finding a way between the bushes. Here I did stop talking. We were determined to get a fair way off the road, and not to make the same mistake we had made at Nauplion. Walls would be nice too, in case of a pother of pigs in the early morning, as at Olympia. After dropping about 100 feet, suddenly, in the light of the moon just rising over the shoulder of the hill, we found the perfect spot: a ruin with three walls up to about six feet, the fourth lower and with a gap where the doorway had been, and level ground inside. It was small: about fifteen feet by ten. Ideal. We unrolled our bags, chomped our bread and sausage, and fell into an easy sleep. As I was dropping off, I heard a dog bark far away across the valley. It was answered by another: and something howled. I would love to think, even now, it was a wolf.

Early morning. I wake first, and do not move, enjoying the quiet sounds. I look up. Far, far overhead, three large birds black, against the sky. And then I realise they are circling, keeping watch directly over us. Might we be breakfast? For they are griffon vultures. I wake Jenny to see them. Not impressed, until I tell her they are vultures. Then she gets up.

A mile or so outside Delphi, and on the road above the ruin where we slept, we could see what looked like a café. We packed up, left our little – well, we liked to think it was a temple, but, clearly ancient though it was, it probably was not – and climbed up to the road. But our having slept there changed its psychogeography for us for ever. We passed the Castalian spring, and I crossed the road for a quick drink of the water of the Muses as it came out of the rock: partly practical – I had a rather dry mouth after the previous night – partly in ironic homage to my youthful literary ambitions. A vine on a trellis shaded the tables on the little terrace of the café: the grapes were swelling. A bent old woman, in black, with bunions, was sweeping the floor with a besom. '*Kalimera.*' '*Kalimera sas.*' '*Dio kafedes, parakolo, kai nero,*' and she went into the back to tell her husband they had early trade. She came back to her sweeping. Then a voice from the back: 'Hey, Aphrodite!' and the Daughter of the Foam called back, 'ἔρχομαι, Socrates' 'I'm coming.' We got our coffee, water, bread and honey. It was good. Made by Socrates, served by Aphrodite, below Apollo's mountain a few yards from the Spring of the Muses.

But I don't know that that concatenation has done me much good.

We walked on to Arachova, and then got a lift sitting on the load of lemons in the back of a lorry going to Athens, to begin our journey home. I have never had so comfortable or aromatic a journey. We bought the driver a drink when we got to Athens, and he chose what I recognised, with delight, given his load, as a *citron pressé* – I could not do its Greek name. Then, newly confident, we took the train to Piraeus, and I asked for the tickets in the Greek in which I was feeling I might even swagger a bit. But one should never get above oneself. The cashier gravely answered me in Greek, and then corrected my case endings, before saying, in English, 'Have a good journey.'

Not much memory of that subsequent journey remains, except sleeping on deck on the ferry to Brindisi and seeing the blue and white Greek flag at the stern against the rising sun, and then a mad dash by connecting trains across Europe. A pair of smelly feet in socks in my left ear were a feature on the crowded overnight train to Milan. A cow heel snatched in Milan as food for the journey – delicious, cheap, and we were hungry. Dozing on our rucksacks as we sat in the corridor on the train from Paris to Calais. And then England, dear England, with our rucksacks solemnly inspected and chalked 'OK' by the Customs in the sheds at Dover, the train in black and maroon livery, and grey coffee in white British Rail cups, and when we got home they said, 'Well, here you are. By the way, there's a lot of post for you, and while you were away...' We were back to old clothes and porridge. And grateful to fold our wings, for a time. But, though we did not then realise it, a mooring line had been cast off.

It was all a very long time ago. But

> Time present and time past
> Are both perhaps present in time future
> And time future contained in time past.
>> T.S. Eliot, 'Burnt Norton', *Four Quartets*

★

From a New World

Come, my friends,
'Tis not too late to seek a newer world.
Push off, and sitting well in order smite
The sounding furrows; for my purpose holds
To sail beyond the sunset, and the baths
Of all the western stars, until I die.
It may be that the gulfs will wash us down:
It may be we shall touch the Happy Isles...

Alfred Tennyson, *Ulysses*

A library offers, if you will risk it, a journey into the past that will change the future. Cutting libraries during a recession, as we see happening all around us as the barbarians reassure us that nothing is being lost, is like cutting hospitals during a plague. If you can get to a library you are free, not confined (unless you want to be) by temporary political climates. It is the most democratic of institutions because no one can tell you what to read and when and how – unless you let them.

Saul Bellow once said, 'People can lose their lives in libraries. They ought to be warned.' Indeed. A great library, if you have any imagination at all, is a humbling, daunting, even frightening thing. Your journey through the stacks can have all sorts of unexpected consequences, and you might not like them. Libraries are places where you can lose your innocence without, as Germaine Greer memorably remarked, losing your virginity. Your comfortable certainties can be most disturbingly challenged. Be careful of what you find memorable, of what lurks in the stacks – and the marks, wounds even, may not show till years later.

The University Library in Cambridge is a familiar place now, familiar enough to grumble about, yet I love it. I found it utterly daunting, even frightening, at first. The stacks were cliffs of learning, unscaleable, with no obvious handhold. At my shoulder all the time was the ghost of that scholar you know you ought to be and never will be, murmuring 'You ought to read that' and 'Why can't you remember what you read last week?' My old friend John Byrom, a learned and humble man, often had a nightmare of the books on the shelves being given voices, and shrieking at him 'Read me! Read me!' But whence does one take the right book? In the end, I found things on those shelves that delighted me, and things too that horrified, caught me – literally fascinated me – with a tale of human cruelty and depravity that in the naiveté of youth I had intellectually known – perhaps – but emotionally had blithely ignored. No ignoring now: you cannot un-know things, for good or ill. Loss of innocence, indeed.

But like a half-forgotten shore, or the Greece of recent memory and ancient myth, the library is now a sort or coming home, changed, only to be perhaps changed again. I now love the things about it that first daunted me, its odd smell, its solidity in bronze and stone and wood, its long corridors, its huge guard books in the Catalogue Room which, when I first started to use it properly, were the only catalogue. They had huge heavy pages covered with little pasted-in printed slips. One saw staff members occasionally, pasting in yet another entry from a sheaf held in their left hands. The Catalogue Room was the key to the place, the nerve centre. You heaved the guard books up from the lower shelves, or took them from the upper, and they dropped heavily onto the sloping, padded, leather-covered reading shelf so you could consult them. That thud was always a sort of pleasure. But my *bête noire* was/is the lady who comes to my elbow when I was working against time to get a list of classmarks from the catalogue so that I find the books I want, and who talks, and talks, and talks in a hard to hear whisper. Once it was understood as bad manners to do more in the Library than politely nod to people you knew, save in the tea room.

I am not alone in this complex and ambiguous memory. Many share it: it's almost written on and in the building. C. S. Lewis, in his unfinished novel *The Dark Tower* – which would have been the fourth in the Ransom series – made the modern Cambridge University Library the setting for his grim tale. In M. R. James' ghost stories, libraries are often places where a chance meeting with a MS or a book can be a warning to the curious and a moment of terror. One of his finest, 'The Tractate Middoth', is set partly in the old Cambridge University Library, a darksome place behind the Enlightenment elegance of Gibbs' Senate House. Anything might lurk, hidden, there.

★

When I was still in the foothills of this mountain range, finding my way to wherever I am going, more classes of books were on the open shelves, and browsing along them in idle moments to see what caught my fancy became a habit. The sudden dark as the *minuterie* at the end of the stack performed its office could catch you on your knees, looking at the bottom shelf, right at the dark end of the stack, and you felt your way to the light. Unsystematic serendipity certainly in the past led me to something good, and I love the quirky little corners where people find quiet and privacy to work – right at the top of North Wing, among the stacks, way above the trees of the gardens of Trinity College, was/is my own favourite place – and I love the happy chancy way in which looking for one thing you find another – but there is another afternoon gone. It was during just such a serendipitous browsing among the books of the Royal Library (when that was still on open shelves) that I found an eighteenth century edition of the fourteenth century *Travels of Sir John Mandeville,* and Mandeville has been my King Charles' head ever since.

★

The Royal Library — well, it was the Bishop of Ely's first, but George I, that unlovable monarch, gave it to the University. Joseph Trapp, first Professor of Poetry at Oxford, commented:

> The King observing with judicious eyes
> The state of both his universities,
> To Oxford sent a troop of horse, and why?
> That learned body wanted loyalty;
> To Cambridge books, as very well discerning,
> That loyal body wanted learning.

Those of an unkind disposition might try to make much of the fact that Cambridge only replied in 1770, when William Browne, Fellow of Peterhouse, (according to Mrs Piozzi, the former Mrs Thrale) made his reply extempore in response to Dr Johnson's — he was an Oxonian of course — triumphant quotation of Trapp:

> The King to Oxford sent a troop of horse,
> For Tories own no argument but force;
> With equal skill to Cambridge books he sent,
> For Whigs admit no force but argument.

The graffiti in the loos were a cut above the usual, too. I once saw a short poem in Greek, in Sapphics, the pencil uncertain on the roughnesses of the wall. 'Hegel boot boys rule OK?' 'I pee, therefore I am.' Someone had added a comment: 'How can you know?' 'Full Marx for Jung people.' 'Is there intelligent life on Earth?' 'Economists have the Keynes to everything.' 'How do we know this is not a black hole?'

★

I remember my first visit, in my first year, to look at the Pied Bull Quarto of *King Lear*. I had absolutely no idea why I should look at it, or what I was looking for, but my Director of Studies, John Holloway, had said it was interesting, so there I was, wearing (as was proper) collar and tie and gown, and for the first time faced with the massive guard books of the Catalogue Room. There were no induction courses for new undergraduates then, nor did anyone think that the gentlemen needed instruction in how to use a library. O but they did, they did: for in Blackpool Public Library, the only one with which I was familiar, there was so little that it could easily be found, and the latest thing on Chaucer – this in the 1960s! – was Kittredge's book of half a century before, and the latest thing on Shakespeare Bradley's classic *Shakespearean Tragedy* (1904). The guard books glared at me, challenging me to take them down and open them on the leather covered sloping shelves. At length, working from first principles, I found 'Shakespeare', and then *King Lear* – and then immediately ran into further difficulty, for while I take it for granted now that everyone can read a bibliographical entry, I could not then, and I had no idea of how the classification system worked nor what the class mark meant. In the end, though, I had a reference, and apparently you had to order the book in the Anderson Room, a place that would later become a place of consolation in a distressed hour and of refreshment in an exhausted one, a place where it was always afternoon. The deep blue leather armchairs reassured with many promises of summer's lease: 'Come now, trust yourselves to our embrace, and sit among these learned men and women, and you may become like them too.' The *sotto voce* conversations between readers and those on the issue desk emphasised the quietude, their sibilants tantalising with suggestion of the words just unheard. The suppressed burr, burr of the phone, like a bee up a flue... There was an elderly don who, it seemed to me later, was always there, always walking from his seat to the desk where books were delivered, and his shoes creaked, CREAKED, creaked, CREAKED – one much worse than the other. And the lotos of scholarship had overcome some, who snored gently, decorously – as in a library one must.

That first visit, they brought me *MacBeth*. I had got the classmark wrong. But I was not going through all that again. So I read *MacBeth*. It is actually quite good.

But now... The library has become for most a place simply of deeds and industry. Busy people, the click of laptops, the urgency of computer terminals and microfiches,

and the insistent subtext of publish, publish, publish or
no job. One is never quite sure that more work is being
done, for we seem to have forgotten about thinking time
in a desperate worship of quantity over quality. Wisdom
and understanding – and God knows our society needs
both – fruit as much from a stock of quiet musing and
unhurried, rigorous thought as from the tendrils of
bibliographies. We have turned what ought to be the
moral and intellectual powerhouses of our culture into
something not far removed from intellectual *ergastula*,
and all in the name of some indefinable things called
efficiency and – save the mark! –'impact.'

For so many years, as salad days passed and the passing
years turned towards the fall of the leaf, physical travel
was impossible and my only journeys were deep into
the stacks of libraries, where one reference sends you to
another book, and that to another, and so on almost *ad
infinitum* until perhaps you end up with a reference to
what you were reading in the first place... You need to be
stern with yourself, or you will end up in the Library of
Babel. In a Garden of Endlessly Forking Paths.

But that exploration, which took me to more than one
intellectual, conceptual, metaphysical impasse, where the
trying to understand, knowing you never would do so,
can be an agony, ended up steering me to other journeys,
physical and mental, for which, looking back, I can see
that hard path upwards on the craggy hill trained me.

On a huge hill,
Cragged and steep, Truth stands, and he that will
Reach her, about must and about must go,
And what the hill's suddenness resists, win so.

John Donne, *Satire III*

One unexpected later consequence was a series of almost yearly peregrinations, far faring, where I was invited to talk to audiences from the stratospherically academic to those who brought their knitting in case they would be bored. Nervously pretending to an authority I did not feel, I have sung for my supper in strange places, even on a storm-tossed boat 300 miles SE of Cape Horn. Some people went to sleep, noisily. I remember indeed one retired 4 star general in North Carolina whose snores came utterly on cue as I was talking about the sleeping conditions on mediaeval pilgrim ships to the Holy Land. On another occasion in the Mid West of the US the Chair said, 'You will have to speak up: we have the two-hearing-aid brigade here tonight,' and added, 'By the way, I am the local undertaker. I have a good business. I'll take you to see my rest home tomorrow.' Perhaps she was sizing me up. But another, young, couple in New Bern, came up to this traveller from an Antique Land and said, 'Thank you, thank you, for coming. We learned so much and you have opened so many doors for us.' There was a seminar at an Ivy League university which I wished many times longer. And what it all adds up to I know not. Yet. If anything.

★

It so chanced that I first set foot in the Americas in the area where the first modern Europeans did, the first raindrops in that storm that overwhelmed the ancient cultures of the Americas. Some things I had written led to an invitation to give some lectures in the US Virgin Islands and New York on mediaeval and early modern travel, and how travel could then be written about, and in the Virgin Islands the interest just then was very much on the first recorded Old World contact. I soon found it was far from a dispassionate academic matter. A local newspaper had a headline the day I arrived: 'Columbus: A Fatal Legacy?'

★

We had left London with sleet flurries in the morning wind. Decanted briefly into the nastiness of Miami, then into a smaller plane to San Juan in Puerto Rico, we finally stepped out of an even smaller plane into a hot and scented midnight at the little airport on St Croix. So this was the tropics.

I fell asleep with the South East trade wind, a steady 15 miles per hour day in day out (save when a hurricane comes) rustling the bug screens and the Venetian blinds. Below everything, there was the ground bass of the white noise of the surf on the reef. The ceiling fan slowly turned, and a gecko had come out from behind a picture to watch me getting ready for bed. This was a long way from London. I woke to find the room barred with a light more brilliant than any imagination. I rolled up the Venetian blinds. Way below was the lagoon, its forests of weeds and coral as clear as on a map. Later, from the same spot, I watched barracuda hunting along the edge of the coral heads, and, one night, a shoal of phosphorescent fish cruised past. I became used to looking up from writing to see the frigate birds patrolling; an osprey hurried by on his way up to Carolina; busy brown pelicans fished; a black heron stood thoughtfully in the shallows. Further out, the white line of the reef, and beyond the deep-water blue of the ocean, with huge swelling argosies of fair weather cumulus sailing above it. On the terrace little bananaquits foraged among the cacti.

The morning sea drew us first – not surprisingly. The stones on the beach were too hot to touch. The water broke with no shock of cold on feet white from English shoes. Coconuts lay in the white sand: one or two were sprouting, and might, one day, be like their big cousins above the beach. Conch shells, some still with the gleaming pink blush unweathered from them, dotted the tide mark. Hot. And so into the water, old shirts donned to protect our backs from the merciless sun as we lay and gazed through our masks at the unconcerned life of the reef. Two large squid flew past, keeping station on their own business, their big intelligent eyes watching us. A circle of broken shells on a sandy patch showed where an octopus lay camouflaged. Angel fish came inquisitively to inspect us as we came near their home – an abandoned drum, encrusted with coral. Later, a friend of our host Morton organised a trip to the Nature Reserve off Buck Island, to the north: and there, in among the reef, there are signposts on the sea bed to help you not to lose your way, and you see big blue parrot fish, and nurse sharks, and barracudas that, so everybody says, do not like people. (But the one I saw had a nasty, thoughtful look in its eye.) Huge brittle stars with delicate limbs like feathers, and lobsters, and crabs who will sometimes come up the beach and rustle among the rubbish at night – a world where man is an intruder, where your shadow passing over the bottom momentarily clouds the existence of the little fish, and then, as you pass on, is forgotten. But there are subtler and more permanent destructions.

★

How people name places reveals a lot. On Tristan da Cunha there is a cliff called Place Where the Goat Jump Off: sensible, no nonsense stuff. Or they tell you who owns a bit of land: Grimsby – Grim's *bu*. Place names also reveal an ideology, consciously held or not. Those given by European voyagers, *soi-disant* discoverers, divide roughly by time and confession. Most of the names given by the sixteenth century travellers are dates: the saint's day on which the islands or cape were sighted. Come forward to the Enlightenment, and the pride of English and French naval power, and places memorialise otherwise doubtfully distinguished monarchs or Societies Royal, or not. Which brings me to reflect on those Virgins.

There were, so it was said, 11,000 of them. Attendants on St Ursula, they were (of course) martyred, in Germany by the Huns besieging Cologne , and it was on their feast day, October 21 in the old pre-1970 martyrology, that Columbus first saw these islands. That was on his second voyage, with seventeen ships. That voyage was much better funded and equipped that his first. His glowing – and highly fictionalised – account of his first, which was printed and circulated within days of a battered *Niña* limping up the Tagus to Lisbon, was a very effective investors' prospectus, and lots of people hoped and believed that a route to the riches of India and Cathay and to their own personal fortune had been opened. With Columbus' second fleet were the first horses to set hoof in America: an introduction that, by one of those malign quirks of history, in the fullness of time enabled the Plains Indians to exploit with greater ease, to devastate, the migrating herds of bison. Other passengers were a number of European diseases to which the Americans had no immunity, and those diseases in the next thirty years caused a catastrophic decline – 90%, some say – in the population: a far bigger shock to the societies and cultures of America than the Black Death was to Eurasian. And also on board were a rag, tag and bobtail of disreputable adventurers like the odious Michele de Cuneo. For every devout and, on the whole, decent Franciscan friar who went west, and often championed the natives against the get-rich-quick crowd, there were many like him. And as I look at the palms by the white sand, the translucent blue of the lagoon and hear the white noise of the surf on the reef, I can't forget him and others, so many, like him, whom I have met in reading. But perhaps there were other sides to them as well, of which we have no knowledge. Nobody is monochrome.

I first came across his letter, which he dated 15 October 1495, when my research had led me into reading a lot of the early accounts of the Atlantic voyages. His was one of the first accounts of these islands. He cared not for any virgins, sanctified or otherwise... he began his letter 'In the name of Jesus and of His Glorious Mother Mary, from Whom all blessings proceed.' And one passage that can still shock me – there are others – runs:

> ...We captured this canoe with all the men. One cannibal was wounded by a lance blow and thinking him dead we left him in the sea. Suddenly we saw him begin to swim away; therefore we caught him and with a long hook pulled him aboard where we cut off his head with an axe. We sent the other Cannibals together with the two slaves to Spain. When I was in the boat, I took a beautiful Cannibal girl and the admiral gave her to me. Having her in my room and she being naked as is their custom, I began to want to amuse

myself with her. Since I wanted to have my way with her and she was not willing, she worked me over so badly with her nails that I wished I had never begun. To get to the end of the story, seeing how things were going, I got a rope and tied her up so tightly that she made unheard of cries which you wouldn't have believed. At the end, we got along so well that, let me tell you, it seemed she had studied at a school for whores. The admiral named the cape on that island the cape of the Arrow for the man who was killed by the arrow.

Columbus, devout Columbus, who signed himself (with a still undeciphered cryptogram above), in Greek/Latin, 'Xρo Ferens' – 'bearing Christ' – 'gave' her to him, he says. An editor of the letter comments:

> Michele de Cuneo was a jolly dog and a good raconteur, in contrast to Columbus and the rather solemn Spaniards who wrote on the early voyages. He didn't care whether or not this was the Orient, or whether its discovery had been foretold in the Sacred Scriptures, [as Columbus most certainly did] so long as he had a good time, which obviously he did. Although his narrative is somewhat confused, it is valuable for personal touches, incidents that nobody else related, and a lively account of fauna, flora and native manners and customs.

So that's all right then.

All places where men have been have their shadows – as dimly we had begun to realise in that trip to Greece years earlier. Columbus first landed on his second voyage in what are now the US Virgin Islands, on St Croix, at Salt River, and our new friend the Archaeologist wanted to take us there. He did not say why.

We drove down there through the rain forest. We parked the Land Rover on a patch of shingly, shelly ground below a grass covered mound. As we got out, I noticed that the ground was covered with shells, and little bones, some of them marked and scored. The Archaeologist seemed pleased I had noticed, and before I could say anything, 'Yes,' he said, 'it is. One of the biggest middens in the West Indies, going back at least a thousand years. Only we do not have money to excavate it.' He went on to tell us that the wind and tide occasionally scour the beach, and uncover one of the many graves made there by those earlier people who called this land their own – if they had that concept. Above, overlying the graveyard, as we realised as soon as we climbed it, the mound was a star shaped fort built by the French in 1617 to protect that anchorage from the English – one of whose ships lies just offshore, by the reef. The shadows of European quarrels had darkened the sun of this place too. Then the penny dropped: this is the very place where Columbus' crew raided the Taino village and carried off the women, this is where de Cuneo was given that unfortunate girl, who had just seen her defender beheaded: the first blood shed by Europeans in the New World. The brochures say the scuba diving is excellent.

As we sat there, we thought and talked of those earlier people, whose race has now left this land, who came there in their big canoes across the windy ridges of the sea to harvest the fish and the conch, and to bury their dead, for years upon years upon years. Now only the wind and tide reveal, occasionally, the skull of one of their folk, its eye sockets filled with sand, mute witness of the temporariness of ourselves and the emptiness of our power. As the sand dries in the sun and wind, the wind makes little swirls of it and grain by grain it escapes, leaving the eyes' hollows to fill again with the next tide.

★

The car number plates call the Islands 'American Paradise.' The native snakes, they say, are no threat to humans. It is almost – without the studio choir doing a wordless *vocalise* – the Hollywood dream of the Caribbean that made our imagination – mine anyway – of the place back in the cinemas of childhood. That sugary dream is still what sells the place to droves from middle America, vacationing from 50 weeks of dull jobs with all the energy they have left. But behind the dream for me lie insistently the ancient cruelty of de Cuneo, and others, and the cries of 'his' girl, and so many like her, and outside affluent residences the barking of Rottweilers, and the razor wire, with bougainvillea rambling all over, on the fences. There is a reality behind the popular dream infinitely more interesting, if a good deal more cruel.

★

Oh, and those lectures? Well, the first was the toughest. The local paper had seized on my lecturing about Columbus and ran that splash story under the title 'Columbus: Hero or Villain?' – which sat rather obliquely to what I was going to discuss. Television picked it up, and the second night I was there they broadcasted a live discussion between me and Wilfredo, a local lawyer who had a formidable library of Columbania (as I later discovered) and deep knowledge of it to boot. The TV people expected, I think, a bad tempered confrontation –'who is this uppity Brit coming to tell us about our history?' – but must have been disappointed since we agreed about almost everything except the amount of credit Columbus gave to *Mandeville's Travels,* that fourteenth century travel account of India and Cathay which, as I said, is the nearest thing I have to Mr Dick's King Charles' Head[4]. As nobody in the watching audience was very likely to have heard of it, let alone read it, the controversy was doubtless muted. Not good television, but the beginning of a good friendship that in the end brought Wilfredo to Cambridge. So far, so good. A book signing at the bookshop in St Croix sold more books than I thought I had written. Even better. Then the lecture, in Government House. Now, warned by this time of local susceptibilities, I had, I thought, covered my back. Judiciously I was going to give due credit to the possibility – no more – advanced by Thor

Heyerdahl that the first Old World people to cross the Atlantic had been Egyptian. I was aware that there was a legend that in the fourteenth century Mansa (i.e. King) Abu Bakr II of Mali gave up his throne to explore the Atlantic, and had never been heard of again, and that some in the Caribbean claimed they descended from him and his ship's company. Certainly, I argued, the resources of that empire then at its zenith would have allowed such an attempt to be made. But there was no evidence, and at that time the possibility of DNA searching was way in the future. I was careful also to acknowledge that in the room there would be some who claimed part Arawak, Taino or Carib, descent, who felt very strongly about the arrival of the Europeans. I was also circumspect about the issue of cannibalism, and how easily excarnation as a funeral rite might be mistakenly seen as preparation for a cannibal feast – as indeed it is represented in the fine copper engraving in Theodor de Bry's *America* (1591).

The room was packed. There were even people standing. You could hear the noise of axes being ground. Wilfredo, a man of reputation in the community, took the chair. He introduced me generously – 'my friend'. The lecture happened. There were agreeing nods, and some people laughed at my attempts at lightness. Questions. Mostly bland, and Wilfredo was a kindly Chair. But then, just as I thought I was safe, came the wild card. A man at the back put up his hand and said, 'You have been very fair in allowing for the possibility of other Old World people getting here before the fifteenth century. But you have completely ignored my people, and I find that insulting.' 'Sir,' I said, 'You have the advantage of me. Who are your people?' 'We,' he said, 'are the Lost Ten Tribes of Israel, and we were the first people in America.' To which I had no answer. So, meanly, I turned to Wilfredo, and said, 'You have far more knowledge than I in this area. What is your view?' And Wilfredo, bless him, took it on the chin and closed the meeting with a vote of thanks.

Wilfredo invited us to dinner at his home. He was a lawyer in medical malpractice, with a big office in San Juan in Puerto Rico, another in Christiansted, another in Miami. Those great responsibilities obviously paid him well. The house was on a hill, in a compound with two friendly Rottweilers to welcome visitors. They licked my hand when I patted them and I do not think they were just seeing if I tasted nice. The terrace looked out over the sea, a view carefully framed by palm trees clacking in the trade wind. Below were the lights of Christiansted, and we were far enough away and high enough up not to hear the noise of the town. The dark of the sea stretched over to where the other islands must lie. I remember the dinner as an elaborate affair, though I recall less of the menu than I do of the immaculate and attentive waiters in white gloves and the surprising ordinariness of the wine. After dinner, we retired with our brandy (decent) through an elaborately locked door into Wilfredo's private sanctum to see his paintings and his library. The paintings were, shall we say, of mainly masculine appeal; the library was, for me, dukedom enough. It had almost every major work ever written on Columbus, his family, and the early voyages to America. It had several relevant early printed books. From this real scholar's library, Wilfredo gave me a little book he himself had written on Columbus' landing in St Croix. Again, the curious nature of the island's imaginative relationship to the first European visitors was apparent. On the one hand, there was a sort of appeal to a legitimating authority in Catholic Spain, for a lot of people descend from Spaniards, and some from branches of great houses – like Wilfredo. But at the same time there is a subtle awareness of how ill that might sit with the history of the native peoples who were supplanted, and of the blacks, who came across the Atlantic with no choice in the matter. We had perceived exactly the same uneasiness when we stood on the beach in the wind at Salt River, and The Archaeologist was saying how layered the site was with different cultures, each overwriting its predecessors, but all making up the problematic present. Once the ghosts are awake, they do not go to sleep again. Be careful what you read, and what you seek to know.

★

Journeys end; business is done. There we were at World's End, as Morton had called the house he and Lila had built, sitting talking far into the night, by the pool – sea water,

of course – as one does when things are coming to an
end. The stars wheeled slowly overhead, and in the light
of the lamp we idly watched a gang of ants trying to lift a
three inch centipede up a vertical wall four feet high. And
dropping it when more than half way up, again, and then
again. We sat there, WASP, Brit, Puerto Rican, Black and
Jew, and thought about success, and failure, and trying,
and about everything else. Five friends on a small island:
the worlds that had made us seemed a long way off in
that island of light in the dark. Bruce, the WASP, with a
German surname, had made his home here after a career
in the military. His family had come from Nuremberg.
Old Morton, the Jew – well, second generation New
York rag trade, made a packet importing cheap cloth
and then buying the factories that made it – could just
recall seeing New York for the first time from the deck
of the steamer that brought his mother and father and
himself and his sister from Hitler's psychotic Germany.
Some of my ancestors – the ones whose remaining silver
cutlery we use on high days and holidays – had been
prosperous Liverpool shipowners, who had made some
of their money on the notorious Middle Passage taking
people like Wallace the Librarian's ancestors to America,
where those of Wilfredo, child of the conquistadores,
had bought them. Amazing Grace. The Cruzan rum
passed round again. 'Plane to catch in the morning,' I
said, stretching, and half rising. 'Yes,' said Wilfredo. 'But
you will be back and we shall talk again. There is much
to say.'

The ants dropped the dead centipede yet again. I sat down again.

*

And so the years rolled by, each with a springtime hurry to get the potatoes planted and broad beans put in at the Cambridgeshire house before the setting out once more across the water with a new sheaf of lectures. Always in Spring, never in the Fall. And some springs were late.

More than once we ended up at a Homely House way up the Hudson Valley, near the painter F. W. Church's Olana, when the late snow was still lying and the creeks were quiet as the frost gripped them. But it is a fickle time of year: the next day might be shirtsleeve weather. The white frame farm house, built sometime in the late eighteenth century, still had a few acres with it, and sat at the top of a slope down to the creek. The leafless sumac bushes formed an underwood along the line of the water, below the tall maples and oaks. Vines in the gnarled nakedness of late winter drooped in festoons from the branches. We were warned about poison ivy, towards which Jenny's sister Morag nursed a vindictive and impotent hatred. Below the house, deer grazed in the late evening when the weather was open, and drank at the creek. Raccoons raided the rubbish from time to time, and groundhogs made nuisances of themselves by digging under Morag and Michael's plants, and below the verandah itself. Once a skunk made itself noticeably at home. At the end of several of the trips, this was our refuge and our stay, a place to unwind, and talk. Walks to Olana were regular – the house has to be seen to be believed, but the view makes it easy to understand why Church, the most accomplished (and far and away the best paid) landscape painter of his generation, set his pleasure dome there. Each visit, we walked through the woods to hear the frogs beginning their mating calling in the still partly frozen swamps. We walked together in the Catskills, we did part of the Taconic Trail, we went to visit iconic Woodstock in a light snowstorm, when 1967 seemed a universe away. Morag's and Michael's friends visited, talk flowed, music played, even in the snow Michael cooked on the barbecue, and wine made glad the heart of man as the Bible says it does. New York and its noise and frantic restlessness seemed a long, long way off, and nobody minded.

The first time Jenny and I went, it was after a busy time in New York and we were exhausted, after lectures at the Explorers' Club, at the English Speaking Union, and a long and inconclusive meeting with a publisher. Memories of that New York trip are fragmented, kaleidoscopic. I hated what I still think of as the radical ugliness of so many buildings, the traffic, the noise, the lack of space. Where Morag had for years been living, a flat at a good address on East 55th, which we back home had assumed had to be glamorous – after all, you could see the Empire State Building – was so small its footprint would nearly have fitted into our living room. You *could* see the Empire State Building, or at least its top, with a bit of craning. A failed peasant like me felt hemmed in, constrained, cut off from light and air and trees and grass. To see a bedraggled squirrel in Battery Park lifted the heart at the same time as it excited concern about how it and its fellows could survive, cut off by traffic and concrete so far from any other habitat. The memories that endure of my trips to that city are oddly skewed: walking through the streets to the east of Central Park at night, with all the lights on, and glimpsing momentarily why so many people love the place; a magnificent hamburger in Long Island City; the tedious horrors of trying to get out of the place by car. But then other memories – old Europe in the New World! – Tilman Rimenschneider's limewood carving of a seated bishop in the Cloisters Museum, his face lined with the pain of memory and the wisdom of old age; and in the Frick Collection, those two old and bitter enemies, Thomas Cromwell and St Thomas More, facing each other in two uncannily powerful profile Holbein portraits that virtually spit at each other across the fireplace.

To get up river was a relief. That first visit to Hudson, the weather was open, the garden greening. I was alone in the early morning in front of the house. Morag's friend Mike turned up in a big pickup. He had been a US Navy Seal in Vietnam. It showed. He guarded the house when they were not there. They hardly needed to lock. He had not known they were coming back, and the car was put away.

He got out, wordlessly, and came towards me. 'Who you, then?' His hands were in exactly the ominous attitude where in a Western one expects the quick draw. Well, all was soon plain, and he came in for coffee. I liked him a lot, and he liked me. 'They tell me you're a shootin' man,' he said. I confessed the charge. 'I'll come round in the morning and we'll have a go at those old groundhogs.' I did not expect him to keep his word, but, oh boy, he did, he did. He turned up with a twelve bore – my own preferred weapon – an AK 47 and a 7.62 rifle. And a knife down the side of his boot. Groundhogs are quite peaceable creatures, on the whole. As it happens, we did not see one – to my relief – but he shot a fox on the other side of the field. Then we had some more coffee and he cleaned his gun.

Came one Saturday afternoon, at the tail end of a late winter. The mornings were still cold, with sharp frost, but the day warmed up to shirtsleeve temperature. We are all outside, beginning the spring tidy up after the cold pressure of the snow has been lifted off the grey grass. Michael puts on the outside speakers for the stereo: a relay from the Metropolitan Opera. Opera – he has a fine baritone voice – has been his and Morag's passion for years. Jenny's sister Morag had introduced her father to Wagner's *Ring* in the old, and very fine, Solti recording – a fine (and valued) parting gift as she had been just about to emigrate, permanently, to the US, and at that time hopping across the Atlantic as easily – and nearly as quickly – as going to Manchester was not a thing one could do. Saying goodbye to a daughter is very hard.

Die Walküre is a long opera. We worked on, but increasingly quietly as the music exerted its power. Even the intrusive and banal interval chat, chat, chat, did not quite break the spell Wagner was weaving. The afternoon wore on, and the sun began to sink in a fiery glory behind the bare trees on the hill. By this time we were all silent, and slowly, one by one, our hands put down trowel and fork and rake, and we sat, scattered round the garden, as that tremendous dialogue between Father Wotan and wayward Brünnhilde built up to its climax as she is cast into her enchanted sleep and Loge is summoned in those rising arpeggios, to surround her until a hero comes who knows not fear. The fire in the music chimed with the blaze of light on the hilltop to the west. Each bare tree seemed edged with fire. Both daughters were weeping quietly. So were their husbands, but biting back, as men too often do, the showing of it. Memories, and love, as delicate and ungraspable as woodsmoke, coloured the dying of the light. The night would be cold.

II

STRANGE SEAS OF THOUGHT

Northabout

I looked at the sky and the earth and straight ahead
and since then I've been writing a long letter to the dead
on a typewriter that doesn't have a ribbon, only a horizon line
so the words beat in vain and nothing stays.

Tomas Tranströmer, *Baltics*

Wagner's *Ring* cycle — well, you love it, live in it, or you hate it. I incline to the former, my wife has no doubts about the latter. C. S. Lewis describes in his spiritual autobiography how as a boy he felt the pull of 'northernness', and found a sort of satisfaction (that only fed the inchoate longing) in the Icelandic myths and sagas, and in Wagner — however odd Wagner's take on that material seems to be. I know what he meant: hearing, whether in good clothes in a theatre in London or muddy from gardening in upstate New York, the All Father putting his errant child, his *wunschtochter*, 'daughter of his will', into her enchanted sleep, knowing it is the beginning of his own twilight, breaks my heart with a terrible pleasure. For those ancient stories from the Northlands, outstaring with a grim heroism fate, Ragnarøk, and the darkness, bring back each time, however long it is since I thought of them, the same strange enveloping absorption in them as when I first read them. They peopled the Northlands for me, long before

I went there regularly, and they colour the long sunlight and the cold grey widowmaker every time I do. For I have long had what Norwegians call the Northern Sickness, for which there is no cure. The Northlands and their saga have always drawn me imaginatively and emotionally since long before I worked as a deckhand, little more than a lad, on a deep sea trawler fishing the south Iceland and Atlantic grounds. (There were several trawlers going out of Fleetwood then on every tide. I used to see them from the window of my parents' bedroom.) As a youth I could have told you where lay each of the roots of the World Tree, the ash Yggdrasil, how Father Odin lost his eye and Tiw his hand.

Over the accumulating years I have travelled a fair bit in the summer light of Greenland, Svalbard and Scandinavia, and the Baltic, and ski-ed under the sharp midwinter stars of central Norway. But those first voyages, almost the first job I had, put aside for good any idea that the north was merely a pretty place, the home of Natural Wonders and Wildlife, as the cruise brochures say: it was and always has been a place of hard work, ever since men followed the animals who followed the retreating ice north, winning a living. And a place, too, of the tensions and feuds of men and women competing for honour and sustenance.

Moreover, the North mattered. For centuries, if not millennia, western and southern Europe relied on the resources and trade of the North and the Baltic. Before the opening of America and of the sea route to India, the Baltic was a major conduit to Europe for goods – and ideas – from the far lands of the East. I rejoice in knowing that without Swedish iron and Baltic tar and timber Nelson's navy could not have kept the sea. Without Polish and German grain, people in France and England would have been hungry. Without the salted herring of Lübeck and Hamburg mediaeval Lent would have been a fast indeed. Without the wealth generated by those Easterlings who worked these trades (and took their cut, of course), we would have no currency we could think of as sterling.

The more you know about the history – which is people's lives, loves and losses and longings – of a place the more technicolour and, well, resonant its landscape becomes both in imagination and actuality. That flood of Vikings – Rus, they called themselves – going East and down the rivers of the country they gave their own name, to the riches of Persia, the Black Sea, Byzantium, the Silk Road that reached to far Cathay, then settling and founding a dynasty that lasted till Ivan the Terrible; the campaigns of the Teutonic Knights – strictly The Order of Brothers of the German House of Saint Mary in Jerusalem, and by no means all of them German – against the Slavs, the Ests and the Letts; the once huge empire of the Poles, now hardly a memory – the intensity of interest gets stronger and stronger as you read more and find out more: almost a hot lust for knowledge and understanding, ever just beyond your grasp, which becomes imperious. And then came my interest in the nationalism of the nineteenth century and its baleful legacy to the next.

And my interest in music. It is easy to forget how subversive music can be. The Poles' mazurka was banned by the Russians when they at last controlled Poland, their ancient, feared enemy. The nationalist music of northern and eastern Europe, of Chopin, Smetana, Dvořák, Sibelius and so on, was a not so coded protest against Austria, against Prussia, against Russia. It seduced me as a youth who then comprehended little of these things. I remember exactly when that interest started, one evening in the Dean's rooms in College. Six of us undergraduates were sitting round the fire, after dinner, and this was the Music Evening of the week. Now, we had no record player – we called them gramophones – at home when I was a boy – few people did – and apart from the Church choir with its energetic and determined choirmaster, the big village where I grew up was pretty much a musical desert for me. So these musical evenings were rain on a thirsty soil. All sorts of new worlds were revealing themselves, leading off each other into an immeasurable distance. I kept quiet because I knew so little. One of us that evening had brought along Sibelius' Symphony no 2, in D major, and the cool greens and dark blues and blacks of Sibelius' music spoke across the sundering seas of a land of forest, of water shimmering below a cold sky, of lonely lakes where the darkness dwells, of a myth of heroes, of betrayal, of death, of loss. And of paradoxical hope. That sense of longing, *sehnsucht,* of a distant light seen and impossibly desired, is the sound I would one day hear in the wingbeats of the migrating swans in their great flocks, of the temporary summer gathering of the waterfowl, the unearthly, spine-shivering, bubbling cry of the curlew. Einojuhani Rautavaara's *Cantus Arcticus* makes that wild music of the empty northland call back, with a sudden clutch at the heart, the experience of being there, of watching the grave courtship of the barnacle geese, of seeing a red necked phalarope whirling about in the shallows to stir up the plankton on which it delicately feeds, of having the crossbills drop bits of pine cone on me as I sat in the snow beneath a tree while they fed, prising open the leaves of the dry cones for the seeds of life hidden in them.

So, in time, to Stralsund, Gdansk, Tallin, St Petersburg, Turku, Helsinki, to the Baltic highway for the rich goods from the warm south and distant east, and the shores where amber was gathered, and traded down to the opulent and luxurious lands below a higher sun. That amber... Once upon a time – way beyond historical memory – much of the Baltic was dry land. Soon after the last Ice Age ended, some 11,000 years ago, where now the water is full five fathoms deep, people lived and loved and hunted and cooked, just as they were doing in Doggerland over which now the North Sea's grey waves stretch as far as the eye can see. Pine forests blanketed the land, and the fossilised resin wept from those huge trees made the amber that with luck you can pick up on the beach in North Germany, Poland, Latvia, Estonia. When I hold a piece, I cannot help thinking of the distant summers of those ancient trees whose branches sang the wind, their trunks bleeding sap from holes bored by insects and birds. And once I did see a piece...

> Pretty! in amber to observe the forms
> Of hairs, or straws, or dirt, or grubs, or worms!
> The things, we know, are neither rich nor rare,
> But wonder how the devil they got there.
> Alexander Pope, *Epistle to Arbuthnot*

But it was too expensive.

Much I have now forgotten of those northern journeys, for some were hopelessly hurried, needing only a couple of clean shirts and underpants. Some things I wish I did not remember. I disliked on sight the glitz of St Petersburg – perhaps because I was prejudiced. For I had read about Peter, called 'the Great', wrecking John Evelyn's beloved garden at Sayes Court when he was in England, which struck me, who love gardens, the height of bad manners. (Parliament had to vote Evelyn special compensation for the damage.) I had read of Peter's advancement of his crony Menshikov to dizzying wealth and power. (Prince, Marshal, corrupt as hell, laden with the loot of Poland... The story goes that Menshikov was making a living on the streets of Moscow selling stuffed buns known as *pirozhki* – nothing wrong with doing that of course, and what he came on to do was far less respectable – when his handsomeness and wit caught, eventually, the Tsar's attention.) I had read of Peter's torture and, in effect, murder of his own son, and the impaling or breaking on the wheel of his associates. And they call him 'the Great'... And then the German empress, Catherine, insatiable if generous, an able woman, but not without blood on her hands... too many others to mention. So I admit the prejudice in my negative response to the (to my mind) vulgar bad taste of the Hermitage. The guides hurry you through the art collection – you have ticked this box, now go on to the next and do not hold up the next party – so you can get to the Impressionists, when what you really want to look at is the Dutch genre painting. That gallery, which I know only from hurried (passive!) visits and the catalogue, strikes me as what rich kleptomaniacs with too much power and no taste would collect and house in a flashy building with lashings of gold leaf and malachite panels – the green stone was brought at great expense from the Urals. But I think I dislike the city for other reasons... that old beggar woman in the road outside the Kazan Cathedral, simply wailing at the sky, her hands cupped in supplication, as the shiny Mercedes and Jaguars with privacy windows swept smoothly by unheeding. One hooted at her. Their slipstream fluttered her rags. In a momentary glance, I saw the depth of long agony in her eyes, incommunicable. Mother Russia, *Matushka Rossiya*.

What hope had she ever had in her whole life in her violence-torn, misgoverned country? Even more I wish I did not remember a well-dressed, well-paid colleague in St Petersburg, whom I had quite liked up to that point, saying with a complacent smile and a shrug, 'Of course, this is the best of Russia. Ten miles outside the town people are wearing newspapers. They cope.' I saw people weeping for the past at the tombs of the Romanovs in the Peter and Paul Cathedral, and God knows there is much more about the horrors of Lenin's and Stalin's evil tyranny to weep for. Similarly, I wish the photos I later saw of the ruins of Gdansk – after the soldiers of the Red Army, these mainly from central Asia, arrived in 1945 – did not occlude completely in memory the pretty, reconstructed, townscape that now is, and when I think of that town, where I have been happy and welcomed, the pictures in my mind are of rubble and destruction. The Russian soldiers had been told they were in Berlin, and had taken a terrible revenge on the idea of Germany.

> When Russians came, together with my girlfriends we were hiden [sic] in the corners of the main train station in Gdansk.[...] They first found one of my girlfriends, a young and beautiful girl. They throw her onto a table in a room. They striped [sic] her clothing off and holding her they brutally raped her many times. We came out of the hiding place when they left. She was dazed and blood-stained. The blood was pouring off her legs.(...) In the evening the Soviets came to my tenement. They started to robe [sic]

watches and other valuables. The time of plundering and pillage didn't last long. They started to shout 'rabotac' which meant that they want to have coitus with women. They dragged all the women who they recognized as suitable for raping. They put them on tables or beds and formed a queue and were waiting for their turn. Me and my sister were also raped.

I do not know who wrote that: it is in a file of notes I made in the museum in Gdansk. Such things were repeated in Berlin, and all over war-torn Europe, and happen as I write below our European radar. Just one more item on the news before we hear about the next celeb's *awful* trauma... Iris Origo in her *War in Val d'Orcia* says much the same for the French forces fighting their way up Italy – particularly the feared Spahis. I wish I did not remember Theresienstadt, the killing factory where not much pretence, in the end, was made of it being anything else. People who became my relatives died there, lambs to the slaughter, sacrificed to a perversion of all that Europe had stood for, but which Europe had made: our parents made. And we might do again.

★

It was to Sibelius' and Rautavaara's Finland we came, in an age still almost of our innocence if no longer wholly of ignorance, to the deep forests and the richness of the summer light. I have a friend who has translated much of the Finnish *Kalevala* (1849) into Latin in trochaic tetrameters – the metre exactly matches that of the Finnish poem. His Finnish wife is distantly related to Elias Lönnrot, who indefatigably tramped round the wilds of Finland collecting, just as they were disappearing, half-forgotten stories and songs, of Lemminkäinen and Kullervo and the Swan of Tuomela and Ilmarinen's Forging of the Sampo. Lönnrot took lots of time off from his job as a doctor, and toured remote Finland, the land of the magic-making Sami (which used to be called Lappland), and nearby Russian Karelia. What he gathered he forged into an epic for the nation that one day would be. For poems, myths, make nations, for good or ill. And some people still see it so. I was reading the *Kalevala* on the plane to Helsinki, and as we landed the hitherto silent girl sitting beside me suddenly said, without ceremony, 'Why are you reading that poem? It is the soul of my homeland.' Her tone was odd: almost as if she felt it was *her* poem, a private thing, and I, a mere scholar, was somehow intruding on a mystery.

There are a lot of lakes in Finland – nobody seems to know offhand how many. There are even more trees. I love trees, and have planted many in my lifetime. Trees are our fellow creatures, with whom we share the planet, on whose exhalations our inhalations depend. In their rings we read the weather centuries ago, of sun and storm, drouth and flood, heat and cold – of what it was like to grow when the world was younger. A forest shares a history, which each tree remembers, records, even after it has been felled. And to me trees have always had different personalities, even within a species, just as they all speak with different voices, from the roar of a big oak resisting, playing with, outshouting a gale, to the whispering chatter of aspen and poplar in the lightest of summer breezes. The femininity of ash, or birch – oh, I know it is all deplorably anthropomorphic, but I understand instinctively why the ancients revered trees, and to label something with a dismissive Greek-derived adjective does not dismiss the idea. Sometimes the ancients gave them spirits, dryads. Who has not been in a wood, alone, quiet, and felt sometimes an antagonism, sometimes a welcome, sometimes almost a Presence? I know one tree in a Cambridge College garden in whose vaulted shade even the most garrulous people fall involuntarily silent, as in a cathedral, a place of Power. Some call it a Portal. It offers a shelter, a haven, a thin place, so to speak, in between the worlds. A distinguished man, now full of years, told me that when he was a young student at that College he used to go there for spiritual sustenance in dead of night. The Ancients knew all about that sense of the uncanny, of some spirit there: *numen inest*. I can fully understand the reverence so many civilised Germans – and central Europeans generally – I know seem to feel for the forest.

Trees demand some reverence from us, for they see many lives of men, good or bad, and when they die they still serve us, if only to keep us warm. Our homes are full of dead trees, in books, and shelves, and chairs and whatever. Boniface, Apostle of the Germans, understood their powerful hold on people's imaginations. He cut down the sacred oaks wherever he went. He heard that at midwinter the folk of Geismar gathered around a huge oak, 'Thor's Oak,' to sacrifice, usually a small child. They boasted that the God of Boniface could never destroy the Oak of the Thunderer. With a few companions he went to Geismar. When they reached the village just before the sacrifice, his scared companions ran away. Boniface went on alone, carrying an axe. Laying it to the trunk of the Oak, he felled it. (An interesting point: so says the Saint's Life, but why did nobody stop him? It would take about an hour to fell a big tree.) Pointing (and probably sweating, for swinging an axe is hard work) to a little spruce behind the felled oak, he said to the dumbfounded people, 'This little tree, a young child of the forest, shall be your holy tree. It is the wood of peace... It betokens endless life, for its leaves are ever green. See how it points upward to heaven. Let this be called the tree of the Christ-child; gather about it, not in the wild wood, but in your own homes; there it will shelter no deeds of blood, but loving gifts and rites of kindness.' Well, there are lots of Christmas trees in Finland, and in that fair country I have received many gifts and acts of kindness. In piety I have even planted the odd tree there myself, where a hollow in the granite has allowed soil to accumulate, and I ask after the health of my plantings whenever I see my friends.

Boniface, as it happens, comes into my story again: but of that later. Thor's Oak: there were other trees, drinking shed blood through their roots. At Frösö ('Frey's Island') in Jämtland, Sweden, work in the church uncovered the stump of a large birch, felled sometime in the eleventh century – about when the first wooden church was built. It was surrounded by bones from a century or so earlier. Animals – elk, pigs, deer, cows, sheep, goats – had been sacrificed, the usual method being to cut their throats so that a spectacular spray of blood drenched the ground and the tree. There were human bones too. Perhaps the bits were hung in the branches: there is evidence from elsewhere for that practice. Those of the new Faith aggressively appropriated this holy place: the altar is exactly over this bloody spot where the Tree stood.

Once the forests covered Europe, from sea to sea, and the survivors recall their ancient dominion – like Tolkien's Ents. The life of the forests – and this is true for me in Germany too, and other places – feels insistent, pressing on you, and the habitations of man merely punctuate their breathing immensity. The trees exhale different scents. Stop. Breathe deep. Listen. They are rarely quite silent. Trees move, susurrate. The silent tiny stir of pine needles catches on their shine the momentary change of light. In the sun the buzz of insects tells how much the work of life is going on. The trees have a secret life. Recent research, indeed, suggests they work not just as individuals but as a mutually supportive community, interacting with each other, supporting the weaker ones, passing nutrients, and alerts, to each other along the nerves of their secret roots, in symbiosis with the mycelia and mycorrhizae that make the very soil a living thing[5]. The largest trees in forests work as central hubs – some call them 'mother' trees, with a question-begging but seductive anthropomorphism – for vast subterranean mycorrhizal networks. The mother tree nurtures seedlings by infecting (is inoculating them a better term?) them with fungi and supplying them the nutrients they need for growth. (Back to that worrying thought again: what *is* an individual?)

A poet friend of mine once said, 'Trees in their community intercede for us.' Stand in a still, cold, clearing, as I try to do each winter, and shades of an older world, the dark, fierce freedom of trees, press on you. For trees are much older than Man, the late comer. High on a Spitsbergen moraine, this last summer, I found their tropical leaves in coal laid down in forests when no Man was and the ancient land was half a globe from where it now is scoured by the Arctic winter storm. As you skirt the forest of Finland in a boat, the green curtain at the edge of the lake parts, every so often, to reveal houses by the shore, and at the edge of the lake their saunas. A smudging of smoke against the green, a boat pulled up out of reach of the waves that can get up, or of the winter's ice, are the only signs of human activity in this immensity. But the waiting trees close in again at the edge of the clearing as we scull past, as they will surely close in wholly when that house is no more.

In the forest depths, where snow or a gale or felling has brought down the trees, the sudden inpouring of light makes the undergrowth shoot up into nearly impenetrable tangles. In late summer you graze on the raspberries and wild strawberries, which can carpet the ground where sunlight can filter through. People say you may be lucky and see an elk – or at least hear the crashing through the undergrowth as that shy animal makes itself scarcer. I heard crashing, certainly, and would like to think it *was* an elk. Later, the first saplings will begin to shade this lower growth out; meanwhile, progress is slow, at times tastily so, through the tangles of raspberry and bramble. In just such a clearing, secret among the woods, suddenly we found the remains of a great house. The roof had long fallen. You could just make out where the levelled parterre had been. Honeysuckle and bramble lolled on the portico steps, the stucco had peeled, and ivy's disjunctive embrace shrouded the neo-classical proportions. We stood silent. Once, said Hekka, this had been the great manor of the neighbourhood, in season full of lights and laughter, where Marshal Mannerheim, one of the founders of Finnish independence from Russia, had regularly visited her grandfather. (Forced by diplomacy to meet Hitler, he referred to him as 'that Bohemian corporal' with the disdain that comes from old lineage and the career soldier's contempt for the unprofessional.) At Christmas, said Hekka, the sleighs had swished up with their bells jingling and their horses steaming, and fur-wrapped guests had been welcomed at the *porte cochère*. Now the quiet forests were taking it back from the passing things of the summer, as they had already taken back where its lawns and walks had been. And Hekka said, pointing to a tangle of young trees, 'And over there was our cherry orchard where we three sisters played.' And burst into laughter.

In Russia they play Chehov's *Cherry Orchard* as a comedy. Hmm...

★

Hekka's laughter, her matter-of-factness, could not quite hide pain, regret, loss: of childhood, parents, their world, the scars. Forests always take back, in their patience, what we took from them for a space and thought our own. That includes what we did, our memories. What else is hidden in these northern forests, in the memory of the trees? Trees near the German border in Holland's eastern provinces are dangerous to chainsaw because of the shrapnel buried in them. Trees in the forests of Finland hold in their flesh bullets from the terrible if short Civil War that divided Finnish society for decades afterwards. They hold the metal hail that came with the three and a half month storm of the Winter War of 1939-1940 against Russia. Trees will drink blood. Somewhere in the Teutoburger Wald in what is now Lower Saxony and North Rhine-Westphalia, lie the bones of 15 to 20,000 Roman soldiers slaughtered when Quintilius Varus led his three legions to utter defeat by Arminius (Herman the German) in AD 9. (Arminius spent his youth in Rome as a hostage, and had had a Roman military education, even being given the rank of *eques*. After he returned to 'Germania', he became Varus' trusted adviser, but meanwhile was secretly fixing up an alliance of tribes that had traditionally been enemies.) The historian Suetonius says Augustus used to beat his head against the wall, saying the while, 'Quintilius Varus, give me back my legions!' Tacitus, writing three quarters of a century after the disaster – or victory, depending on where you stand – says that many officers were sacrificed by the Germanic forces in their religious ceremonies, or cooked in pots and their bones used for rituals. (No worse than what Varus did. His reputation stood high with the Senate for the harsh way he put down revolt: and crucified defeated rebels in droves on the patient trees.) Others were ransomed. Some more common soldiers appear to have got away with merely being enslaved, one of those things that could happen to anyone. But, reassuringly, we are told the walking in the Teutoburger Wald is excellent. A website says, 'Battles have now been replaced with peaceful relaxation on the Hermannshöhen (Hermann Heights) trail. The ridge of the Teutoburg Forest offers amazing views.' And that, perhaps, is the right perspective?

★

Almost everywhere, in Finland, through the trees, there is the glint of water, and the light seems to rise from it. In summer nights there is a peculiar luminosity to the northern sky, and as autumn shades the hemisphere there is a quiet that seems to reach to the pale stars. The long summer daylight allows plants to photosynthesise almost without a break, till the dark returns with the departing of the migrating birds. And the forest has not had it all its own way since man came. Open pastoral and arable country smiles with the passing work of men. Occasionally you glimpse elegant Classical mansions, often from the time of Gustavus Adolphus III of Sweden. Wood has been cleverly disguised, with paint and moulding, to look like Italian stucco. For this was rich country, a place of constant coming and going. The King's Road, the old trade route along the south of Finland from Sweden to Russia, was a major artery of trade at least from mediaeval times, and the many fortresses show how important were its security, and its tolls. The trade of the middle ages and the tolls of the Road gave some towns, like Lohja, the wealth, and the pride, to build substantial stone churches – about the decoration of Lohja my editor has stopped me, alas, from being enthusiastically tedious[6]. But the road was far older than that. Two thousand and more years ago people lived and hunted along this seaboard. They carried their goods along the lakes, smelted their iron with the charcoal they made from the trees on little pitsteads that are now merely placenames (like Rautaniemi) – and left their dead in clusters of burial barrows in the forest. I stumbled upon two barrows, once, on my morning walk.

Some lake shores are steep, glacier-scoured granite elbows sticking out of the sleeve of trees, where only mosses and lichens have yet colonised. Here, given the right wind, the waves will crash in a surf no boat would risk. Other gentler shores shelve gradually out to deeper water, fringed with a shading of reeds where big pike lie waiting for the unwary perch: the sunlight flashes on their barred flanks as they turn below the boat. Taking the boat out, and trolling or spinning with a light rod along the edge of the reeds, every so often, on the breeze, you catch the rumour of woodsmoke. Someone lighting a sauna, maybe; or, if it is rich with the aroma of juniper, it might be someone smoking one of the big trout or *siika* the lakes do produce. I remember one such smoking, by the lake. What Barrie the Classicist took out of the makeshift cabinet was of a rose-pink succulence that would have made a glutton out of the most determined dyspeptic; and there was a dish of green peas (for they were in their brief and wonderful season), cooked whole in their pods and eaten with lashings of butter, and the little potatoes that grow in the northlands. (On the bus going to Lohja, bags of fat green pods of peas were offered round like bags of sweets.) The woods offer fungi, too, of an indescribable range and profusion. I remember a fillet of reindeer, dressed with a cream sauce of freshly gathered chanterelles...

★

I have been persuaded on occasion to have a sauna: and always get nervous when I catch the scent of newly kindled birch logs on the afternoon wind. For I know what pressure is coming. But when in Rome... People seem inexplicably to jump into a sauna at the slightest provocation: Barrie – the friend who translated the *Kalevala* into Latin – even asked his future father-in-law's blessing in a temperature of 100 degrees C. The lakes do warm up in summer to a temperature just tolerable to me for swimming. Some people enjoy it. By late August it will be dropping a couple of degrees every day, and wimps (me) should avoid the water. Yet that cold water after a sauna is, I have to admit, invigorating. On the few occasions I have been persuaded to take a sauna – usually by telling me I would have no dinner if I did not – and it was certainly interesting to see one's body steaming off the lake water while having a cool beer and watching the sunset over the lake. But I say this without much enthusiasm. *Chacun à son goût.*

*

An early autumn morning, and we wake up in our room. The golden wood walls smell of cut pine: for the house is new. A warm thick mist outside, luminous with diffused sunlight. A woodpecker is drilling somewhere. The lake, a few yards away, swashes quietly on the pebbles of the little beach. The clear bright water shades into the mist only a few yards out. The ground is covered with gossamer, for this is the time of year when the minute young spiders spin a strand for the wind to lift them off and carry them off to wheresoever it listeth, which shall be their home. Each strand is picked out in the dew. On a juniper bush a web suddenly drops its dew as its delicately piebald owner, sensing a presence nearby, runs to the middle and makes her web vibrate. The sun begins to burn off the mist and be warm on my back as I sit on the step and break my fast. The whole land becomes too bright to look at. But before us lies Helsinki airport, and landing a few hours later to the Babel of Heathrow, for we have promises to keep.

I like Helsinki, and wish I were not leaving. It embraces the sea, takes it to its heart. The town started as yet another station on the King's Road to the East and its anchorages were in time protected by a fortress on one of the islands in its harbour: Suomenlinna, 'the fortress of Suomi/Finland.' I went there once, taking with me a *muikku* pie from a market stall as lunch. *Muikku* pie is good peasant food for a journey, a hard rye crust round a tight bunch of little fish. A sea wind puts an edge on your appetite and I chewed my pie as the ferry back to Helsinki came past the dry docks and a collection of old boats, past the yacht club where Arthur Ransome swung *Racundra's* compass. Even that tame trip across the harbour, as the end of even the smallest of journeys should, reminded of landfall and departure – here is a new place, a place to take rest in, a place where wings can be folded. For a space.

★

You can't quite get away from the *Kalevala*. (Why should one?) Sibelius's music illustrated a lot of it. Akseli Gallen-Kallella painted a set of murals of it in the Museum's entrance hall.[7] First impressions, the sort of careless glance that to my shame too readily I give, suggested a scaled-up Arthur Rackham on some extraordinary stimulant. But read the paintings closely, and something subtler, insistent, appears: a fierce nationalism, a desperate desire for Finland's freedom from Russian rule, a desire which in the end led to the Civil War – in which Gallen-Kallela fought with some distinction.

His illustrations of episodes of the *Kalevala* haunt the mind long after those complicated stories, with names so easily forgotten – after all they belong to an unfamiliar linguistic family – are remembered as a series of mere happenings. But for Finns his paintings told a story related organically to what being Finnish meant. The frescoes made for the 1900 Paris World Fair were openly political. In *Ilmarinen Plowing the Field of Vipers,* one viper wears the Romanov crown, and what clearing the vipers from the field means is obvious. But for me his most extraordinary painting, *The Defence of The Sampo* (1895/6), is in Turku, once the old Swedish-speaking capital on a shore facing Sweden across the western sea. With the inexorable slow uplift of the land after melting of the weight of the deep ice sheet, the town is now high and dry a mile from open water. Now, nobody quite knows what the Sampo was, or looked like, but Ilmarinen the smith forged it with great labour, a task set him by the witch Louhi, in return for her daughter's hand. Louhi is mistress of Pohjola, a dark and terrible place in the most extreme North.

> Ilmarinen, worthy brother,
> Thou the only skilful blacksmith,
> Go and see her wondrous beauty,
> See her gold and silver garments,
> See her robed in finest raiment,
> See her sitting on the rainbow,
> Walking on the clouds of purple.
> Forge for her the magic Sampo,
> Forge the lid in many colors,
> Thy reward shall be the virgin,
> Thou shalt win this bride of beauty;
> Go and bring the lovely maiden
> To thy home in Kalevala

After many days of work, he made the Sampo, which brought riches and good fortune to its holder:

> On one side the flour is grinding,
> On another salt is making,
> On a third is money forging,
> And the lid is many-colored.
> Well the Sampo grinds when finished,
> To and fro the lid in rocking,
> Grinds one measure at the day-break,
> Grinds a measure fit for eating,

Grinds a second for the market,
Grinds a third one for the store-house.

But Louhi steals the Sampo. As a result, so they say, bitter times fell on Ilmarinen's land, and desperately Ilmarinen and Väinämöinen set off to win the Sampo back. They manage to steal it from Louhi's stronghold, but Louhi pursues them and in the shape of a hideous gigantic bird fights Väinämöinen. He overcomes her, just, but the Sampo is destroyed for ever. There is a cost in victory, even when it is of the light.

The symbolism shrieks. The battle for the Sampo is the battle for what a free Finland might be. Patriotism is noble thing – if we are clear about what it *is*, exactly, to which we are being loyal. But as Edith Cavell said before the bullet put out her light, 'it is not enough'. And Wilfred Owen and millions of others found out the hard way it is not always sweet to die for the *Patria*. A noble ideal can so easily become the camouflage, the refuge, of the scoundrel, and then the road to the mass-produced horror of the last century lies wide open, even inviting.

★

In Helsinki, where Aleksanterinkatu and Mannerheimintie meet, there stands a bronze statue by Felix Nylund of three naked Smiths. They are forging something: it is hard to see what, but we know, of course, it is the Sampo. But the bronze does not move, and their work will never be done. Some in Helsinki say that their motionless hammers will ring on the anvil when a virgin goes past. My friend Barrie Fleet turned a neat epigram:

Incus illa trium fabrum, non tacta, silebat;
Tu si praeteris, num tacita manere potest?

The three smiths' anvil was silent, untouched;
But if *you* pass, silent surely it cannot be?

This civilised nation, which values a good education for all, and musical literacy, as should be, would appreciate that, for they broadcast weekly on the radio a Latin digest of the News: *Nuntii Latini.*

★

From Helsinki to Estonia, across the Gulf, was once a tricky journey where wind and the short steep seas that can get up in those shallow, rock-strewn waters could play havoc with boats and their plans. When the blanket of the political dark descended upon Europe, getting into Estonia became politically difficult as well, to say the least. But with the thawing of that ice, it is now, for the time being, the merest step to Tallinn and Estonia: hydrofoils delete the distance. But this is not travelling, it is merely getting there, like a parcel.

Being already in the eastern Baltic it seemed silly not to grab the chance to go to Tallinn, only a few months after

Estonia got back precarious independence from Russia's suddenly relaxed bear hug. That first visit was brief, a toe in the water, you might say, and curiosity: what would an ancient Hanseatic town so recently under Soviet rule be like? But an old and half-acknowledged wish also drove me, at least.

For Tallinn already had a curious resonance for me, if not for Jenny. She cared little for – indeed, rather deplored – my interest in maritime history, and the fact that Tallin – Reval until the first Estonian independence in 1918 – had been the main Russian naval base in the Napoleonic wars, and that Nelson had almost blockaded it, aroused deep misgivings in her of yet another informative monologue. The real point, though, was that I could not think of the place without thinking of Arthur Ransome. I read and re-read his *Swallows and Amazons* books as a child. Too young to realise that fiction and reality are different, and that the present is always, I had written to him when I was eight asking if I could meet John and Susan and Titty and Roger, (they were based on real people, as it happens) and where the Lake was. I got a charming hand-written reply, which I still have, saying the 'secrets are secrets, and must be kept, so no more questions.' He was one of my childhood's formative writers. But later I came across his wonderful *Racundra's First Cruise,* one of the best of sailing books, and his loving descriptions of bringing her into Reval in 1922, and of the town, had really taken me. (And I so wanted to go to the island Moon as well – but that is still in the future and I may not now have time for it.) Then, even later, I found out about his work as a war correspondent, and probably for MI5, during the Russian Civil War. He had walked through the opposing lines with Evgenia, who had been Trotsky's secretary and became his wife and 'The Cook' on *Racundra*, and they set up a first home in Reval/Tallinn. 'Sailing in there is always, for me, like coming home, and I hardly know how to give a picture of it as if I were seeing it for the first time,' he wrote. Equally difficult is seeing behind the images and emphases earlier reading has formed for you. My first walk through the stone gateway defended by a huge dumpy tower which the badly-printed tourist brochure coyly said was called 'Stout Margaret', then up that steep hill to the fortress, was coloured by the images Ransome's writing had formed in my mind those many years ago.

We took the hydrofoil from affluent, affluent Helsinki, across the grey waters. Many Finns were doing the same, most just for the day. At least in Estonia vodka is cheap, and its sale not limited to government outlets, and getting through the long winter darkness you do need something to warm you up. And the languages are closely related – sometimes confusingly. For example, *hallitus* in Finnish means 'Government', while in Estonian it means 'mould', which of course grows on the top of things like mousetrap cheese and old bread. Which is joyous. As we landed, the passengers quickly dispersed, many off to the right towards the railway station, most left to the grey town. Before us the Old Town of Tallinn towered up on its limestone rock, seeming – seeming – untouched by the surrounding scum of war and occupation. ('But the changes are inside...,' says one of Joseph Conrad's characters, acknowledging the darkness at the heart.) Long before those proud, forbidding walls that enclose the citadel high above, there were the wooden huts and palisades of an ancient people. The ancient Est legends, no more or less 'true' – whatever that means – than other such legends give you an imaginative cross-bearing on a people finding, like the Finns, in a memory an identity for the future. Friedrich Reinhold Kreutzwald collected (like Lönnrot) these legends and forged them together as the *Kalevipoeg* (1857-61), the poem that would make the Ests a nation. (We have been here before...). In The Beginning there was a woman called Linda, born from the egg of a grouse: a smallish bird, to be sure. She refused both sun and moon as suitors, and instead took up, naturally enough, with a handsome young giant Kalev. After their wedding, which lasted seven days, he carried her off on his sledge to this wild place by the shore. Their son, Kalevipoeg, the poem's hero, cleared parts of the country of its rocks so that it was fit for corn and pasture. He slew the wild beasts, and resisted the Christian invaders – the Danes, in the thirteenth century, who were getting fed up with constant raids by the pagan Vikings based in Estonia. When Kalev died, full of years, Linda built a grave mound for him, the hill of Tallinn. She gathered rocks in her apron, and when she placed the last stone on his mound sat down and wept. Her tears made Lake Ülemiste, south east of the citadel. But communist rule left a tidemark of malfunctioning ugliness round Kalev's grave.

Behind the huge fat tower the Coast Gate leads into a comfortable mixture of buildings: some mediaeval, some Renaissance, some nineteenth century Russian neo-Classical. Hanseatic merchants' tall houses jostle each other as if bidding at a market. Many are late mediaeval, some have elaborate Renaissance frontages you might see in Delft or Amsterdam or Copenhagen. They butt up against churches of that peculiar narrow-shouldered German Gothic, or respectfully keep their distance before the confident Baroque. The Town Hall reminds you of any solid north German or Danish town. Climbing higher, the wall the Teutonic Knights built in the fourteenth century dominates a long steep alley. Many of them were English, who, like Henry Bolingbroke – who had a future as Henry IV – or Chaucer's fictional Knight, would serve with the Order for a few years to get military experience on what was technically a Crusade. The Order brought the Gospel of the Prince of Peace, the Suffering Servant, to this heathen part of Europe on their swords' points. (The guidebook we had that first trip, printed before 1989, tried to score a cheap point, explaining the military architecture purely in terms of the nobles' oppression of the town. Which is practical and historical nonsense.) High up in Toompea, the citadel, where the Ests' timber stronghold had been long centuries before, the Russian Orthodox cathedral, dedicated to Alexander Nevsky, cheered on by a crowd of late eighteenth and early nineteenth century palaces built by the Russians, luxuriates in a flourish of onion domes and outfaces the lovely late Gothic Lutheran Cathedral,. But this town was then no museum, no place dying when the tourists wheel off to their roosts in the evening. The shops sold necessaries of life – when they had them. (Mahogany Art Nouveau shelves recalled an age of plenty and elegance, but held, say, only a couple of cans of peaches.) Palaces were lived in, divided up into flats where lived the poor. Lack of money to mend the gutter sent a winter's water pouring down the bulging stucco. No-one then had time, or money, to stop the hole in the roof of the former ballroom. Decay was everywhere. But the place felt, and smelt, alive. People, we thought, live here, make love, have children in these buildings, who play in the grass in the unweeded courtyards and on the gracious steps where once walked Grand Dukes, even the Tsar himself.

Further round Toompea –'cathedral hill' – there was a cafe where the more energetic tourists went – the ones who had made it up the steep cobbles from the lower town. It was expensive. But from there you look over those grey cliffs of dreary communist-era flats that then encircled the old town, over the harbour, out to the Baltic – the 'finest view to be obtained in any of the Baltic

capitals,' Ransome wrote. 'I cannot believe that any man
who has looked out to sea from Reval castle rock can ever
be wholly happy unless he has a boat.' When he saw it,
beyond the precipitous drop to the walls of the lower
town, beyond the tall spire of the church of St Nicolas,
patron of seafarers, the wide bay out to the island of Wulf
would have been full of ships coming and going, or lying
to their anchors, schooners with main and fore courses
set slipping away north to Helsinki, or west to the open
horizon that led to the old distant towns of the Hanse. It
was a place and a view dramatic enough to be where the
roads to the ends of the earth began.

My eyes were beginning to water in the northerly wind.
We became aware of a small waiting presence just at thigh
height: a girl, who could not have been more than five,
reaching up and offering us, as she surely did everyone
else, one of a bunch of wilted roses. We buy one; then,
seeing the hunger in her face and remembering how little
there was in those beautiful shops, we gave her the packet
of chocolate biscuits we had brought with us. Her eyes
grew round, she stuffed them in the pocket of her thin
dress, remembered to thank us with a grave little bow –
then dropped the roses, and dashed off round the corner.
Later we see her with a yet smaller child, licking the last
chocolate smears off their fingers.

For we saw real shortage, even hunger, which no
quantity of chocolate biscuits would relieve. Ransome

had described a busy market in the lower town by the theatre, where you could buy baskets, pots, pans, a samovar, where you could choose between competing sellers of poultry by prodding the breasts of their birds. 'You can walk between rows of boxes full of pike, some of them still alive in bath-tubs, big perch (two- and three-pounders are not the rarity they are at home) and baskets full of the little shining *killos*.' In another part, stall after stall of vegetables; in yet another, you could buy hunks of meat wrapped in newspaper, dripping blood, and the printer's ink becoming unreadable in the red wetness. A long time ago... nothing like that.

The old lady must have been over 80. Perhaps: she might have been much younger. She stood in an angle of the wall, out of the wind, at the corner of Kirikuplats, opposite the Cathedral of St Mary, the Toomkirik, that watches over all Tallin and much of the plain of Estonia. Her brown coat had holes at the elbows. The wind was rasping across the gulf of Finland with the first chill of autumn. Her bunioned feet were bursting her canvas shoes; her hand was held out, cupped, but without a word said or a look exchanged: a beggar too proud to beg. Give if you wish. One does.

Those two, the child and the woman, said a lot about Estonia. The one was beginning her life in poverty, but with all the dignity the other has retained through all the turmoils that have racked her unhappy country. That old woman (if she was as old as we thought) would have been just in her teens when Estonia declared independence from Russia in February 1918. She would never have known a country in peace and plenty – and in the Middle Ages it had certainly been a land of plenty. She might remember men, a father perhaps, perhaps a lover, who fought in the War of Independence (1918-1920). The new state had to fight Bolshevik Russia to the east and the Baltic German forces (the Baltisches Landwehr) to the south. The Tartu Treaty (February 1920) ended the fighting: Bolshevik Russia 'unreservedly recognised' the independence of Estonia and renounced 'in perpetuity' all claims to its territory. Hmm... The child knew nothing as yet of such things, but her thin dress and skinny limbs were the bitter fruit of broken treaties, broken promises, broken hopes.

That brief first visit left bitter-sweet impressions, of a town full of surprises, contrasts, a place between. For example: I opened the big door of the Cathedral on a choir rehearsing Bach's B minor Mass for a broadcast. Nods welcomed us inside: step over the cables, quietly, and find a seat. Listen to the ancient harmonies that tell of another world where war shall be no more and human pride and folly shall be redeemed. Facing us was an elegant neo-Classical tomb, its lapidary Latin impeccable in all the pride of marble: one Admiral Greig. He was not one of those many Scotch soldiers of fortune in the eighteenth century whose country had been taken from them by polite treachery, and by the butchery after Culloden.

He had been seconded like several other officers by the British Admiralty to help Catherine the Great build up her navy to counter the threat from Sweden – the British had no interest in a Sweden that dominated the Baltic and its exports, crucial to British iron working and naval supplies of tar, and masts, and rope. One Gustavus Adolphus had indeed been quite enough. Greig served Catherine the Great well, finally as Admiral of her fleet, against the Turks and the Swedes. The dust that lay in that tomb would have known Reval as a major naval base, the town full of his sailors and all the things sailors desire, the harbour a forest of masts, the yards a bustle of ships being refitted and readied for war. But above that polite marble, rank on rank of wooden funerary coats of arms, with the exuberance and flamboyance only German heraldry and sixteen quarterings can offer, covered every inch of the walls. These are the last proud statements of the dead who can feel no pride. And half way across the church, facing the Baroque pulpit, some notable two centuries ago built himself a comfortable balcony, with a fireplace against the Baltic cold, and sash windows – to be shut, I suppose, when the nearby preacher became too tedious or too loud. But in the square outside, the grass grew between the cobbles and people were mending cars, or lounging in corners out of the wind. Washing hung beneath the stained, elegant facades of a lost time. There was a sense of a place caught in a sort of suspended time, waiting, in between states of being. A few tourist buses regurgitated their loads at the gate, by the street market: mainly Germans. For already there were the beginnings of a tourist industry, and accommodation was plentiful, cheap and clean. You could buy Agfa film where you could not buy much fish or many loaves. In shops of a dignity and elegance most English towns demolished in the 1960s, the spaces on the shelves made home seem a land of excess. Which, however accustomed to it we may be, it is.

Coming down the hill that first time, we wandered to what looked like a huge building site in the middle of the old town. My hackles rose, for I get nervous when I see such sights. For in so many old towns, heirs of all the ages, that have taken centuries of lives to grow there has been so much wanton destruction in the name of modernity and money. But soon it was clear it was no building site. The vaulting of mediaeval cellars and undercrofts stood naked to the sky, faintly greened by weeds. It was a bombsite, like those where happy childhood afternoons slipped by for many of my generation. On the fence a notice, in three languages, recalled that in December 1944 the Soviet air force bombed Tallin, destroying much of its housing and killing hundreds. One building lost in that pointless raid was the 'Golden Lion' hotel, where Graham Greene had stayed, where he began to plan *Our Man in Tallin:* what became *Our Man in Havana.* (After the Soviets came in, making the town inaccessible to outsiders, he changed the location to one that you could get to.) And this bombsite, with the temporary flush of rose-bay willowherb, and the broad leaves of coltsfoot, was the war memorial. We wondered how the ethnic Russians in Estonia felt about so public a statement. Most, sent there by the Soviet state through no fault of their own, know no other country. Forty percent of the population, under the new constitution they had no vote, no voice in the future. The past, here as everywhere, reverberates ominously still. There is no escape.

★

We came across an unprepossessing door, a mere hole in a whitewashed wall: the Church of the Holy Ghost. ... But inside... A stupendous altarpiece, made in Lübeck in 1483 in all the pride of late Gothic prayer, is background to a grandiloquent Baroque pulpit that would hardly need a preacher. At the Reformation, someone who had visited Italy, and looked with taste and discernment at Italian Renaissance carving and painting, put in a gallery running round three sides of the building. On each of its many panels is a painting, in a sequence starting at the south east corner with the creation of Adam, that tells the story of man's Redemption. The sun, peering each day into each corner of the church through the clear southern windows, has darkened some panels beyond recognition, for there had been no money to conserve what in Western Europe people would have gone many miles to see. But the woodwork had the polish of love on it, and the lady who was cleaning when we went in managed, despite the barrier of language, to make us feel this was her place of hope and freedom of new life.

★

Ransome had been right about that view. Once more high up on the ramparts, we could lean over the stone parapets and look down on the backs of wheeling and fluttering swallows as they hunted insects in the updraughts by the walls. By that little cafe with a view over the sea, artists were displaying their paintings. Some were rather good. As we looked as if we might buy one, the young painter came over. 'A better bargain in dollars, sir,' he says in flawless English. As it happens, we had dollars, and the watercolour was more than worth the price he was asking. As the money changed hands, he volunteered, 'A bit more towards my ticket to the States.' We registered polite surprise. 'This country is finished,' he explained. We shivered slightly in that thin wind, and hoped that that little girl would not grow up to think the same.

I was once in another town, Stralsund, very soon after the reunification of Germany, where the old had not gone and the new had not yet arrived – just like the first wetness on everything as a frost begins to break but the earth is still hard, unyielding to the tread or spade. I had exactly the same feeling there, of a place in between, where people were uncertain of what they were, what they had been, what they would be. Bizarrely, a historical re-enactment society, in uniforms from the time of the Napoleonic wars, was marching and countermarching, and bivouacking in the square, and dragging the lighter field guns of that time about, and drilling with muskets that fired black powder which momentarily clouded the air with its pungent smoke... People were *living* it, an alternative chosen reality, a flight from now. I found that as inexplicably uncomfortable as I had Tallinn. Create a myth that then becomes the truth to which you will be true. Worship a false god you have made in the image of what you would like to be. Thoughts swirled towards Napoleon and dreams of Rome, fostered explicitly in painting and dress and furniture... The Nazis and dreams of the heroic German past, of blood sacrifice, of Heinrich the Fowler hammering the Slavs, preferably with the noisier bits of Wagner in the background... The baleful myth of the American West that never was, as if real geopolitics could be seen in terms of the *Gunfight at the O.K. Corral*... What happens when the last credits die away and the lights go up?

And then... we went back to Tallin, a bit more than a decade later. Cliché dictates, 'never a good thing to do'. 'There is no single street in Reval given over to fine shops and the parade of fools. Everything is decent, homely and unflurried,' wrote Ransome. He could, then. The glossy guidebook, available in several languages, is entitled *Tallinn: a Medieval Pearl on the Baltic Shore*. If only. The traffic was dire. Many of the Communist era blocks had gone, indeed, and high rise buildings were beginning to dominate the sky. Clearly the town was 'doing well': many of the shops, much smartened up, had a full range of designer gear to catch the tourists decanted each day from vast floating hotels. If this is Monday it must be Tallinn. A smart and pricey restaurant had supplanted the little café by the Cathedral. Nearby was a shop where two beautiful and elegant young women sold Baltic amber. Guides with little flags led knots of people round Toompea, along the two roads up the hill, Luhike Jalg, ('Short Leg') and Pikk Jalg ('Long Leg'). One informative blog post says, 'For centuries there was only one way to Toompea – Long Leg, the oldest street in Tallinn from the 11th century. Short Leg dates back to the year 1320, connecting also Toompea with lower town. Today you find nice cafés and excellent handicrafts and art shops along Short Leg. Long Leg is a place to watch the local artists working and you can even buy some of their paintings.' Indeed: I remembered the man in the cold wind by the Cathedral, and wondered how he was getting on in America. The cafés round the Raekoja Plats – I think of it involuntarily as Rathausplatz – had geared themselves up for the influx of comfortably-off visitors: no longer just cabbage soup or cabbage soup. The beggars were not much in evidence. The signs of the party culture were everywhere: thanks to firms like Ryanair, Tallin, like Prague, has become one of the stag night capitals of Europe, a distinction it might well deplore but which seems to pay well. Advertisements are common for what are, in effect, brothels. Money reigns. Today, Wikipedia tells us Tallinn is almost Europe's Silicon Valley, with the highest number of startups per person in Europe, and birthplace of hi-tech companies like Skype. 'One of the top ten digital cities in the world.' Affluent, certainly: but increasingly that cold wind from the east has a bite.

The memorial bomb site is now a memorial garden. So that is better. But the roar of the bombs has not quite died away, never will.

★

I climbed the high tower of St Olaf's Church just as a thunderstorm was starting. The spiral stair — 232 tight steps, and no passing places — leads breathlessly to an open gallery below the final spire. Steel mesh over the openings stops the unwary from falling and the suicidal from trying. The wind of the storm tore at the tower, buffeting it so one could feel the shock, and drove the hail to form little drifts against the walls on the floor inside the mesh. The crash of the thunder resonated with the structure, and all around I saw the lightning connect a wet heaven to a wetter earth. The tower rebuffed the big wind. 'The noise of the thunder maketh the earth to tremble: so doth the northern storm and the whirlwind' (*Ecclesiasticus* 43, 17). It was exhilarating. And far over the sea you could look beneath the storm and see the bright sky and approaching sunlight. Hope, our duty. But I still wonder what happened to the little girl with the wilted flowers.

★

Heartland

Europe is so well gardened that it resembles a work of art, a scientific theory, a neat metaphysical system. Man has recreated Europe in his own image.

Aldous Huxley

Much have I travelled in the golden realms of the New World, from the roaring falls of Niagara to the silent glaciers of Tierra del Fuego, but though in many of them people share a version of the language I speak I have never felt as at home there as I do in places where I have no words to speak: in Finland, or Poland, or Albania, or Romania, or Russia, or Hungary, or even those parts of Germany or France with impossibly thick accents. And to the mystification of many friends, I do not see New York as the pinnacle of our civilisation. I get out of its noise and dirt as soon as I can. Don't misunderstand: I recognise in towns and cities a little miracle. For though I am a pretty pessimistic sort of chap, often with good reason, I do remind myself from time to time that 99.9% of the enormously complicated things that human beings make, from railways to sewers to sewing machines to satnavs, actually work, and make and rely on a net of interdependence. A town is one of the most complicated things of all, and it is the trust between people and in things that makes it possible. That little old lady I saw last week in a morning market in Paris, her mouth perpetually in a *moue*, her basket on her arm, looking disdainfully at the cauliflower she (and the stall holder) know she will soon buy after this ritual – the fact that she is there depends on so many unrelated things all going right. The chain from her shaking her head even as she samples some cheese leads back through so many links to someone near Parma bringing a cow in for the milking. It is well to remind oneself that through all the horrors that fill our history books and our newspapers someone, somewhere, was patiently growing the food, getting in the harvest, singing the children to bed, cooking a meal for sharing with family or friend.

Even so: I don't like towns, and I never feel I belong in the New World. Perhaps it is because I don't know the stories the land sings. I have no ghosts of my own there, and do not connect emotionally (save with impotent indignation) to the tribulations of the native peoples at the hands of colonisers – though too often it is forgotten that their own societies were just as far from being lands of paradisal innocence as any other the world has seen. Perhaps it is because as well as an almost personal pride in, affection for, Bach and Laon Cathedral and Shakespeare and Dante and Tolstoy and all the rest, I increasingly sense in 'Europe', in ways I cannot explain, a communal, not consciously articulated, memory – inheritance indeed – of joy and gladness and beauty, of suffering and evil and sorrow, which the place itself, so to speak, remembers. Place matters. And has made me, and you, what we are. You can't understand history without geography. Abraham Ortelius' frontispiece to his *Parergon* (1579), his maps of the ancient world and ancient history, has the legend '*historiae oculus geographia*' – 'geography is the eye of history.' The landscape we know, where we dwell, where we grew, is as much part of who we are as our family, our profession or our faith. And not just for individuals, for place is important in a deeply grounding way for peoples and communities, and when such grounding is lost something goes out of the light. Ask any refugee. For generation upon generation, migrating birds and animals and fish return to the places where they first saw light like their ancestors when the world was young: do it long enough, and they acquire enough individuation for us to label them with a defining and dignified Latin taxonomic adjective. (I doubt they care.)

Europe – *Mitteleuropa* – is our common heart, and we, the heirs, cannot escape its beat even though we fool ourselves into nationalism and worse. ('Nations' in the usual modern sense are Johnny-come-latelies anyway.) In 1919, Halford Mackinder summarised his greatly influential theory, which has affected geopolitical thinking from Beijing to Washington to this very day:

> Who rules East Europe commands the Heartland;
> who rules the Heartland commands the World-Island;

who rules the World-Island commands the world.

Mackinder, *Democratic Ideals and Reality*, 1919, p.150

But there is a truth more profound than mere power and rule (and paradoxically, as we all know, those with the most power have the least freedom.) The roots of our values and tacit assumptions – the idea of the individual's value, the idea of freedom, the notion that the universe's mysteries can be explored, if not explained, in rational thought – reach deep into ancient soils on shores washed by the Mediterranean, and the tilth that grew them is the community of Europe, from the hierarchs of Byzantium to the hermits of Farne, from the schools of Italy to the hard men of the north who made the whales' road their path to what is now Russia and the Caspian. Anyone affected by what used to be called in the 1960s 'Western Civ.' – they chanted 'Hey hey hey, Western Civ. has had its day' – has spiritual and intellectual roots in this little spot of earth. The very fact that that silly sentence could even *be* chanted was a tribute to that which its chanters rejected.

★

Those two young ignoramuses who had wandered round Greece long ago, when all their world was summer, even then were beginning to be aware of how ignorant they were: the place was forcing it on them, teaching them, often by hinting at things just outside the corners of the

vision of which they then were capable. The Kindly
Ones, as the ancient Greeks sometimes called the Furies,
the pressures of old past and ancestral guilt, were just
below perception. We sort of knew that we ought to be
alert on many levels to what we were seeing, but were
not quite sure what it was, or how. Decades and much
reading later, we came to be leading study tours in Italy,
in Austria, in Bohemia (why not use the old name? The
mentalité is very much alive), in France, in Italy, and so
on. We did our homework, and cased the joints first,
of course. After all, at your back – or the back of the
audience – you always listen for the voice that will show
you, remind you of, your ignorance. The awareness of
ignorance grows exponentially with age, unless you are
Mr Toad. And there are indeed a lot of those.

These stages of the journey to I know not what (shall I
find out one day?) happened, as these things do, quite as
much by chance as by anything else: an invitation here, a
lecture there, a chance meeting somewhere else I had never
previously heard of, a conference in a place to which I had
not hitherto been: Szeged, Vlore, Constanta, Ponte de
Lima, and so on. Quite unsystematic, serendipitous, were
the wanderings, round the Baltic, round Italy, the old
Austro-Hungarian Empire, France, Iberia. But four cities
(for me: others will have other candidates) have come,
over the years, imaginatively to summarise for me, like
synecdoches, parts standing for the whole, our common
European heritage in all its ambiguity, confusions and

tension – what it means to be European (add subset of English, French, Croat, Polish – etc. etc. – as appropriate) and to inherit that entail of glory and guilt. First, Rome – well, how do you summarise what that city has meant? Educated Romans saw themselves as heirs of Troy's Fall at the beginning of history; when Rome in the West came to its own Fall, out of its debris came the states and polities who in their turn sought a foundation on that ancient touchstone. Rome was the *point de départ*, the foundation myth, the ghost behind Charlemagne's Holy Roman Empire, behind the self-images of Renaissance and Augustan, behind Napoleon's Imperial paraphernalia and the unwittingly parodic Fascist salute – and the 1955 Treaty of Rome that for a time seemed to offer a Europe united in purpose and values and civility. Then, Florence, that intellectual powerhouse of late mediaeval Europe. What happened there changed permanently the way we could think and altered the way we can see. Next, Vienna, indissolubly linked for me with Mozart, and Haydn, Beethoven and Schubert, Schönberg and Mahler, but also with the revolution (for good or ill – and I am more than a little sceptical) in our thinking about ourselves. But it is also speaks of the Holy Roman Empire, Charlemagne's politic invention when he persuaded Pope Leo III to crown him Roman Emperor in Old St Peter's on Christmas Day 800. *Bella gerant alii, tu Austria nube!* – 'Let others wage war: thou, happy Austria, marry.' For those Hapsburgs, the later incumbents of Charlemagne's title, had real talent for marrying shrewdly. Their Holy

Roman Empire – Voltaire remarked that it was not Holy, not Roman, not Empire – lasted until Napoleon made the last Emperor dissolve it in 1806. And Vienna guarded the March where Old Europe ended and The Beyond began. Finally, Berlin, where the Power State reached its hubristic and cataclysmic apogee. Berlin stands for me as the epicentre of the world we ourselves have inherited. I came gradually to know I had to go there, one day, whatever my (real) nightmares about the horrors that had been orchestrated there, for ghosts of that place walk in memories that became grafted onto mine in my later, second, life, and they had to be faced, or their darkness might lead to despair. Without passing the Slough of Despond there is no road that leads to Bunyan's Sunlit Uplands. It seems to be a rule of life that you have to go down to the depths before you can scale the heights. The Fall of Troy marked for Rome the beginning of history and her own greatness; that of Rome the challenge of the Lost Domain for the Renaissance. For us the Long War of 1914 to 1945, interrupted hopefully by that hopeless peace, is like a Second Fall: nothing could ever be the same again after the Fall of Berlin. Troy, Rome, Berlin... the Apple has been bitten, and shared, and cannot be unbitten. We inhabit a mental and moral world unimaginably different from even that of my parents' generation. I have got to know many places in Europe on the actual ground over the years, and some I have come to love, to delight in, to know well. But I find I cannot escape the emotional gravity of those symbolic cities.

A journey into Heartland Europe – not just the place, the physical journey, but the mental, to the *ding an sich,* all it has been and is, and meant – can be a journey to the heart of darkness, as well as all the other glorious things it most certainly is. You have to go through the Lion Gate to whatever awaits you, you have to make the Shepherd who reared the abandoned baby tell the truth, even if it cost you your eyes. Yet perhaps in that blinded state you may find a way to the light. 'Europe' holds the precise delicacy and devotion of Botticelli's *Adoration of the Magi* – he painted himself as well as assorted Medicis into it – but also the command of Lorenzo surnamed the Magnificent, patron of arts, letters and philosophy, that he paint the tortured and mutilated corpses of the members of the Pazzi conspiracy of 1478 which Lorenzo had had hung from the walls of Florence's Signoria. Europe is heir of the *Völkerwanderung* and the onslaught (you would see it as that if you were settled on a nice farm) of the Easterlings. It inherits the horrors of the Thirty Year' War in which 30% of the population of what is now Germany died, of the terrible industrialisation of conflict and murder in the 20th century. It spawned the ultimate denial of all human values and imperatives except the will to power in Communism and Nazism: both perversions that turned dreams into nightmares. Yet Europe also is heir to, defined by, the sanctity of men and women like Augustine and Francis and Teresa and Philip Neri and Dietrich Bonhoeffer and Maximilian Kolbe, by the music of the spheres netted in the counterpoint of Bach, and by

the miracle of Gothic stone taught to aspire to Uncreated
Light.

The past is insistent. The air trapped in the box and bottle
I dug up in the garden last week was old air, air of a past,
lost, less polluted world. (I am told that people in the
USA do buy cans of Hebridean air, after all.) Between
the enamel of the Alfred Jewel (an *aestel* that may have
pointed out the notes for a choir to sing) and the crystal
lie molecules of the air of King Alfred's time, the air
that never heard a Norman voice, trapped 'like a flower
between the pages of a book.' And places remember...
They hold in themselves, like the trees of the waiting
forests, the ancient past that made them. In a material
way, obviously: I was once knocking down a wall built of
clunch, the soft limey stone of much of Cambridgeshire.
A big lump fell, and split to reveal inside it, perfectly
preserved, the burrow of a recognisable lugworm, the
sort that as a boy I used as bait to set my nightline, and the
mould of the ancient lugworm was there too. Sometime
between 145 million and 66 million years ago it lived in
the ooze of those warm Cretaceous seas that with time
and pressure formed the lump of chalk that I feel as solid
ground under my feet each day. It burrowed through the
limey mud that was the shells of trillions upon trillions
of living creatures falling over millions of years to the
bottom of the ocean as their lives wore out. Somewhere
on the evolutionary tree the worm and I are related.
(Now the stone has an honoured place in my Cabinet of
Curiosities, which is where I put those odd things I find

that interest me or mean something to me, if to nobody else. Like my little boat carved out of cork.) But places hold more than fossils. They dimly hold feelings and passions – almost as if fragments of the past snagged on some places, like bits of grey wool hanging on a bit of barbed wire or a bramble where the sheep have passed. You do not need to know that 240 Cathars were burned alive at the stake there on a single day, 12 March 1244, to feel there is something terrible in the *feel* of Montségur. My wife's daughter, just in her teens, barely aware of what had happened there and with all the insouciance of the young, was so oppressed by feel of the stark walls of the castle that she could not go further in: she had to leave. There are many other such dark places, like the vast sunny summer fields of Flanders, with corn white unto harvest, with now only the occasional poppy nodding among the heavy ears. But there are other places, too, liminal with light, where the walls between the worlds seem very thin: Florence's San Miniato al Monte, Brixworth, Delphi, Little Gidding, Iona, an ugly little church in Norfolk, a pool shaded by alders where the young stream escapes from the prison of the rock and the tiny shrimps dart in the inch-deep clarity as they sense my footfall. Someone before me threw a coin in that spring.

The voices of the past never quite, quite die away: nor will ours. I was once persuaded to join a choir singing Byrd, Tallis and other great renaissance liturgical composers in a church which is all that beautifully remains of a grand late fifteenth century Abbey. The choirmaster, a charismatic leader, drove us hard, and by the end of the first morning he was getting out of us things we did not know we could do. But not good enough. He stopped us. 'You are singing music that could have been heard in this building four and half centuries ago, and the echoes have not died away. Join your voices to theirs. Live up to them.' Dramatic image, you might say: but then I began to think – and, not paying attention, made a lot of wrong notes – of how the Fibonacci sequence – 1,1,2,3,5,8,13,21,34,55 and so on *ad infinitum* – seems to be one mathematical key to so many of the patterns of life from the complementary right and left spirals on a sunflower head to the harmonies of music to cell multiplication in embryos, and how energy is, so I am told, absorbed in the reverse ratio: ...21,13,8,5,3,2,1,1, and so on... it *never* reaches zero. Sound is energy. It's rather like Zeno's paradox of Achilles and the tortoise, who have a race where Achilles sits in the shade until the tortoise has crawled half the distance, then runs to catch him up, then has a nice snooze again, and then runs... he never, ever, overtakes him. Some say the radio calls of Spitfire pilots are still bouncing through the upper atmosphere, trapped by the Heaviside layer, and getting fainter and fainter. So Jeffrey's remark has a good deal of truth in it. But: if the sounds of ecstasy, glory and worship never quite die away, so do not the shouts of anger, the screams of pain, the Bedlam noise of our quarrels and hatred.

At Binham in Norfolk was once a rich and powerful Priory, a dependency of St Alban's Abbey. For those who care about such things, its Northamptonshire stone in the west window may be the earliest example in England of bar tracery, first used at Reims. All that remains of the pre-Reformation building is the nave, which was saved from the sixteenth century ancestors of the Taliban because it would serve as a parish church. The painted rood screen was cut down, and turned into other bits of church furniture – good wood is dear – but the paintings on the screen dado had their faces and particularly their eyes viciously scratched out, and were whitewashed over. Improving Biblical texts were painted over that. Time and Norfolk damp at Binham have had a slow revenge, for the whitewash is now peeling, and the saints peep shyly out. I had, appropriately enough, a mild toothache when I first recognised St Apollonia through the whitewash, for she is the saint who deals with teeth. But Binham is stranger than that. My friend Clive Wilmer, the poet, went there late one drizzly Sunday, and could not get in, for the door was locked. But he heard voices singing inside, and thought, 'Oh, choir practice: they will not want to be disturbed.' He turned away and as he was walking back up the path he met the vicar coming to the church. They chatted, and Clive said he was reluctant to disturb choir practice. The Vicar looked hard at him. 'Oh, you have heard them too, have you? We have no choir. Look.' With that he unlocked the door, and the church was empty.

World is suddener than we fancy it.

World is crazier and more of it than we think,

Incorrigibly plural.

MacNeice's lines chime with the remark of that great scientist (and fine writer) J. B. S. Haldane: 'The Universe is not only queerer than we suppose, but queerer than we can suppose.' Michael Polanyi has a thought that when I read it went straight to the heart of what I could not say: 'We believe more than we can prove, and know more than we can say. A knower does not stand apart from the universe, but participates personally within it.'[8]

★

Watching a herd of reindeer on the tundra, or a flock of sheep on the hills of the North country I still call home, or in the clear water of the North Atlantic watching the weightless *corps de ballet* of a shoal of fish, the murmuration of the starlings – everywhere a mystery that will not go away from my thought. I have hived a swarm of bees many times, each time enthralled by the way the buzzing chaos of little bodies, like a mix for Christmas pudding, will suddenly order itself, and with one consent all in perfect order stream after their queen into their new home. Each on her own is a poor weak thing, able to do one job and one job only, while the hive itself is far greater than the sum of its parts, and by community changes not just its number but its nature. It seems to plan, to remember, even to remember different people. I had one hive that for a whole summer never forgave me for dropping a frame; another that my son could work without gloves or veil, and I could not. Then, there was that curious experience... On a day of early summer, when the sun was warm on our young backs and The Flowers that Bloom in the Spring, (Tra la), offered the hope that they bring, (Tra la), Of a Summer of Roses and Wine, I stood on top of a tall building with my metallurgist friend Michael, who had just completed his PhD. We looked down on the green by the river below. The day was warm, the grass was dry, and couples sat saying whatever it is couples say to each other in their springtime. Suddenly, Michael said, 'Look! It's a perfect lattice!' And so it was: each couple was, pretty exactly, evenly spaced from the others. But then, another couple, having just got their drinks from the nearby pub, came onto the green, and stepping carefully to avoid invading the space of the other couples, made their way to the off-centre. And sat down. Not a perfect lattice any more. For about ten minutes, we half-watched, idly, talking of this and that, he wondering how many papers he could get out of his thesis, enjoying being able to be out, after a spell of rotten weather, enjoying a pint in a beautiful place. But then Michael again interrupted himself: 'Look! My godfathers, it's a perfect lattice again!' Now, for that to have happened, every one of those twenty or so couples had to have moved, made an adjustment to maximise the space between itself and all its neighbours. Consciously? I doubt it: it would have been far too complex to work out. And then I remembered I had seen, when I was hiring out deckchairs for Blackpool Corporation, but then without noticing its significance – the naïveté of youth again! – the same thing happen on Blackpool beach in high summer when the tide was relentlessly coming in, squeezing people in the deckchairs into a smaller and smaller space of scuffed up sand. But they kept their distance as best they could. Perhaps the legal idea of a corporation helps. But does a corporation, which can legally be guilty of crime, override the moral individuality and responsibility of each member? We are too fond of thinking in and of groups: 'they' (= not 'us') is one of the most divisive words in language. But if we stop using that word, we are forced to recognise that 'they' are Charles, and Jacob, and Josef, and Wolfgang, Sennacherib and Hector, Agrippina and Mary, Plato and Friedrich, and Francis and Adolf, and Mao: all cousins one with another, all different. But an aggregate of individuals interacts, like the starlings, into something else and singular, and makes the vast swarm darkening the sun that those outside its swirling energy see as one. More and more insistently the thought presses itself upon me that what happened a long time ago in a faraway country of which I knew little, as someone once said, actively constrained – constrains – my options not only in terms of action but also what I *was*, what I could think, and feel, far into the future – a sort of meme from which there is no escape. This burden of the past, this load at our back, is in our very genes. From studies of mitochondrial DNA, if what the biologists are saying is right, that all people of European descent, for example, descend from one of seven women[9], who are themselves related, it follows that the men and women who measured the paths of the stars and sought to catch the glory of the infinite in nets of words and music are our relatives, our cousins. We share in the vision of Bach and Dante and Shakespeare and Sophocles and Homer even if we do not know them. The glory and the grandeur are in each of us. But so is the grubbiness and the greed, so are the monsters like Stalin who during the Terror imposed an official quota of murder – 'fulfil it or be part of it' – on each little local cell of the NKVD, or like those urbane and polite industrialists running big corporations which made a lot of money out of making, say, Zyklon B (but *clearly* had no idea what it was being used for) or out of using slave labour – like AG Farben, or Krupp. They are also our relatives – and, given the circumstances, pressures and opportunities, any one of us could have been them in our measure and our time. It is difficult to push away the feeling that there is something in that ancient, primeval idea of collective identity, that somehow an Abraham implies, contains, everyone who descends from him. Nobody is a continent entire unto itself. Molecules from Caesar's last breath are in the very air I breathe. 'A king may go a progress through the guts of a beggar...' Where is the dust that has not once been alive? Atoms whose dance made my millions upon millions of ancestors still dance in me and will dance when our species is extinct. So I acknowledge that I inherit the guilt as well as the triumph of my cousins: both made the world that made me. And if I am my past, I am also in my turn making a future. Original sin is not a daft idea... Marx's analysis of the constraints of economics, of history, of ideology unperceived affecting not only choices but what we are, points in the same direction. Our villainous ancestors – from whose crimes we still benefit – are present everywhere. It's fashionable for politicians of liberal persuasions to say that we must apologise to the descendants of those who suffered ancient wrong because we ourselves are guilty. That's too facile, but many advantages we innocently enjoy in life are indeed built on the suffering of nameless dead others. No Tate Gallery without long-dead slaves working the plantations under the Caribbean sun. Somewhere at the bottom of humanity's tree is some wholly innocent person. But none of us could be that person. Nor would want to be.

At the end of T. S. Eliot's *Murder in the Cathedral,* the Knights we have *seen* kill Archbishop Thomas challenge the audience: who was responsible? Who killed the Archbishop? Well, the knights did it... there can be no argument. We 'saw' it. But guilt? The Second Knight argues that the murder was necessary and brought about 'a proper subordination of Church to State': the status all politicians must seek in order to curb the subversiveness of all earthly power inherent in the Gospel. 'We have been instrumental in bringing about the state of affairs that you approve. We have served your interests; we merit your applause; and if there is any guilt whatever in the matter, you must share it with us.'

The thought often comes to me, 'In this place things happened which I do not know but they made me, however infinitesimally, what I am.' Memories, not ours, held by places... but we make them our own, for others' memories can be grafted to ours so intimately that we *remember* – there is no other word for it – them.

★

Träumerei

Some call it a City of Dreams, thinking of balls and glamorous hussars and sensuous waltzes, without getting the reference to Dr Freud. No ordinary dreams, indeed: *Träume*. Daydreams and nightmares and obsessions and all that lives beneath the surface.

Reading has made it that I now find it difficult to go to Vienna and not 'remember' Mozart being kicked downstairs by Archbishop Collaredo's servant, or Napoleon's cannon troubling the dying sleep of Josef Haydn, or Beethoven trapped in the besieged city in his chaotic, none too clean, room by the walls, and writing the Pastoral Symphony because he could not get into the countryside he loved. (I have been to see both the staircase and the room, as it happens. The room is now spare, tidy, antiseptic.) Equally it is impossible now for me not to 'remember' crowds cheering a little man with a moustache clipped so as to remind all who saw it that he had worn a gas mask in the trenches of 1914-8. He is striking an absurd attitude in an open car as he returned in triumph to the city where he was a sort of art student. If only people had laughed... And those photos of Jews being made to scrub the very cobbles on which I am walking. Laughing people, just like you and me, stand watching them... I was not there but I can 'see' it, feel it, alarmingly: from both sides.

Like so many cities I have come to know in the Heartland (but more intensely), Vienna plays a polyphony of memory and associations in my head and the past is woven into, colours, the present. It is too easy to agree wearily with Gibbon that 'History is indeed little more than the register of crimes, follies, and misfortunes of mankind.' It is much more, much more, complex.

★

Go back a long way, to a more innocent/ignorant time. In the last heady days of freedom after leaving university, and before I was claimed by regular daily work 0800-1700 and fourteen days' holiday (excluding Bank Holidays) ('and think yourself lucky, my boy!') a year, I hitchhiked and walked to Vienna. Why? Partly, I suppose, it was because I had heard tell of the Kunsthistorisches Museum, which happened that year to be running an important exhibition on mediaeval art. I certainly had found a growing interest there, but much more, I think, it was because discovering the music of Mozart and Haydn was taking me into a world the existence of which I had never suspected, and of which I desired passionately to be an inhabitant. Vienna was a sacred space for their sakes, and to some degree has so remained as I have aged, but with much more now in the way of sombre bass notes. So, like that earliest journey to a landscape suffused with the memory of Antiquity, this journey was – though I would not then have so seen either – a pilgrimage, to ancient wells.

I was alone, impecunious if not quite broke, with much enthusiasm but little discrimination, and with a brand new degree of which I was quickly ceasing to be so proud as experience forced me to recognise that ignorance could not always be covered by bluff, and least of all to yourself. I found a student hostel in which to stay in a warren of little streets behind the Kunsthistorisches Museum, and rapidly got used to the uncostly pleasure of spending an hour or more reading, with a single cup of fig-tasting Viennese coffee – quite unlike, and much nicer than, anything I had ever had at home in England – in one of the many comfortable coffee houses where everyone Viennese seemed to go. I found a cheap place

to eat – *gerstensuppe, kaiserfleisch*, potatoes, cabbage, bread
pretty well every night – and settled into a sort of routine.
I went on the tram to Grinzing and sat on my own in
a *heuriger* and drank their wine and ate the black bread
and ham that went with it. People said I should. I spent
hours in the Kunsthistorisches and discovered Brueghel.
I 'did' the usual sights, the Stephansdom, the Hofburg,
the Prater, Schönbrunn – and one day walked all the
way along the hot grey streets to the Danube and back
simply because I wanted to see that great river. Some
weeks earlier my friend Inge and I had seen it rise from its
spring at Donaueschingen, near where she lived, and after
many, many miles and much history it poured that and
the other waters it had gathered to itself into the Black
Sea. I was determined to go there one day. (I did, decades
later, and paddled between lectures, with my trousers
rolled up as my father used to in summer Blackpool.
Anticlimax, as ever.) I returned from that hot walk not
much the wiser: it is a big river, certainly not blue, and
that is about all I found I could say. I walked – again a
long way – to Schönbrunn, and to my delight found that
in the delectable little theatre that very afternoon they
were staging Paisiello's *Il Barbiere di Siviglia*. I scraped a
few schillings together and sat on a little gilt chair as if I
had been an Archduke to listen to an opera Mozart and
Haydn and Beethoven must have known in a theatre that
also they must have known. That added a curious spice
to my genuine enjoyment, as if one was sort of coming
home. The *chinoiserie* in the palace I found not to my taste;

but the story of the six year old Mozart jumping off the piano stool on which he had been sitting to play to the elderly Empress Maria Theresa, and running over to her, jumping on her lap, and giving her a big kiss delighted me. In fact, much about Schönbrunn delighted: the view from the Gloriette at the top of the hill, the vast formal gardens, and though I don't like zoos, I went to the world's oldest, built in 1752. It is an echo of the Emperor Franz Stephan's Enlightenment enthusiasm for all branches of science and there, still, is the rococo pavilion where he and his beloved wife Maria Theresa had breakfast when they were there on a summer morning. I love to think of them enjoying their chocolate watched by assorted parrots, ostriches and other rarities. I like knowing that the zoo got its first giraffe as a gift from the Viceroy of Egypt in 1828[10] The giraffe was so popular that not only did it attract record numbers of visitors but also giraffe motifs appeared on everything from clothes to cakes, and hairdos. But I am still sorry for the lonely giraffe.

I was beginning at last to know at least *some* history, and so was becoming dimly aware of the crucial place Vienna had held for centuries in Europe's history: the bulwark city against the East — after all Austria is Österreich, the Eastern Kingdom, and who knew what lay beyond, what could come from the gates of the dawn? At the second siege by the Turks, in 1683, it was indeed a close run thing. All the West held its breath, for had Vienna fallen... an account of the spectacular victory of Stahremberg and

Jan Sobieski, King of Poland, was in print, in London, *within a week* – 928 miles on horseback, *and* a crossing of the Channel. Someone was worried. Is it true that the croissant was invented to record the defeat of the Crescent of Islam, and taken to France by Maria Theresa's unlucky daughter, Maria Antonia? Is it true that Vienna's taste and reputation for coffee resulted from the Turks abandoning their baggage train, with all their coffee? Did a Capuchin monk in Vienna invent the cappuccino? I don't know. I was told so. I do hope so.

★

Patrick Leigh Fermor's memoir of the Vienna to which he walked in the 1930s describes making a bit of money by selling his sketches door to door. I wish I had had such initiative, and talent, on my first lonely visit. I was pretty nearly broke by the time I started to walk and hitchhike back to the imperatives of work and about-to-begin career. Who knows, if I had been so gifted I might have knocked on a door too, to have it opened by a French maid, and hear a dulcet voice within call out, 'Soon, *schätzli*.' Nobody called me 'little treasure' when *I* was a young man. My height of luxury on the return trip from Vienna was a farmer's wife near Zürich allowing me to sleep on the hay in her husband's byre with seven cows munching nearby. No breakfast.

★

It was only after many, many years that I went back, not now alone, with much more metaphorical (and real) baggage. There was an academic meeting every other December at which I regularly gave papers on matters that seemed important then, and the city became quite familiar, seen as it were from the underside rather than from the superficial guidebook angle: 'This is what you should look at, this is what is Important, and is Good For You'. It felt oddly pleasing when I heard the receptionist say to Jenny when I was leaving the hotel one morning with my briefcase spilling papers, 'Is Herr Doktor working today?' Not a tourist...

It is chastening to return to a place after many a summer and realise how dim your younger self must have been. I know I went, on my first visit, to the Jesuit Church. But all I remembered were the columns spiralling up like the sticks of the golden barley sugar we bought as children when Rationing ended. The *trompe l'oeil* of the ceiling, the magnificent Baroque of the interior, left no trace in memory; and lack of curiosity had not led to questions about *why* the columns so spiralled. I did not know they were called 'Solomonic', were supposed to be like those that made the gate to the Jerusalem Temple, and that the first two examples were brought to Italy by Constantine the Great. Solomonic columns have been important bearers of meaning, shall we say, or signifiers, in Christian architecture ever since. Nor had I then realised that church's tradition of singing one of the great

Masses each week in its proper liturgical context, not as a concert piece: the first time I encountered that was on a dark December Sunday when snow was blowing its soft, cold, fugitive kiss in our faces as we walked across the Donaukanal to the church. It was Schubert's Mass in G that lifted up our hearts. Again, I had been into the Stefansdom, but had not noticed that here, in the south aisle, Mozart had married his Constanze. Memory held no trace of the strange carvings on the West door to this soaring Gothic building, or that it had a pulpit (1515) of such surpassing workmanship that the very stone seems to breath – or crawl, in the case of the handrail where salamanders and toads frozen in stone fight a never endable battle between good and evil. On the panels of the pulpit, in bas relief, Anton Pilgram (or perhaps, some say, Niclaes Gerhaert van Leyden) made the four original Doctors of the Church, Ambrose Augustine, Jerome, Gregory, each life size. Each is in one of the four different temperaments, sanguine, choleric, melancholic, and phlegmatic, and in one of four different stages of life, and so vividly done they seem to take flesh from the stone and lean out with the urgency of their message. It may be humbling to revisit and see what you overlooked before, but it is a joy as another bit of the jigsaw of this puzzle of existence slips unto place. Perhaps you only see things when you are ready for it? Why do I now find that Canova's cenotaph in the Augustiner Kirche for Maria Theresa's and Franz's fifth child, Maria Christina, Duchess of Teschen, moves me almost to tears?[11] It did not use to.

And it is wildly out of key with the soaring Gothic of that lovely interior. (Someone was playing Schütz on the organ – equally anachronistic but gorgeous – when I was last there.) But what are we missing *this* time round?

People too. I had seen Franz Josef's bedroom in Schönbrunn before, but only on later visits did I begin to understand the quiet tragedy of that hardworking, Spartan, monarch's life. He was married to a woman whom he adored, but who did not adore him and spent as much time away from him and Vienna as she could. He was enormously conscientious if not perhaps very bright, he was well meaning – he made it a rule that for a part of each day anybody, but anybody, could come and talk to him with a problem or request. People had tried to assassinate him, but he took the risk of authority in the humbleness of his humanity. His bedroom was – is, for it is a sort of shrine to a lost past – simple to the point of ascetic: an iron bedstead in which he rarely slept for more than six hours. There was evidence in that room and on his desk of unremitting toil in keeping *au fait* with the management of a huge and increasingly restive empire, and, most touching of all, the nightcap for his magnificent *favoris* that were imitated all over the empire by men young and old. For the simple servant of the state had also to inhabit the pomp and majesty of the Imperial rôle, and even moustaches must be disciplined and curled. The long reign saw him grow in the affection of his people but his life became more and more shadowed: an anarchist murdered Sisi; his and Sisi's son committed suicide at

Mayerling in 1889; in 1914 Gavrilo Prinzip shot his (very able) heir and the slide began into the terrible conflict, the end of which he did not live to see, from which our Europe has never recovered. Franz Josef, and many others, could not understand the stirrings of change, the demand for political freedom, that industrialisation and a mercantile economy would necessarily engender. They saw stability, even if authoritarian (and who, then, saw much wrong with that?), as in the best interests of all. So there was an extensive system of surveillance. Strauss the Younger can make jokes about the secret police in *Wienerblut* (1899), an operetta which he tactfully set at the time of Prince Metternich's dominance, and his repression of dissent, after the Congress of Vienna in 1815. But nobody could miss what he was implying.

It is pointless, if tempting, to be nostalgic about a past we never knew. (Nostalgia is not what it used to be.) Some of modern Vienna, certainly, makes a good, if tacky, living from nostalgia. In the Hofburg, the guides talk of Franz Josef's Empress Elizabeth, Sisi, as if she were still alive and still beautiful, and still speak of the Kaiser und König with respect and honour. But it is all over a hundred years of blood and iron ago, before the Fall. Young men in cloaks and fake hussar uniforms accost you in the streets with leaflets about 'Classical Concerts', and if you fall for it you get nearly always a pot-pourri of the Strausses, Lehár, perhaps Lanner, and at the end, always, the Radetsky March. Jobbing musicians have to earn a living, and we should not begrudge it them. Let the audience clap and stamp enthusiastically to the Radetsky March at Vienna Phil. New Year's Day concerts: they don't have to remember Radetsky and his bloody clobbering of the Italians in 1848 and 1849. Strauss the Elder knew how to please the court, though: give them a good tune and a thumping rhythm and people will soon forget. His son had had his knuckles rapped for what looked like support of the radicals in the years around 1848, when all Europe looked as if it might explode into revolution. He had been given to understand that his job was to keep the people dancing, humming his endlessly repeating melodies that spoke to a cheerful feeling that all was right with the world. Happy people, distracted by pleasure, rarely revolt or support revolt. Strictly, Come Dancing... He delivered in spades. On the other hand, I think I can see why, why this almost Ruritanian fantasy past appeals to visitor and native alike. More than once, in Romania, in Hungary, in Bohemia, in Serbia, I have had people say to me, 'Under the Hapsburgs we had a hundred years of stability and prosperity. What have we had since they fell?' It is not quite Harry Lime's question to Holly Martens[12] on the Great Wheel in the Prater, but... A City of Dreams.

As Alexis de Tocqueville remarked, revolutions happen when things are getting better. Meanwhile, like Franz Josef, do the very best of which you are capable. Alexander Pope, a wise poet, remarked,

> Of forms of government let fools contest:
> Whate'er is best administered is best.

★

Appropriately enough, in a city so resonant to me with Mozart's and Haydn's and Beethoven's and Schubert's exploration of the potential of the new-fangled fortepiano and pianoforte, on the Ring there is a smart shop full of Steinways. I do not think it was there on my first visit. Given their price, one does wonder how many they sell each day, or week. It must be enough to pay salaries and cover the rent of such a prestigious address, but you never see anyone going in. The pianos, mute, polished to mirror brightness, stood there asleep, despondent, waiting for the prince whose touch would wake them into life. That Ring of course has nothing to do with Wagner's: it surrounds the city on the line of the old ramparts, bulwarks turned into boulevards – the two words are related. But cross the wide boulevard, and make your way towards the Gemäldegalerie, and THE Ring comes to mind... That gallery is one of my personal favourite museums. The Bosch 'Last Judgment' altarpiece, displayed so that you can see not only the front of the triptych but also the fine grisaille back, Murillo's 'Dice Throwers', and the Cranachs had fixed themselves firmly in my memory on my first visit all those years ago, and it is always good to visit old friends and see how differently you can see them now. Crossing the streets now – not then – buttons you can press to stop the cars help you, beeping away. But near the Gallery is a street called Nibelungengasse, and someone has had a very good idea.

The sound is not now a monotone 'beep beep beep', but, pitched slightly differently, the 'tink, tink, tinkety tink' of the Nibelungs' hammers on their anvils in Nibelheim. I so hope that it was an official with a taste for Wagner allowing himself some unusual levity.

In the U-Bahn station in Karlsplatz, you enter the loos to Strauss and the red and gold of the décor recalls the stalls of the Opera across the road. You urinate to the 'Blue Danube' waltz and the 'Trisch Trasch' polka… which gives one to think more seriously of Sir Toby Belch's remark to Sir Andrew in Shakespeare's *Twelfth Night,* 'Why dost thou not go to church in a galliard and come home in a coranto? My very walk should be a jig. I would not so much as make water but in a cinquepace.' The rhythms are insistent. But, on the walls, there are splashes of dried blood, traces of where druggies have been shooting up.

★

Walking across the cobbles of the square by the Schotten-stift, I saw a grille in the ground. My mind flicked back to the Carol Reed film of *The Third Man,* and Orson Welles'/Harry Lime's fingers slowly relaxing their grasp, as death catches up with him. And (I think) I have found the elaborate little structure where Lime gets access to the sewers.

★

The Kunsthistorisches Museum holds many memories for me. It also holds two disturbing ones, both of a sort of mental watershed. I think of a winter afternoon, with Mihaela from Bucharest and her husband Cesar, exploring the riches of the special exhibition of Goya. Goya was a painter of whom I knew little, and she much, and she is a great teacher. But *The Third of May, 1808,* on loan from Madrid's Prado, that terrible testimony of man's inhumanity to man, needed no teacher. (Then out into the Advent cold, the Christmas Market's cheerful lights offering *gluwein,* and then hot chocolate with cream. Cheerfulness keeps up the offensive.) I think too of another, earlier, visit, when I first looked properly at Peter Brueghel the Elder's 1564 *Procession to Calvary.* It is a full, busy, painting. Since Jan Van Eyck a century earlier, it had been usual to show the procession to Calvary with a multitude of figures dressed in modern European fashion in a familiar landscape – exactly what you get in the 'all times are now' world of the roughly contemporary Mystery plays. But looking again at it, this painting disturbed with the quotidian acceptance of our inhumanity. It is beautiful, and beautifully composed. It is a busy, almost in parts a happy – certainly an excited – scene. You hardly notice what is going on. Christ, fallen under the Cross, is tiny at the centre. The expectant crowd is rushing to form a circle round the little hill. A lolling youth has hitched a lift on the shafts of the cart carrying the two despairing thieves to their execution. Two boys quarrel. Bottom left, a man has just robbed a woman. Bottom right, the Maries and St John mourn. The Magdalene is painted in the height of fashion, looking every classy bit what she was thought to have been. While the crowd is excited, who notices the grey, fustian-clad, fallen figure at the centre? They have just come for the free show of watching a man die slowly. Oh, it's just another execution... Did they sell fast food and play music at Calvary, as they did at Smithfield or Tyburn Tree? (There a favourite was 'Greensleeves.') On the site of Tyburn now the insouciant traffic roars round Marble Arch, for they have somewhere to get to and drive calmly on. Auden's poem, 'Musée des Beaux Arts' says it all: '...About suffering they were never wrong, the old masters... the torturer's horse scratches its innocent behind on a tree.' That time, when that painting really drew me in, I thought of that photograph of people laughing at a Jew scrubbing the Viennese cobbles, or of Ovid's advice that the way to begin to seduce a girl is to sit close to her and press her thigh at the amphitheatre: while the sand of the arena was growing dark with blood and the corpses were dragged out of the Porta Libitinaria with meathooks. Or all the folk enjoying themselves in Hogarth's engraving '*Idle on the Road to Execution*'. Or the apparently insatiable taste, now, for details of the Nazi or Soviet horrors.

Then, change the viewpoint: a handful of years later I enter one of the museum's rooms where a group is being talked through a painting, and, unobserved by her, I stand watching my wife talking her group of students through a painting of the Brueghel she loved. She is animated and excited as I have too rarely seen her and the rapport between her and her audience is palpable. Just by her right shoulder, sitting at her easel, with her back to the group, is a girl, about the age of our daughter, obviously an art student, raptly copying, in oils, Brueghel's enigmatic 'Hunters in the Snow' – what do they want with that fox as they pass that inhospitable inn with the broken sign? – a large print of which hangs on the drawing room wall at home. Jenny's choice.

★

There is a small and rather expensive antique and art shop quite near the Albertina Gallery. We were looking in the window – not that we intended, or could afford, to buy anything, but looking is half the fun. Next to us, a young woman with her young daughter. Suddenly my eye fell on a large box wood phallus, right in the window. The daughter must have seen it at the same time, for she said to her mother, 'Was ist das für, mama?' – 'What is that for, Mummy?' To avoid embarrassment, we moved off before she could reply.

★

Lecturing at one December conference in a room in a grim barrack of a school, in Birgittenau. There was a porn shop on the corner with an inventive window display of improbable garments, quite unsuitable for this weather. It was near where Hitler, having twice been refused entry to study at the Academy of Fine Arts, dossed in the public dormitory for men at Meldemannstraße 27. Nobody cared, then. (In the very years when he was in Vienna, by a strange coincidence, in the light of what they all caused, so were Trotsky and Stalin – both on the run – and one Josip Broz, who worked at the Daimler factory in Wiener Neustadt, earned a good wage and apparently was having a very good time. He is better known as Marshal Tito.) Patterns of red, green and blue ornamental cabbages in the iron hard frozen ground made patterns round the brick church. The reciprocating spirals the florets made on the flowerheads recall Leonardo Fibonacci of Pisa and that sequence that has his name, and how it links with the Golden Ratio, and harmony, and the beauty of pattern in cell divisions. Did Hitler the inattentive art student know about those ancient rules of harmony and proportion, the very rhythms and patterns of being?

But then, into these grey thoughts on a grey day of hard frost... According to James Boswell, Oliver Edwards, who had known Dr Johnson at Pembroke College, Oxford, some 49 years earlier, once remarked to the good Doctor, 'You are a philosopher, Dr Johnson. I have tried too in my time to be a philosopher; but, I don't know how, cheerfulness was always breaking in.' So true – for me anyway. That afternoon, an afternoon of grim, grey, grumbly weather, walking from grim Birgittenau – grim in aspect, grim in association – up past the Stefansdom to where I was staying, I heard music, and saw a little knot of people just where the Stephansplatz turns into Kärtnerstrasse. Tourist guides call the street the 'Music Mile' – which it isn't by a long chalk, but there are five-pointed marble stars set in the pavement commemorating famous composers. (Once I saw a group of very young students playing with passion a Mozart quartet, right over where his star was. It must have been deliberate. And they were good.) There was a man with an accordion wheezily but not unpleasantly playing Strauss waltzes. In the ring formed by the little crowd, a few couples, mostly elderly, hatted and be-Lodened against the cold, were waltzing in the street with expressions of their youth on their faces. The eyes were young. More joined in as I passed. Cheerfulness indeed. It keeps happening.

★

What the Doctors ordered...

Florence in December was a city of tired flowers. The swallows of summer had long gone, the winter flocks of starlings had moved in, and the bats of summer gloamings were hung up upside down somewhere like bits of old rags, hibernating. It is Advent, the expecting season, and the deep tenor bells – all ever so slightly differently pitched – of Florence ring out for the Offices that, day by slow day, darkening to midwinter, will lead us to the Great Antiphons that herald the Nativity. (The bells are never quite in time with each other. I like that.) There is frost in the air. The fumes of the wasp-voiced motorscooters are trapped in the bowl of the hills, so you cough as you walk, and, days later, from Fiesole, in this still anticyclone, we could see the brownish haze that often sits over the old city from whose flowers so many things fruited that made the Europe we know. So bad is the pollution that I am not sure John Milton's 'Tuscan Artist' *could* this evening 'Through optic glass [view the moon's orb] at evening from the top of *Fesole*/ Or in *Valdarno*, to descry new lands, rivers or mountains in her spotty globe.' In 1638, Milton met old, blind Galileo, confined by the Inquisition to his house in Oltrarno save to go to Mass. Milton's powerful defence of free speech, *Areopagitica,* recalls this meeting and warns of the consequences for England if it bows to censorship, 'an undeserved thraldom upon learning.' Then, now: censorship can take many forms, even masquerading as liberal and 'progressive' – a word that begs many, many questions – political correctness. Sometimes nothing is so illiberal as the liberal conscience.

That December visit long ago was my first: not Jenny's. She knew the city well, knew that the bobbles on the Medici coat of arms represented the pills by which that family, originally apothecaries, had made an honest living before they got big ideas about money and power. She it was who had persuaded me to make this winter journey at the end of a long and gruelling term of teaching, and who had planned our route and contacted the hotel she knew of old. We had made our way up from Pisa on the slow train, passing through Prato where our friend Morton, our host in St Croix, had bought a factory to supply seersucker cloth for his New York business. (And had been a generous employer, as he told us.) As we paused at that station I suddenly remembered, 'But this is where Francesco di Marco Datini lived!' and wanted to get off into a sort of acted-out parenthesis and go and look at his remarkable business archive which has survived from the fourteenth century[13]. Each of his account books begins 'In the Name of God and Profit.' He traded in cloth and what we call 'art', and other commodities, and slaves. But Jenny firmly demurred, pointing out that we had a short enough time in Florence anyway and needed all there was if she was going to show me what I ought to see: both of us had developed a mission to inform.

And so to Mussolini's Santa Maria Novella Station, and then through the traffic and past the church to the first sight, in the streetlights, of the wonderful geometry, rising up into the dark, of Alberti's new façade for that Gothic building. Crossing the piazza, the Corsa dei Cocchi, a light rain damped our faces – welcome after the heat of the train – as we made our way to our hotel. We passed the obelisks which mark the *metae*, the turning points, for the *palio* Cosimo I de' Medici instituted. They stand (to my mind incongruously) on Giambologna's bronze tortoises. We found the hotel: our room was in a building that was standing when Marsilio Ficino, Niccolo Machiavelli, Agnolo Poliziano, Cristoforo Landino, Sandro Botticelli, Leon Battista Alberti, Pico della Mirandola, and other names I revered from my reading walked this way – but they would not have seen the obelisks or the tortoises, for they came after their time. But then, that weight of past and memory is not unusual in the centre of this city. It does not go away, just becomes mere matter of fact, as familiarity telescopes time, and the Quattrocento is merely yesterday.

Ours was a room with no view, except across the narrow street to another building that also reached back to memories of sunlight that Giotto saw. (He worked just round the corner.) The floor was tiled, red terracotta. The bed was vast, heavy carved dark wood. There was a marble topped washstand just like my grandmother's. On the ceiling, only to be seen and enjoyed when lying on your back, plump cherubs sported in, and with, flowers, perpetually arrested in motion, and round the moulded plaster ceiling rose a celestial chariot parted the clouds in a perpetual dawn. Not far away was the palazzo where the Florentine Academy had its meetings, a body which made John Milton so welcome as a member when he came this way in 1638 and 1639. In the Via Giglio, that first visit, I noticed an understated plaque:

Qui, nel palazzo dei Gaddi
è tradizione che soggiornasse negli anni 1638 e 1639
John Milton
trovando a Firenze
l'Italia dei Classici.
(There is a tradition that here, in the Gaddi Palace,
John Milton stayed in 1638 and 1639, finding in Florence the
Italy of the Classics.)

That sent a minor shiver down my spine, for I revere
Milton. Most of the things we value in Florence, the
art works and architecture, were there when Milton
was 'Finding the Italy of the Classics...' His poetry, the
poetry of a blind man who remembered sight, is poetry,
as it were, from memory.

We returned many times to Florence over the years. But
for that first visit to the city where Forster set one of his
better novels, where Lawrence and Browning had written
poems that I had begun to enjoy bent over my sloping
wooden desk years before at school, I had primed the
pump, so to speak, by reading guidebooks. For centuries
Florence has of course been guidebook country. It
must be one of the most written about places on earth
– as well as written on, about and in. Like all places, it
is a temporal palimpsest, but here this shouts at you: so
literally, no writer or scholar can be unaware of those
who preceded him. And the city is beyond question one
of the intellectual epicentres of the Europe we inherit.

Reading old guidebooks may be a minority, even geeky, taste, but as I have got older it is one I have developed with less and less furtive enjoyment. I have preferences. Murray's guide – *A Handbook for Travellers in Northern Italy: embracing the continental states of Sardinia, Lombardy and Venice, Parma and Piacenza, Modena, Lucca, and Tuscany as far as the Val d'Arno* – of which the 4th edition 'carefully revised and corrected to the present time,' came out in 1852 – is still very serviceable to the discerning traveller. It gives a glimpse of a mental world lost for ever, but which is in our ancestry – which is why I read such books.[14] Many owners before me read, thumbed, spilt things on, my copy. For Florence drew English visitors in droves from the seventeenth century onwards. Many stayed for months, years even. The ex-pat English community, and the temporary Grand Tour (and after) one in Florence was very large: the oval of the English Cemetery, opened in 1827, holds many among its cypresses and miniature obelisks, their only visitors birds and the cats and the occasional tourist who has run out of other sights.

★

Behind Santa Maria Novella is the Spanish Chapel. For years I associated Browning's 'Soliloquy of the Spanish Cloister' with the Green Cloister outside it. I loved that monologue poem and knew it pretty well by heart. (I like Browning: I respect a man who tries to wean his wife off her addiction to laudanum with the best Chianti. A good poet too.) I saw the wit of placing that outpouring of pent-up unmotivated venom towards a gentle, saintly brother monk in that serene rectangle of green surrounded by the cloisters where a man might walk, or work, or read. (But why is it that real saintliness and goodness so often draws down on itself a terrible hatred? Is it a sort of fear? Browning was uncomfortably right.) I tried to quote bits of it to Jenny as we walked round. But as I had not explained I was quoting, she thought I was being personal, so I stopped. The marks on the Giotto and Uccello frescos of the 1966 flood, when the grossly swollen Arno swirled through the old city, reminded of precariousness. Our gentle rivers only seem tame. Like us.

★

A quiet afternoon, the winter light fading outside so that the flame of the rank of votive candles casts a stronger pool of light in the church. We were both very quiet, and went across the piazza to find a coffee. We had been into San Marco, because Jenny loved the luminous paintings of Fra Angelico and he had been a member of that Dominican house. Here too in the time of Lorenzo il Magnifico the beautiful aisled library was one of the favourite meeting places for Florentine humanist scholars like Agnolo Poliziano and Giovanni Pico della Mirandola. There they had on hand the precious book collections the Medici had assembled, with their rare Greek and Latin texts, some saved by Greek refugees from the swelling tide of Ottoman power. That morning, at Mass, I had knelt to my devotions, and been utterly distracted for its duration by seeing to my left memorials recording Poliziano, Pico and Savonarola. My thoughts went off at many tangents; not least to the first time I heard Poliziano's name, in a first year lecture at Cambridge, when I felt hopelessly ignorant as I had no idea then who he was or why he mattered. But that was not what had made us quiet. It was walking round the now deserted convent, and looking into the little cells, each with its fresco by Fra Angelico or one of his pupils, and suddenly finding ourselves in Fra Girolamo Savonarola's cell. His stool stood there: uncomfortable enough, in all conscience, but now the name of a distinct type of undesirable but often expensive stool. The crucifix before which he had prayed was there. On the table was one of his books, with notes in his handwriting. And then we noticed on the wall a small painting: a view of the Piazza della Signoria, with in the centre a pyre, and on it Savonarola, on whom the Church had turned and on whom the Florentines had taken a terrible revenge after his brief period of austere and theocratic power with himself as the passionate ayatollah. The painting is contemporary with the burning: the few people in the piazza don't seem particularly interested, and most are not even looking, turned away, talking among themselves, probably of business. An innocent horse is doing what looks like a *capriole*, a difficult manoeuvre. A couple of men are bringing up extra faggots. Yet Savonarola's preaching had caught the imagination of, for example, Botticelli. Niccolò Fiorentino made a bronze portrait medal, with on the reverse a Latin inscription, 'The sword of the Lord is swift and speedy over the earth.' At the height of his persuasive, inflammatory, preaching the Florentines had made bonfires of their vanities: literally, in this very square where we had sat that morning with our morning coffee – where a few months later they made a bonfire of him. Never did Walter Benjamin's words strike me with more force: 'There is no document of culture that is not at the same time a document of barbarism.'[15]

The train of thought would not let go. My mind flashed back to our Sunday Schools in Lancashire, where we were given little coloured stamps each week to stick in our books, and if we got enough we had a prize at the end of the year. Each of us remembered the one with Savonarola burning, and I remembered Miss Murphy explaining to us nine year olds that he was a martyr a long time ago. (Not that we really knew what that was.) And here we were, where he had lived and prayed and preached and suffered.

And paradox plucks on paradox. In one of these austere cells, Cosimo de' Medici, whom I can't help thinking of (unfairly) as the original Godfather, would come for his retreat. It was adjacent to and as simple as those of the friars, and like them it had a fresco by Fra Angelico or his pupil

Gozzoli. Retreat he did quite regularly, relinquishing the running of the growing family business, and the bank, and the buying of votes to influence the city's politics, for a time when he could say with the Psalmist, 'I am a worm and no man', and 'Enter not into judgement with thy servant O Lord, for in thy sight shall no man living be justified.' I am sure – I know – some people in politics do that now. For it is hard and inevitably compromising calling.

As we were finishing our coffee, a man came in with two little black and white dogs, almost exactly like the dogs, the *domini canes,* or 'hounds of the Lord', in the fresco Andrea Bonaiuto da Firenze painted in the Spanish Chapel of Santa Maria Novella. As we were so close to San Marco, I asked him if by any chance the dogs were Dominicans. He looked at me mystified for a second, then burst into a laugh. 'No, they are not holy dogs. But they have learned obedience, at least.'

★

And hither we came, Jenny and I, much later but in due time, leading those study tours for a visiting American faculty during their spring break – and later still in my own journey I came, alone, to academic conferences. Those tours were, I suppose, the enfeebled descendants of the Grand Tour, with the same aim of improvement of mind and taste... and that made us the heirs of former and more learned cicerones. It is curious how differently you see things when you are trying to see them, as it were, for others to see. Almost like being an impresario – to be kind – or a salesman, to be less so. But we so wanted our charges, many of whom had not been even to Europe before, to love what we loved, to feel our own excitement – but 'twas new to them – about things where the inside was bigger and more enthralling than the outside. I don't know that we succeeded, and I am certain that for some if this was Thursday then this must have been Florence. (I actually overheard that remark in a café – thank Heaven not from one of our people.) But in some cases also I am sure that a life was changed, a perspective altered for good, just as for us the same sort of thing had happened, was happening, and still happens. You cannot make it happen, though: for a teacher to try is almost to guarantee failure. You have to set out your stall to the view, and hope that the browser will buy and take what you offer to him or herself. Teachers and lecturers never see the end of the stories they may start, for each journey is unique.

So there were great frustrations as well as great joys in these later visits, to Florence, to Vienna, to Prague, to Rome and the other places to which we took our victims. One of them said, with a metaphoric ambition the confidence of which I envied, 'You are trying to graft onto willing stocks who only have a fortnight free from the shackles of work the scion it has taken half a lifetime to grow.' I think I grasped what she meant, and tried to cap it by talking about old wine in new bottles. Too true: we took them once to the opera in Prague: a crass (and musically mediocre) production of *La Traviata*, with spectacular and pointless nudity which shocked some of the ladies from the Mid-West. But for one young lecturer, now a firm friend, this was the very first experience not only of opera but of live theatre. Asked at the interval what he thought of the production, he said, 'I don't know what opera is, but I am enjoying this and if it is all like this I shall come again.' Whether he referred to the ladies of the chorus, the dancing or the music, or all three, is uncertain.

Despite the planning stage of trying to persuade our American colleagues not to take on too much and travel too much – often an uphill, defeated struggle – we loved those trips and the camaraderie that came out of them. But keeping the party more or less together when we took them on a walking tour was like trying to herd cats. One lady, vague, with scant idea of where she was in the town, got left behind because she was a passionate cat lover and had been waylaid by a couple of Florentine moggies of dubious appearance and probably of morals. Overwhelmed with concern for them, she was trying to find somewhere to buy some cat food. Eventually Jenny found her in a shop trying to explain, by sign language and mewing, what she wanted. Then, walking along the Lungarno, we lost Tim Bywater, who organised the US end of these tours. In the end I spotted him, leaning over the wall below the Ponte Vecchio, oblivious of our absence. I joined him, and leaned over the wall too. 'Enjoyed the trip so far? Happy with the reaction from your colleagues?' I asked, tactfully, looking down at the early summer Arno. He did not reply immediately, and I followed his gaze to where a swirl in the water suggested a fish. For clearly the scholar had been overtaken by the Yellowstone Park Ranger he was in the summers, who had taught Bill Clinton to cast a fly, and for the moment the fishability of the river, not the study tour, was at the front of his mind. Oddly, I had never thought of fishing the Arno. But I suppose...

★

We took one tour group to the opera: Verdi's *Falstaff*. The audience was mainly Italian, and the opera house in a big Italian city had been, a century and more before, a place where political passions could run dangerously high. Verdi's operas for example often had a political subtext: these were the years, after all, of the Risorgimento. More than once his audience chanted, 'Verdi! Verdi! Verdi!' – a code, as everyone knew, for Vittorio Emanuele Re D'Italia, but about which the authorities could do nothing. There was no chanting at this *Falstaff*. But later I looked up what I half-remembered from reading Tobias Smollett, bad-tempered and vastly entertaining, who came to Florence in 1764, on the entertainments of Florence, and found more than I had bargained for:

There is a tolerable opera in Florence for the entertainment of the best company, though they do not seem very attentive to the music. Italy is certainly the native country of this art; and yet I do not find the people in general, either more musically inclined, or better provided with ears than their neighbours. Here is also a wretched troop of comedians for the bourgeois, and lower class of people: But what seems most to suit the taste of all ranks, is the exhibition of church pageantry. I had occasion to see a procession, where all the noblesse of the city attended in their coaches, which filled the whole length of the great street called the Corso. It was the anniversary of a charitable institution in favour of poor maidens, a certain number of whom are portioned every year. About two hundred of these virgins walked in procession, two and two together, clothed in violet-coloured wide gowns, with white veils on their heads, and made a very classical appearance. They were preceded and followed by an irregular mob of penitents in sackcloth, with lighted tapers, and monks carrying crucifixes, bawling and bellowing the litanies: But the great object was a figure of the Virgin Mary, as big as the life, standing within a gilt frame, dressed in a gold stuff, with a large hoop, a great quantity of false jewels, her face painted and patched, and her hair frizzled and curled in the very extremity of the fashion. Very little regard had been paid to the image of our Saviour on the cross; but when his lady-mother appeared on the shoulders of three or four lusty friars, the whole population fell upon their knees in the dirt. This extraordinary veneration paid to the Virgin must have been derived originally from the French, who pique themselves on their gallantry to the fair sex.

Love him or hate him (and I incline to the former), he can be vastly amusing and very observant:

> Just without one of the gates of Florence, there is a triumphal arch erected on occasion of the late emperor's making his public entry, when he succeeded to the dukedom of Tuscany; and here, in the summer evenings, the quality resort to take the air in their coaches. Every carriage stops, and forms a little separate conversazione. The ladies sit within, and the *cicisbei* stand on the foot-boards, on each side of the coach, entertaining them with their discourse. It would be no unpleasant inquiry to trace this sort of gallantry to its original, and investigate all its progress. The Italians, having been accused of jealousy, were resolved to wipe off the reproach, and, seeking to avoid it for the future, have run into the other extreme. I know it is generally supposed that the custom of choosing *cicisbei* was calculated to prevent the extinction of families, which would otherwise often happen in consequence of marriages founded upon interest, without any mutual affection in the contracting parties. How far this political consideration may have weighed against the jealous and vindictive temper of the Italians, I will not pretend to judge; but certain it is, every married lady in this country has her *cicisbeo*, or *serviente*, who attends her every where, and on all occasions; and upon whose privileges the husband dares not encroach, without incurring the censure and ridicule of the whole community. For my part, I would rather be condemned for life to the galleys than exercise the office of a *cicisbeo*, exposed to the intolerable caprices and dangerous

resentment of an Italian virago. I pretend not to judge of the national character from my own observation: But, if the portraits drawn by Goldoni in his comedies are taken from nature, I would not hesitate to pronounce the Italian women the most haughty, insolent, capricious, and revengeful females on the face of the earth. Indeed their resentments are so cruelly implacable, and contain such a mixture of perfidy, that, in my opinion, they are very unfit subjects for comedy, whose province it is, rather to ridicule folly than to stigmatize such atrocious vice.

★

A curiosity – more than that, once upon a time. In the nave of Santa Maria Novella (which church is, unusually, aligned north-south rather than east-west) a sinuous bronze line is set into the pavement of the long nave. If you look above the rose window, in the green fascia, there is a hole through which a sunbeam at midday strikes the bronze line. Sometime after 1571, Cosimo I de' Medici engaged Egnatio Danti to make this meridian line. Depending on where the beam strikes the bronze, you can tell not only noon but the date – and just at this time the reform of the old Julian calendar by the Gregorian was a hot topic. For some of our charges, the maths of the meridian was much more entrancing than the majesty of the Madonna's church.

★

Florence, graceful, artistic Florence, was about Power. And Money, which is the same thing. (It's interesting that the word 'rich' is etymologically related to *rex, reich*: power and rule.) You can feel it once you get behind the froth of art tourism – and that does take time. Money: Florence's bankers financed Edward III in the family quarrel he started which we call the Hundred Years' War. They financed the Papacy's move to Avignon. The art was the result of money and patronage and conspicuous display of status and wealth. The *palazzi* thrust their pugnacious bulk at you. Their dark grey rusticated walls, grim to the world outside whatever the delicate elegance within, remind that a *palazzo* for a long time was also a fortress. In other cities several *torri* mark the strongholds of many noble families, refuges against brawls that could escalate in minutes into streetfighting between factions – we would say gangs. (As in *Romeo and Juliet*.) Florence has only one building with a tower. That shows how thoroughly the Medici came to dominate the place, by money, mayhem, murder or machination as suited them. You get a sense of ancient blunt power, even in a city heavily tidied up and made for a time the capital of the new Kingdom of Italy. In front of the Palazzo Davanzati a whole warren of small streets and houses where the poor lived and worked was swept away to make a more dignified space: not the only one. Long ago though that was, I can't help feeling indignant. For I would have been one of the poor cleared away, my life worthy of only short and simple annals. Only the church made some provision for them, for the unfortunate, for the women exploited or abused or abandoned. The lovely rhythm of the colonnade of Brunelleschi's Ospedale degli Innocenti (which is the model for Cambridge Railway Station, as it happens) had a revolving shutter where abandoned or unwanted babies could anonymously be deposited. The church brought them up, in many cases giving them a trade or skill, often music. Literally, a *conservatoire*.

Santa Croce, where Rossini and Michelangelo are buried: heretically, it is not my favourite church, but there Byron was 'dazzled, drunk with beauty', and so was Stendhal, so I must be stupid – *pazzo*. When the Franciscans came to the city to minister to the poor and destitute, they established themselves at Santa Croce long before they built the huge church. There they could be in amongst those to whom they ministered. For in that quarter, outside the old walls, were the warrens of poor hovels. The poorest people were relegated to a suburb well known to be far below the flood levels regularly attained by the Arno, a short river violent when the Apennines shed their melt- or storm-water. People drowned. It happened. It always had done. The poor stayed here, 'living and partly living, /Picking together the pieces, / Gathering faggots at nightfall, /Building a partial shelter, /For sleeping and eating and drinking and laughter.'

In 1966 the waters of the Apennines swelled the Arno to spectacular heights. Cimabue's huge crucifix in Santa Croce was not moved in time and the waters of the flood engulfed it. The paint with which Cimabue had shown the Saviour, his body twisted in agony, began first to soften, then to flake off the saturated wood. The egg white used to fix the gold leaf gave up its strength. Mud inserted itself into the crevices, and the dry wood of the Tree, sawn from trees felled on the high hills long winters before, warped. More paint flaked off. When the waters left the face of the earth, the face of Christ was half gone, the painted body racked and broken.

I have seen that crucifix several times. The first few times it left me in art-historical overdrive. But then, late in time, I saw my wife standing in front of it, her eyes wet. That is what it is about: her clearer vision had humbled my scholarship. She said the painted flesh glowed with life in its death. I bought her a miniature, pale imitation of what it had been. It sits on her dressing table. Challenging.

★

The chapel of the Pazzi, next to Santa Croce, is a perfect building whose shape and dimensions sing a harmony around you as you stand at the focus of its acoustic. The family were bankers before they were ruined after their conspiracy. Italian surnames, like Roman cognomina, are hardly flattering: Botticelli means 'little barrel', 'Flaccus' means 'floppy' – poor Horace – and 'Caesar' means 'hairy' and 'Cicero' 'chick pea' (I hate chickpeas). *Pazzo* means 'nutty' or 'crazy.' Which they must have been to try in 1478 to assassinate Lorenzo de' Medici and his brother Giuliano. They finished off Giuliano, but had scotched the snake not killed it, merely wounding Lorenzo. (Poliziano saved him by shutting him in the sacristy: who says that scholars cannot be practical?). Five of the conspirators, including Francesco de' Pazzi and Francesco Salviati, Archbishop of Pisa, were hanged from the windows of the Palazzo della Signoria. They tortured Jacopo de' Pazzi, head of the family, then hanged him next to Salviati's decomposing corpse. He was buried at Santa Croce, but the body was dug up and thrown into a ditch. It was then dragged through the streets and propped up at the door of Palazzo Pazzi, where the rotting head was used as a grotesque door-knocker. Then it was thrown into the river. Children fished it out and hung it from a willow tree, flogged it, and then threw it back into the river. (It is too easy for us to forget that we live in a world from which so many ancient stenches have been banished... Our forebears must have had much more tolerance.) Meanwhile, just down the road, Marsilio Ficino was doing his great work on neo-Platonic philosophy and Pico would soon write his *Oration on the Dignity of Man*.

The shadows, once noticed, are hard to ignore. The tourists (and scholars) who crowd the Bargello in the Palazzo della Signoria to admire Donatello's David, or those cabinets of that high and epigrammatic art form, the medal, or go to have a drink in the Piazza in the easy sunlight, could easily forget (if they knew it) the smoke on the wind and the smell of roasted human flesh from the pyre that burnt Savonarola, for so short a time the darling of the Florentines. X marks the spot, as they say: the site of the pyre is recorded in the pavement. Florence in its beauty holds together the worst of human nature as well as its ability to glimpse, and adore, *l'amor che muove il sole e gli altri stelle*: 'the Love that moves the sun and other stars'. Botticelli, 'Little Barrel', could move easily from those Madonnas and infant Christs, or from painting Simonetta Vespucci as Venus, to those graphic sketches of the tortured Pazzi bodies noisy with flies hanging from the walls of the Signoria.

★

Years, years, later, my lady and I were in the Uffizi: the office from which the state was run. She wanted to find her favourite painting, a self-portrait by Fra Lippo Lippi, a print of which she had had on the wall of her College room. (By an odd coincidence, a print had been on the wall of my home, when I had no idea what it was, but liked it.) It had, of course been moved – lent to another gallery, I think. So, somewhat cross, more than a little disappointed, with hot museum feet, but having paid to get in, how were we to get our money's worth? (That matters to a Lancastrian.) Both of us love the Quattrocento, so we gravitated to where the Botticellis and the Verocchios, the Piero della Francescas and the

Venezianos might be. But of course you get sidetracked...
I find I never have the singleness of purpose to stick to an
agenda, as one ought. And – however *did* I miss this on
previous visits? – I find myself stepping, almost, into a
painting. You can't actually go in, now, to the Tribuna,
as you could in the eighteenth century, but even looking
in from the doorways was a startling delight. You see,
the hold Florence had on generation upon generation of
English is epitomised for me not by E. M. Forster's novel
or Lawrence's or Browning's poems, not by the graves of
Elizabeth Barrett Browning or Fanny Trollope or Walter
Savage Landor or A. H. Clough in the English Cemetery,
but by Zoffany's extraordinary *tour de force* of a painting,
The Tribuna of the Uffizi, (1772). I remember being shown
a slide of it (when slides were bang up to the minute),
and being astonished by the panache with which it brings
together almost a catalogue of 'Famous Works You
Ought By Now to Recognise', and portraits of many of
the men of fashion then in Florence. Identifying, in time,
both the works of art and the people looking at then –
no women, of course – was a source of slow pleasure as
well as a wonderful reminder of my own delight in seeing
those paintings for the first time. For a lad like myself,
growing up when and where I did, near Blackpool,
could have virtually no experience of art. Art books
were horribly expensive. Printed on heavy coated paper,
the pictures were usually black and white, and although
a library might have, say, E. H. Gombrich's *The Story of
Art,* there was little to point you towards it. The nearest

serious art gallery was Manchester, and that was then a longish journey away. To be sure, the Grundy Art Gallery, founded in 1911 by two brothers, both painters, John and Cuthbert Grundy, offered *Aircraftsman Shaw* [aka T. E. Lawrence] by Augustus John, *Sanctuary Wood* by Paul Nash, *The Yellow Funnel* by Eric Ravilious (who has since become a favourite of mine), but what I remember from the rare teenage visit are *The Roofs of Ambleside in the Rain* and a collection of netsuke. Quite unlike *The Tribuna of the Uffizi*; and by golly, when I did get my eyes on such contents as that painting brought together I realised just how much my youth had missed. Zoffany's painting became a sort of summary of many discrete hours of pleasure: Raphael's *John the Baptist*, flanked by two Guido Reni religious paintings, is just above the optical centre; the head of Titian's *Venus of Urbino* is at the lower centre. On the walls, three deep, are miniature pastiches of canvases by Caravaggio, Carracci, Correggio, Lotto, Perugino, Rubens. Neatly, religious paintings occupy the upper register, while homage to feminine beauty is offered at the sides and bottom. And then I began to get to know some of the people in the painting – 'Oh, *that's* what he looked like.' (Some more than others, of course.) Piero Bastianelli, the custodian of the Uffizi, presides over the gathering. George Finch, Earl of Winchelsea, Thomas Wilbraham, and James Bruce the African explorer – about whom Dr Johnson was impossibly rude and whom I respect greatly – admire, as connoisseurs, the seductive curves of the *Medici Venus*, modest and shy in her nudity, and the original of so many modern garden ornaments that you can buy in Garden Centres. (Well, a gnome would be worse.)[16] Lord Lewisham and Sir John Dick, consul at Leghorn – he met almost every person of quality taking that short sea route from France to Italy to avoid the testing crossing of the Alps – are being shown a Raphael Madonna, while Lord Edgecumbe and Charles Loraine Smith gaze rapturously at the bottom of one Grace in a Roman statue of the Three Graces, Euphrosyne, Aglaea and Thalia. Among the statues – a Roman copy of Praxiteles' *The Dancing Faun*, the Three Graces, the Wrestlers, the Knife Grinder, an Etruscan chimaera, a Greek torso – are other members, permanent or merely passing through, of the English community. Titian's voluptuous *Venus of Urbino* is being shown to Sir Horace Mann by Thomas Patch. Now Mann (1706-1786) was British diplomatic representative to the Grand Dukes of Tuscany from 1737 to the end of his long life. As Britain had no diplomatic representation at Rome, Mann's job included keeping tabs on the activities of the exiled Stuarts, the Old and Young Pretenders: a sad job, as the glamorous Bonnie Prince declined into bibulous obesity and pointless *affaires de coeur*. George III, a nice man, allowed a pension to live on to those who would have taken his throne from him.[17] I had got interested in Mann once, as I was thinking about writing a book about the Young Pretender's wife, Luisa von Stolberg. Rome knew her as the Queen of Hearts. Then Patch: himself no mean painter and one of the English founders of serious art history, he made a living painting caricatures of the

English visitors as souvenirs. That tradition is alive and well: so many young artists in the city in summer offer to do your portrait in chalk While U Wait. Some are quite good. Jenny had one from her first visit with her brother. I said I thought she had improved as she got older.

George III paid Zoffany well, but his delightful queen Charlotte disliked the painting, and Horace Mann too damns with faint praise. He wrote to Horace Walpole – and there is another old friend whose wonderful letters allow you to look over his shoulder into his world – on 23 August 1774:

> The one-eyed German, Zoffany [Mann refers to his squint], who was sent by the King to paint a perspective view of the Tribuna in the Gallery, has succeeded amazingly well in many parts of that and in many portraits he has made here. The former is too much crowded with (for the most part) uninteresting portraits of English travellers then here.[18]

★

> At evening, sitting on this terrace,
> When the sun from the west, beyond Pisa, beyond the
> mountains of Carrara
> Departs, and the world is taken by surprise...

D. H. Lawrence watched the swallows with 'spools of dark thread sewing the shadows together' over the evening Arno, and then the sudden flutter of the bats. It was a poem we 'did' at school all those years ago. But I feel he missed the real show. We came out of the Uffizi into a luminous December gloaming. It had been a clear cold day, with promise of more to come, and the dying light edged the darkness of the buildings seen against it with a glory. Then we noticed: against the bright evening sky, a cloud swirled and swooped, swift, now dense, black, now open. Thousands upon thousands of starlings in their daily winter murmuration, just like the winter starlings at home. The storm of murmuring birds sweeps over like an overmastering wave, almost with the sound of surf, and they rush over with the wind in their wings, then sudden, down they go with a communal sigh into the gardens of Florence to roost.

We walked to a favourite, unpretentious, restaurant in Via delle Belle Donne. (I do wonder how that street got its name all those years ago.) We had to pass through the Piazza di Santa Maria Novella, and as we turned the corner by the old cemetery we heard them: a ceaseless chatter and gurgle and all the other delicious noises starlings make. They roost in the trees, crowding the branches so that they bend under their weight, and quarrel, and push each other off (it seems) and re-arrange themselves, and do it again. Noisily. I love them, and I love them as they do the same manoeuvres over the level vastness of the winter Fen which the house where I write this overlooks. They finally come together with a great rush of wings and die down, a *djinn* going back into its lamp, into the hedges and sedges and ditches that piece and plot this land.

Starlings caught Dante's imagination too. In *Inferno* V. 40ff. the starlings he must have seen over the roofs of the beloved town, of which he came to despair, fly while the world dures and as long as he is read:

> *E come li stornei ne portan l'ali*
>> *nel freddo tempo, a schiera larga e piena,*
>> *così quel fiato li spiriti mali*
> *Di qua, di là, di giù, di sù li mena...*
>> (And as in winter time the starlings fly
>> in great tight flocks, even so the gale blows
>> The cursed souls, here, there, down, up, low, high...)

The swirls of doomed lovers on the winds of Hell – you *see* them in Dante's lines – those who loved too much, too unwisely, without moderation, qualify for me for ever, after reading that, the winter flight of starlings, their passion till all passions shall be still. As in Tchaikovsky's swirling music, when Francesca da Rimini leaves the ceaseless dance to tell her tragedy. Ecstasy infinitely prolonged is hellish.

Dante's eyes would have looked on Santa Maria Novella (but without Alberti's façade), outside the city walls, and perhaps even the predecessors of the trees in the cemetery. The starlings on whose roosting we intruded – but they cared not – may even descend from ones he watched.

★

I walked briskly, for the late afternoon wind was chill, round the corner into the Piazza della Signoria. Two women, in the colourful dresses and headscarves gypsies love, walked confidently in the other direction, chatting happily. Their voices had no trace of the cringing whine that I have heard so often when I have had to run the gauntlet of women begging outside the churches. I find it hard not to give. But it did cross my mind to wonder if these two women were going off duty, for I have been told by more than one person that begging from soft-centred visitors is big business in which the Mafia has a hand. I don't know. I worry, impotently.

★

In a narrow little street is what has come over the years to be my favourite restaurant. Good peasant food, and lots of it: bean soup, excellent pasta *al dente*, fine generous *ossabuco*, and good house wine. After one conference, when I had persuaded some colleagues to go there for the third or fourth time, Mario saw us coming in and raised his eyes almost resignedly as he greeted us. 'The same table, signori? And the same wine? And grappa after your meal?' Yes indeed, we chorused: and at the end of the meal he brought not just glasses of the spirit but put the whole bottle on the table. 'No charge, signori. You come again.' It had been a good conference.

★

High over Florence the church of San Miniato keeps its watch, as this holy place has done for over a thousand years. From its terrace all the populous city is spread out before you. The early morning light, with the sun rising behind the church, picks out the details of Duomo, of Santa Croce, and far over the city the hills of Fiesole are clear. It is indeed a fair city, that 'now doth like a garment wear /The beauty of the morning; silent, bare... /All bright and glittering in the smokeless air... The very houses seem asleep.' But we are not. At the other end of the day, as the sun begins to decline into the west and the heat of a summer day begins to ease, the monks chant Vespers in the old Gregorian mode, and those ancient patterns of sound, once heard each day from Iceland to Jerusalem, collapse time and space. The old is new again. They are not barefoot, as the friars Gibbon heard in Rome in 1764 'as [he] sat musing amidst the ruins of the Capitol, while the barefooted friars were singing vespers in the Temple of Jupiter.' (And so *The Decline and Fall of the Roman Empire* was born.)

Each time I have been to Florence this place has drawn me. I always follow the pilgrimage route – which we found by pure accident. I begin at the Ponte Vecchio and walk up Via di San Gregorio to the Forte di Belvedere, which lives up to its name, then from there along Via di Belvedere to Porta San Miniato and Via del Monte alle

Croci, then up the unrelenting steps – not as fast as on that first eager visit, for knees are less willing – alongside the green of olives and orchard to the right. Then, at the top, you face the flight of broad marble stairs to the terrace before the west door, a humbling climb to the church. The Southern Steps, 200 feet wide, up to the Temple at Jerusalem, were mnemonic and penitential. These echo them under this western sky far from Palestine.

At the beginning of the path up the hill, unobtrusively, on the left, is a tablet with lines from Dante's *Purgatorio*, 12, 97ff.:

> *Come a man destra, per salire al monte*
> *dove siede la chiesa che soggioga*
> *la ben guidata sopra Rubaconte,*
>
> *si rompe del montar l'ardita foga*
> *per le scalee che si fero ad etade*
> *ch'era sicuro il quaderno e la doga;*
>
> *così s'allenta la ripa che cade*
> *quivi ben ratta da l'altro girone;*
> *ma quinci e quindi l'alta pietra rade.*
> (As on the right hand, when you climb the hill
>   Where above the Rubaconte sits that church,
>   Which overlooks the city ruled so well,
>
> The steep rise of the hard slope is broken
>   By stone stairs carved in rock in other days
>   When weights and records were not yet rotten;

Just so, steps eased the steepness of the cliff
    That from the higher circle plunges sheer,
    Though on each side the high rock presses close.)

These are the steps of Humility. We walk where Dante walked, both in reality and in his poem, where he moves from the circle of Pride in Purgatory up the steps to 'that church which dominates the city.'

We took our students there, of course. Most went up by humble bus. Fair enough, for it is a fair step. But few were unmoved by the building, surely one of those in-between places where the worlds embrace – the sort of place that George Macleod, the visionary soldier and Church of Scotland minister, who founded the Iona Community, called 'thin' places. The sun shining through the clerestory runs through the marble zodiac on the floor and sends a ray precisely to the Fishes on the pulpitum on the very day of San Miniato's dedication festival in that Sign. Bill McMurrin, architect and distinguished designer of many beautiful buildings that grace his native state way out West, came out into the light, past the usual beggar at the door, and stood silent in the sunlight looking back at the façade. 'I can go home now,' he said. 'There can be nothing better than this.' He turned and silently gave the beggar some dollars, and made his way across the lofty marble terrace to where the city of this world was spread before him.

There is a way down, a wandering path through a paradisal garden, where in summer the goldfish flash as they turn lazily in the water and the roses open to welcome the sun to their bosoms. The lemons are little suns in their green night.

★

On the threshold on the church is inscribed 'Hic est Porta Coeli' – 'Here is the Gate of Heaven.'. The little shop nearby, which sells perfumes, icons, cards and very good gungy cakes, has a notice saying 'Hic est *Torta* Coeli'. Their chocolate ones are indeed heavenly.

★

And then. Death came quickly, almost before we had time to register his quiet footfall. As I watched beside her bed that last night, she slept away, and the years drained away from her profile. I saw once more the girl I had courted, who had... well, no matter.

As virtuous men pass mildly away,
And whisper to their souls to go,
Whilst some of their sad friends do say
The breath goes now, and some say, No:

So let us melt, and make no noise,
No tear-floods, nor sigh-tempests move;
'Twere profanation of our joys
To tell the laity our love.

I knew, I held her hand, when she slipped away. Oddly, she felt more alive than ever, as if some sort of spring, power if you like, had been released into the room. I placed a late rose from our autumn garden between her cold hands, and called our children.

So now she journeys on, in a different sphere, and who knows what she sees now she has passed that bourne from which no traveller returns. 'No longer mourn for me when I am dead. Live on, you have work to do. Your journey is not over.' Almost (not quite) the last things said.

They were long and lonely years, travelling alone to many places, deeper into the interior, accepting every invitation or commission, piling on the work, wandering affably and pleasurably in and out of lighted rooms of talk and laughter and attempts at high thinking before returning to the silence of the enduring dark. But the road goes on: there is no option not to take it, even when your fellow travellers drop out.

★

III

INTERMEZZO: THE DOLDRUMS, OR, GOING NOWHERE

Forgotten Kingdoms

Over every mountain there is a path,
although it may not be seen from the valley.
Theodore Roethke

They say that ships becalmed in the Doldrums, neither
north nor south of the Line, used sometimes to stay there
for months, even years, while the tar of the caulking
melted and the fresh water grew foul, foul. Going
nowhere, except where the chance feeble current might
drift you... Keep the men busy...

★

'What should I do in Illyria? My beloved, she is in
Elysium.' Arriving, alone, at strange airports at dead of
night, is like being shipwrecked into a new existence.
You have no bearings. Perhaps, as I did when I went
to Albania, so soon after she died, you might seize on
anything to get some bearings – even the black two-
headed eagle of Byzantium, facing both east and west, on
the badges worn by the police. It is at least *something* you
know in this strange land, though Byzantium is only a
memory, if even that, except for oddballs like me. Once
Byzantium's writ had run there among the Ἀλβάνοι,
and the country's name in Albanian, *Shqipëria*, 'Land of

the Eagle', may refer to this well-endowed bird. But to
the immigration people the badge was just a badge, with
no echoes, and they were simply impassive, unglamorous
as only they can be – and, as in Romania, you realise that
their jobs under Albania's *ancien régime*, a mere dozen or
so years before, might have been less anodyne. No one
was waiting for me: did I seriously expect there to be?
I came out of the ultra-modern, and beautiful, Mother
Teresa Airport into a warm darkness pulsing with the
busyness of cicadas in the surrounding palms and olives.
'What country, friends, is this?' 'This is Illyria...' And so,
once upon a time, it was. The language is one of the most
ancient in Europe.

The long drive south across the central plain into the
unknown dark started on smooth tarmac. At increasingly
frequent intervals it was punctuated by half-built
roundabouts, aggressive potholes and stretches of, in
effect, cart track. I came along that road in daylight on
my way back home at the end of that journey: after a
few times it was no strange sight to see a donkey cart
turn across two lines of lorry traffic, or to see at the side
of the road, stalls, under bamboo shades that sieved the
sunlight, selling fruit and vegetables, or budgerigars,
of all things, far from their ancestral Australia. Brakes
slammed on as we came to an unmade stretch at speed.
But that first night, the headlong headlights picked up
those same stalls, now deserted, and an extraordinary
number of petrol stations, many with big yellow signs
promising 'Kastrati'. One could feel threatened: but no

cause, for the company is named after Gjergi Kastrioti, Skanderbeg, the national hero, who for four long decades in the fourteenth century held the Turks at bay. (He used that eagle on his seals.) The Albanians have always been an awkward lot to their would-be rulers: the beaches, and, inland, every hillock, every coign of vantage, are littered with domed concrete pill boxes – some 900 in all – just big enough for one man and his gun, dating from times when Enver Hoxha's Albania was beleaguered and had no friends except an awful lot in China – and Hoxha fell out with those in the end. To attempt a landing or attack, had anybody wanted to take over so poor a country, would have been rather like putting your hand into an angry beehive. The Albanians were a handful for the Venetians, they revolted against Byzantium a thousand years ago, and they were testing for the Caesars before them. But the Turks won in the end, and many folk converted to Islam. It is the usual story, I suppose: most people, who like Gallio 'care for none of these things', accept, reluctantly or not, *cuius regio, eius religio*. The country now – 30% Orthodox, 10% Catholic and the rest in theory Muslim, the statistics say – shows many signs of that long Turkish dominance, in vocabulary, food and customs. Tall slim white minarets aspire to the sky. Mosque and church in some villages nod to each other politely enough across the shared street. In Pier, church outfaces mosque, each flaunting new paint. And relaxed Muslim villages can grow some lovely wine... I found it a strange, and attractive, place. But I only saw the surface. And my heart was empty.

The darkness paled in the west as the car began the climb over the coastal hills: the loom of the lights of Vlore (anciently Valona). One reason I was in Albania was that there was a conference on language, silent, spoken and written, which sounded interesting, and they had asked me to speak. The other reasons are now of small concern. But it was the first time I had travelled abroad since her death, and so something of a watershed. It felt very strange to be checking into a hotel in the small hours, alone, with no sense of the place or people, with the porter dishevelled and confused by sleep. The next morning I woke to the sounds of horns and motors, which shall bring... well, not Sweeney anyway. My bare feet relished the cool of the marble as I padded across the room from the large and lonely bed I had hardly disturbed to open the shutters. The new hotel overlooked University Square in one direction and the Adriatic, or more properly the gulf of Valona/ Ragusa, in the other. Across the square was the University building, now home to high thinking and serious scholarship: once it was the Communist Party HQ, devoted to different ideologies and other imperatives. Below, in front of me, was a plinth, the marble paving round it parenthesised by weeds. On it were two bronze feet. Nothing more. Ozymandias was here... Here stood for all time the statue of Hoxha, whom we Brits had helped to power through our support of his fierce (and brave) partisan resistance to the occupying Germans. They say – the guidebooks – that his shade like Montezuma's exacts a terrible revenge on those who, full of sybaritic thoughts, pursue frivolity in this his land. But I saw little sign of it — I may have been lucky: the food was sumptuous and imaginative, and with a supply of all sorts of fish straight from the sea and, with the profusion of fresh vegetables and bracing local wine, how could it not be? You can see why some people see Albania now simply as an ideal holiday resort.

Yet it is hard to joke about Hoxha. Though he said he was a Stalinist, Hoxha's real roots were in the centuries of Ottoman rule — after all, it only ended in 1912. Some have called him an 'Ottoman dandy'; certainly his inner circle seems to have been far less motivated, whatever its members said, by Marxist-Leninism than by the age old Balkan ideology of revenge: *gjak per gjak* — blood for blood. Aeschylus' *Oresteia* all over again... For four decades, Hoxha ruled Albania with revenge murders and government purges at a whim, in an atmosphere of shadowy fear, rumours and recrimination. In his last years he and his wife seemed to be running the troubled, isolated, country by themselves. Just so, in Romania, Ceaușescu, the shoemaker's son who made good, and his ambitious chemist wife declined into the prison of their own personal tyranny. Lord Acton's first law of politics is the cost of power. That is what Shakespeare's history plays explore so devastatingly. It felt apposite to be lecturing on them in a room overlooking Hoxha's bronze feet.

They were rebuilding Vlore: wholesale, fast. Wipe out the past – but it will lurk in the shadows of memory, and grudge. One common sign, on plots of land by the road, by the sea, on buildings, says 'Shitest': there is no comparative to this superlative, it merely means 'For Sale'. Land speculation was in full, uncontrolled swing, and they told me, quietly, that lots of people have fingers in that pie. A serious effort was being made to cash in on the tourist boom of a then more affluent EU – to 'catch up' with Durrës. One hoped they would not. Having seen what has become of Dyrrachium, which the Venetians called Durrazzo, where once upon a time the emperor Diocletian decreed his stately pleasure dome – probably even then of dubious taste – the prospect of vulgar jerrybuilt ugliness and the reduction of the local people to an exploited urban helotry hardly attracts. You glimpse what might have been: a few two storey houses with pierced shutters and outside stair, and vines lolling over trellises, remain in Vlora's centre: houses for living in, for taking one's ease in the cool of the day as the sea wind stirs the vine leaves. They probably go back to King Zog's time, if not earlier, but their days are numbered as the rash of ten storey hotels breaks out alongside them[19]. The infant conservation movement hardly stood a chance: it lost a major battle when the city fathers welcomed building on the site of mediaeval Vlore, which itself overlies much, much older remains. Nobody could regret, though, despite their historical interest, the passing of the slum blocks of flats jerrybuilt under communism, the depressing reduction of the inhabitants of the Socialist Paradise to interchangeable units of labour. Yet even there, where the unmade roads reach through the sighing pines to the shore, you can see where someone has occasionally tried to make a hovel Home and Beautiful, with paint and flowers. But for most of them, grey, cracked, ugly, why bother? For we are trained to expect nothing...

The beach stretches for miles, and to walk out of the surf, warm to my white English feet, into the edge of the trees is for a moment – only a moment – to imagine oneself as *heureux qui comme Ulysse a fait un beau voyage*. But alas there was no longer a Penelope weaving her own story at home. Only a couple of lads on a smelly scooter, no Nausicaa, came out of the trees, and in the sand broken glass glinted, and in the trees the plastic detritus of modernity. (There were no plastic bottles when Odysseus was a lad – might he have tried to send a message home from Calypso's isle?) Yet: turn round, look along the bright highway to the westering sun, and there a boat is poised, with two men standing, fishing, black silhouettes against the light. Sea, sunset and a picture as old as Time. Odysseus knew this.

In the town, along the sea front, platoons of toilets, blue Portaloos decorated on the doors and sides with large white silhouettes of women with crossed legs and men with hands folded modestly over their crotch. Nothing if not clear what they were for. Palm trees, with nuts and wide boles, reminded deliberately – they are deliberate trees – of Monte Carlo and the Promenade des Anglais. For before the war when Europe went mad this had been a fashionable resort for the well-off Albanians, and ever so much easier to get to than the French Riviera. An echo of a world away. The smell of the sea is clear and sharp across the empty beach. Inland, in the town, the smells are different: the sweet reek of Marlboro cigarettes, gas, oil, bitumen. In cafés beneath the slow dappled shade of welcome eucalypts men sat at little tables, with tall glasses of mountain water and little cups of thick coffee, playing chess and backgammon. No women. Not here, anyway: but along by the hotels affluent Euroclones frolic in and out of the sea nakedly unabashed by the erstwhile customs of the country. The old men's eyes show something: offence? or interest? or memory? Perhaps all three. The vast gap between what was so recently normal and what is and will be is everywhere apparent. In the country alongside elderly women in black with white headscarves, teenage girls sell vegetables and fruit at the side of the road, and herd sheep as their mothers did before them. But those young wear the Europe-wide fashion of tight jeans bleached if they had sat in something nasty, with frayed knees. How did they afford them with what they must earn? The little house with its roof of terracotta tiles nestling in the cool trees of its garden by the sea is elbowed by the concrete cuckoo next to it. Donkey carts, some with awnings, go by, the animals' faces full of thoughtful care, their delicate hoofs raising little puffs of white dust. On the wide promenade, which was still being finished, motor scooters, some very old, perhaps going back to the fashionable vehicles of the 1960s young – how I wanted one! How I loved the wind in one's hair, and dreamed of a girl (I had one in mind) who would grace the pillion – dart in and out of the traffic like foraging wasps. The old ladies a-sidesaddle on the pillion no longer look like Audrey Hepburn in *Roman Holiday*. Perhaps they did once; perhaps they still do inside. But again, perhaps they look just like their mothers did riding sidesaddle on the backs of depressed donkeys, whitescarved, their old feet in wrinkled black stockings – as one still sees them high in the hills.

It was busy. Old Italian buses snorted along, frustrating the new BMWs and Mercedes driven by the sort of sunglassed men who drive new BMWs and Mercedes everywhere. But there were also lots of older, beat-up Mercedes, with the scars that show the unflinching machismo of their drivers in facing the traffic. To be driven at 120kph in a Mercedes with a cracked windscreen on a two lane highway, overtaking slow, overloaded lorries, or those puttering three wheeler carts, what I call lawnmower carts, straight into the path of oncoming lorries – that is white knuckle stuff. The driver had a badge on his dash which had been sent him from Lourdes. I was glad. We not only escaped disaster, but I also found the experience, after a time, even exhilarating: rather like the matador might feel as the bull charges and he turns lithely aside at the last moment. On the seafront at Vlore was a rink for dodgems: one wondered what possible attraction they could have when the real thing was so much faster and more exciting.

Our University hosts gave us *conférenciers* a day up in the hills. The bus, unremarkably like any tour bus anywhere, crossed the thin coastal plain with its long unfenced plots of land, its plane trees, and the sea wind stroking the bamboos in the ditches. The wave of pressure runs along the line, and the tall screen bows, and rises, alternately yielding and then resisting. I would much rather have been walking, getting the feel and the smells of the country, but nobody official seems to allow for that. (I had to wait.) The bus began the climb up to Llogara Pass in a series of unceasing, determined hairpins. Here the Ceraunian Mountains divide into their western and eastern ranges. And then pennies began to drop. I had read about this part, years before: Ptolemy, Strabo and Pausanias all mention them as formidable obstacles, and how the road, once gleaming limestone, white and unmetalled as it climbs the high pass to over 1000 metres, was visible far out to sea. It was a well-known mark for sailors. Julius Caesar got his legions over this pass in 48 BC when chasing Pompey, while his galleys commanded the Gulf of Valona. (What we would now call Combined Ops. He was good at that.) Indeed, it beats me how those legionaries did it, carrying about 90lbs without the benefits of a modern pack frame, or Vibram soles, climbing 3000 feet in the heat, with only a mess of *frumentum* and sour wine to look forward to at the end of the day, and then be ready to fight, or build a temporary entrenched camp, or whatever.

The brilliant light dulled as we got higher, and all of a sudden a hill fog, clammy as any Lake District offering and welcome after the heat of the plain, rolled up the hill and enveloped us, and the air was suddenly silenced. A brief lifting allowed a steep glimpse under the skirt of the cloud to the turquoise sea and the curving strand – no, that word is not too precious – far, far below. And then the fog rolled in again, and the pines sighed and began to drip small beads of moisture. The temperature was perfect, for me. On the way down into the sunlight there was, thank goodness, at last a chance to get out and walk. In the sun-dried open patches between the trees bees bustled among the late flowers and lizards lounged on the hot rock. Below the woods, innumerable terraces, neglected – and when were they ever not? – clambered dizzily high up the steep limestone hills. These are the labours of men, stone upon stone, mattock stroke on mattock stroke, for thousands of years in this place, for it is certain that these terraces reach back to Antiquity. Still these are where the grapes and the olives and the crops grow, and the odd horse grazes, while a belled brown cow forages in the dry fields of late summer, or ambles past the scarecrows set to deter blackbirds from the ripe fruit. (There were no pigs, for this part is Muslim.) Apricots, figs, melons at their best, and stooked millet in the fields made a pattern as old as the settlement of Man as a farmer. Children herded indignant turkeys – newcomers indeed – with long bamboos. Long-nosed sheep, driven without sheepdogs, superciliously flocked by. In the distance, a lime kiln smoked, exactly of the pattern that lies derelict in my own north country. Wood of olives and the pines from high on the vertiginous slopes fuel it.

We went to an inn, for on the morrow the group would disperse and I would be on my own. Farewell lunches are occasions to indulge, in sentiment if nothing else. In a very short time in that sort of academic situation you have got to know people very well on a very narrow front. We had all worked hard, listening to and commenting on papers good, bad and a few as usual incomprehensible and therefore clearly very, very clever. With so many people coming from so many different angles, everyone was being made to think outside comfortable boxes. That is what such meetings are for. We were eating fresh young lamb, and chips done in olive oil, and polenta, washed down with wine from the vineyard (so the owner told us) up the hill. Just higher up the hill from the terrace someone had stretched a cloth banner across the village street congratulating everyone on the end of Ramadan. We celebrated with them and for them. With pleasure. The conversation was good. After all, the conference was on 'The Said and the Unsaid,' and we could do both very well. My Egyptian colleague, Fatima of the lovely eyes, told me how dangerous things were getting in Egypt, and, almost in tears, how impossible that country's problems seemed. She wondered how long she, a woman, would be allowed to hold her University post, and how she would provide for her family, what work her son would ever find as he grew up. She even told me, as she sipped her wine, how she sometimes hated wearing the *chador* – 'for my mother says I have beautiful hair.' Her hand went to her brow, hesitantly – but then she thought better of it. Or perhaps I was imagining what her utterly beguiling gesture meant. (Her name in Arabic means 'captivating.') Bledar, the conference organiser who had invited me to be there, earnestly asked me if he thought there might be any chance, ever, of his coming to Cambridge to study, 'for we have so small a library here, and our English section is among the smallest. I love reading, and poetry, I love your literature, but to make a living I have to make do with critical theory.' (Poor man!) Elena, from Ukraine, a fine Renaissance scholar, said she was desperate to get a job in the EU, for 'nobody in my country cares any longer for anything but money and business, and yet literature is where humans discuss the real questions, who they are and what they *mean*.' A group who had come from four continents, twenty countries, and four religions (and some few from none) found a moment out of time when just being, and being together at a meal, was enough. Too soon we had to go back down the hill, to jobs, to status and competition: in a word, to our threatened profession, the job of which is to ask awkward questions of those in authority and power. For some of us, that was already risky. We promised, as one does, to meet again. We meant it. We never did. For a time, we corresponded, some of us, and followed each other's work. That languished with the years. Our single strands had briefly come together to make a braid as strong as death, and then frayed apart again. But the memory is warm. I shall not go back.

★

Invitations came quite often. When you are alone you accept them, for not having to cook your own dinner is always welcome. And talking about Shakespeare was one of my passports – not least because I am interested in how and why his work had such a huge following in Europe and particularly central Europe – a common ground in every sense. For just as epics make nations, great literature can be potent in unexpected ways. Homer's story of the wrath of Achilles and the loss of Troy's greatest defender was for ancient Greeks the foundation story; for Rome, Virgil's overgoing[20] of Homer's *Iliad* and *Odyssey* became an authorising myth – and for those who read more carefully, a warning about power. The states that in the early middle ages eventually crystallised out of the break-up of Rome's Empire all – England, Scotland, France, Spain – claimed their royal house derived authority by descent from Aeneas, Father of the Roman people and Prince of Troy. The family trees of Elizabeth I, in the British Museum, and of Henry VI, in the Society of Antiquaries' Library, both trace

descent from Brutus, grandson of Aeneas. And just as
Virgil's Latin had to be made to do all and more Greek
could do so that Romans could feel they had, so to speak,
come of age, just as making the vernacular languages of
early modern Western Europe do all that Virgil's and
Cicero's Latin could do, just so two centuries later when
Europe was once more in the ferment of revolution and
post-revolution, Shakespeare, of infinite linguistic and
conceptual resource, was the challenge: translated into
French, and into German – Schlegel's version became
standard – at a time 'Deutschland' was beginning to mean
more than just an area made up of over 300 little states
where all sorts of German was spoken. And at such a time
of the breaking and making of nations, the nationalist
movements of Bohemia, of Hungary, or Romania
took on the same challenge as a signal of nationhood.
The rise of nationalism that culminated in the 1848
revolt had one literary consequence: many scholars
attempted to translate the works of Shakespeare, already
acknowledged as a genius of towering stature (as in
Germany, with its own identity crisis and its own culture
of translation of the major works of the western canon).
In Hungary, for example, totally different from anything
Shakespeare knew in climate, geography, history,
language, a Shakespeare Association, still flourishing,
was founded in 1864 – a hundred years before the Société
Française Shakespeare – on his birthday, in the run-up
to the crisis that in 1867 established the Dual Monarchy
of semi-independent Hungary and Austria. The
philosopher Johann Gottfried von Herder had remarked

decades earlier that Hungarian was a dying language as it was linguistically isolated and had no epic to define its identity, and without such an epic Hungary could never be a real nation. If Shakespeare could be translated into Magyar, then Magyar was no dying language. If he could be translated into Czech and Slovak, then Bohemia might claim its own identity from Austria.

Busily, then, to Prague, seen first on a day of driving rain years, years before, with Jenny as we shepherded our wet and grumpy charges on one of our study tours. The World Shakespeare Conference is in some sense a hiring fair. But I was neither hiring nor interested in being hired. So I felt somewhat old, and lonely. But the people-watching was as much gentle and affectionate fun as ever. One of the doyens of Shakespeare Studies, whose slight resemblance to the Droeshout portrait of the great man is enhanced by a careful little beard and studiedly dramatic carriage, courteously listened to the thoughts of the shoal of young people who spanieled him at heels, an affable dolphin among charming minnows. (Conferences mix everything, including metaphors.) The hooves of the hobby horses made the usual noise as they came out of their stables: the aging *enfant terrible* still attacking a position long abandoned, or that passionate and logorrhetic exponent of the *idée fixe*, with glittering eye and skinny arm. The young gave papers ranging from the awful to the excellent – but then so did their elders. A feast of jargon and a flow of cool... Everyone was very polite about it, openly at least. But some of the plenary lectures, especially those that reminded us of what life under a totalitarian regime had been like, and how important are stories and drama to the business of being human, were actually greatly moving. The gritty business of jobs and reputation for a moment was put in perspective by what it was ultimately all about – and how lucky we in the West have been! As Churchill retorted to someone who asked what use studying Shakespeare was when there was a war on, 'There is a war on so we *can* study Shakespeare.'

Mozart conducted the premières of *Don Giovanni* and *La Clemenza di Tito* in the wonderfully restored little theatre where they held the plenary sessions. And they did not tell us the significance of the building. Once I had found out, I made sure that over those few days I sat in a box in every tier, and in the stalls as well. It would have been good to have an opera, but all Prague could then offer – underestimating the market, as usually happens in such places – was musical lollipops. At one hell of a price. But perhaps they were right, for the awkward fact is that for most visitors Prague is simply the pretty party town, the place for stag or hen weekends. The first hoardings you see on leaving the airport provocatively leave no doubt about that. A plethora of bars compete to offer unlimited booze, and 'Thai oil massage' on the first floor. (There seems to be a fashion at the moment in Prague for absinthe, which is said to make the tart grow fonder.) In the Old Town Square, a host of faces gawp at the astronomical clock, as well they might, as it performs its complex drama each hour, but most visitors are clearly insensitive to, indeed ignorant of, the crucial events in European history that took place to the chiming of that very clock, in front of these very buildings, in this very square, in this very town. Here were the first stirrings of the cataclysm of Reformation, with the preaching of Huss and the first Defenestration onto the hard stone of the Square. Two centuries later, here was the opening of the most terrible conflict Europe had up to then seen, the Thirty Years War, which depopulated whole swathes of Germany and lasted so long that almost nobody could remember what they were fighting about. The White Mountain, site of the first battle, is a mile or two away. When I went there, with my head full of thoughts of James I's daughter, the tragic yet manipulative Elizabeth, who was Queen of Bohemia until the disaster of that battle, I found it surrounded now by a depressing, dull housing estate. Elizabeth, at whose wedding the King's company of players (including Shakespeare) played *A Winter's Tale* and *The Tempest,* is immortalised less by politics than by Henry Wootton's perfect poem to her:

> You meaner beauties of the night,
>   That poorly satisfy our eyes
> More by your number than your light;
>   You common people of the skies;
> What are you when the moon shall rise...?

(They called her the Winter Queen: queen for that one winter, then widow for year after impoverished and impotent year.) You can still see the window in Hradcany from which the Hapsburg envoys were hurled in the second Defenestration. They landed, some say, in a pile of straw, and some say a dung heap. The Catholics said the angels held them up lest they dash their foot against a stone; the Protestants, who favoured the dung heap version, that they ended where they belonged. A compromise might be that the angels guided them to a soft landing. That providential dung heap has since been moved. But the tourists either do not know or do not care: they flock across Charles Bridge, lined with stalls selling souvenirs, they take photos of their children standing with arms spread out, grinning, in front of the great crucifix on Charles Bridge, or cuddle each other below the memorial to St John of Nepomuk at the point where he was flung into the swollen Vltava for refusing to reveal the secrets of a fourteenth century Queen's confession. (There is an awful lot of silver to polish on his shrine in St Vitus' cathedral.) I overheard two young Brits asking why that man was on the Cross, who he was. They do not know about the grey paint of the houses underneath the colour wash, the scars of the dreadful years after 1968 of 'normalization' which sometimes come to the surface as Czechs let themselves remember. The parents of Helen, my colleague, were in Prague that morning when the bitter breeze from the north east killed the buds of the Prague Spring. They opened the curtains of their hotel on Wenceslaus Square to see the grey tanks drawn up, silent, watchful. (T34s are surprisingly small.) My friend Ludmila and her husband Dolibor told me a lot about that awful time. Ludmila knew too well what it was to be the child of parents who had been declared non-people by the Communists. Denied education, denied healthcare, denied employment, she garnered the anguished and impotent sympathy of all but they dared not do something for this ragged, hungry child, this sad adolescent who is now a University professor. And bitter. And as we walked to find a restaurant they knew in the old Jewish quarter, deeper wounds were palpable: for in the pavement were set brass stars, with the names of those deported or simply shot under the Nazis. It was all very well to go on that last evening to a grand reception at the US embassy, in elegant gardens in a spectacular house: but the Ambassador was descended from Czech Jews who had fled Hitler with simply a suitcase, and the house had been built by one of those rich and cultured Jews who made so huge a contribution to European civilisation. And then Europe went psychotic, as it could again, so easily. The goblins, as Beethoven knew, never quite go quiet. And some of those who did well under the old regime are still there, comfortable, even powerful. One sometimes wonders with whom one is shaking hands. But, as Ludmila said, there may be such a thing as remorse, and even, perhaps, forgiveness. 'But I find that hard.'

I went on a tour – it sometimes helps one to get bearings – in the pouring rain, billed as showing us the Prague of

Rudolf II and Dr John Dee, in both of whom I have long had a certain interest. But it amounted to telling us where something had been in their time, before they pulled it down to build something else, and I think I knew more about those two remarkable individuals, the one a notable patron of arts and sciences and the other one of the most learned men in sixteenth century Europe and Elizabeth I's favourite *magus,* than did the chap leading his diminishing and dissolving straggle of wet people. In St Vitus' Cathedral (bits of which were indeed there in the sixteenth century), we found a welcome refuge from the storms without. Two Japanese ladies asked me what a particular bit of carving meant, and as I told them I suddenly thought, 'they would not ask that if they were not Christian', and – a stab in the dark – I said, 'Are you from Tokyo Women's Christian University?' Delighted smiles, and lots of bows, and then – the strangest coincidence – they said they had been to Cambridge, and had stayed at my College. We exchanged addresses, and weeks later there arrived in my College pigeonhole a copy of the history of their university and its links with the College. In Japanese...

Later, alone again, I wandered, drenched and dripping, into the Bethlehem Church, as I wanted to see where Jan Huss used to preach, and found myself in the middle of a University Graduation ceremony, being courteously ushered to a seat as the graduands touched the mace and bowed to the Chancellor. The last night my colleague

Stuart and I wandered through the darkening street, after
the Embassy bunfight – lots to drink but nothing to eat
– enjoying a now quieter townscape, free of cars, that
cannot have changed that much for a couple of hundred
years. Except it must be less smelly and is probably
more colourful. We found a little restaurant in a back
street, Kamzikova, just behind that gorgeous theatre. It
wasn't bad, if a little dark. Thank Heaven, there was no
background music – you would not need it in Prague
anyway, for *Ma Vlast* never quite leaves your head. As
we were starting to eat, in comes dear Dieter Mehl, and
joins us. Three elderly Shakespeare scholars, a picture
of respectability and what eighteenth century England
would have called 'bottom' and the Romans *gravitas*. And
then my eye was caught by a framed notice, and being
curious, I got my glasses out and read it. It told us we
were sitting in what about a century earlier had been one
of the classiest brothels in Prague – U Goldschmeidů,
'Goldsmiths' – which was called Gogo by its famous
visitors. Franz Kafka and the Emperor Charles I were
regulars. The reputedly uxorious Otto von Bismarck,
the notice claimed, apparently regarded the house as a
home from home when in Bohemia, and together with
other Prussian officers, he spent the night after the Battle
of Sadová there. They say that he ran up the steep stairs
as many as six times, with a different girl each time... (I
always thought battles were tiring.) The place was then
luxuriously furnished, with armchairs and large mirrors
on the ground floor. Girls led their clients from there

up the steep stairs to higher floors where were themed rooms – Gentlemen could choose whether they would be serviced in the Turkish, Persian, Japanese or Doctor's room – or others. The lady of the house apparently sat with a cash register on the first floor, with a large and lazy dog lying beside her, who was a favourite with all comers as well as with the residents. An antique piano near our table was the same vintage – might have been the same – as the one on which Gustav Mahler planned some of the *Kindertotenlieder.* The famous brothel is only recalled by the original wood stairs up which Bismarck ran like a chamois. Well then... we had little to contribute, three loquacious individuals at last silenced.

I had spaghetti. It was quite good.

★

Travelling alone without a purpose is infinitely less useful and perhaps less rewarding than staying at home and cultivating one's garden. But academics, a depressed and poorly rewarded profession, have one great advantage: they have a network, which reaches across the world, of similarly depressed and impecunious colleagues with whom they can on occasion meet and talk and remind each other of the importance of what they are doing in their lonely towers, which are not made of ivory or even any passable substitute. For while it is increasingly clear that human beings are not the only intelligent species on this planet, and not the only ones to have language and self-awareness – all of which moves the moral goalposts sharply – what does (so far) seem unique to us humans is that we make sense of the world by telling each other stories about it. This puts the discussion of the stories we tell, in the humanities as in the sciences, at the very centre of our understanding of what we are.

And so we meet, and talk, and write, and the busy world tries to ignore the leaven we are. But the yeast works away unseen, unheard, over centuries with a dream of whatever truth might be. It is well, if difficult, to keep those high thoughts in mind when, on what will clearly be a hot day, at an impossible hour you are standing waiting to board a full flight on a budget airline to yet another conference. Some sort of cheer.

Like Hungary, like Bohemia, Romania took on in a serious way the challenge of Shakespeare. Two of my colleagues have published books on his place in the cultural memory of what, when he was writing, was a Turkish province. So once again the study of a dead white early modern man, writing for a very specific and quite peculiar market in a country off the coast of Europe, bad-temperedly reinventing itself – rather like now! – became my passport and meal ticket.

Nobody except a few historians and politicians thought much about Romania in the sixties, when almost the only thing we encountered from there was a tin of tomatoes at the grocer's. Then with slight twitching of the Curtain at its southern corner came cheap package holiday holidays on the Black Sea, the only difference from Spain being that the cheap wine was different and there was no flamenco. Then...

It is difficult now, as the world darkens, and my own night draws on, to recall how one felt in those heady years when, as it were, a puff of wind blew away the Soviet Empire, and Communist states, one after the other, fell away like the seeds on a dandelion clock. 'Bliss was it in that dawn to be alive...' – I know exactly what Wordsworth meant, when he looks back bitterly at the hopes disappointed by the French Revolution. We felt hope, certainly: as if a terrible blight, a dark shadow, had lifted. Suddenly, it seemed as if the more civilised Europe, the work of centuries, of my beautiful, big, heavy pre-1914 atlas, might be about to return. But ghosts don't walk like that. They come back as pale gibbering shadows of what they were. There was also a recognition that all the markers that had been there all one's adult life had gone: the world was suddenly very uncertain. One prayed that someone in the US or Europe would have the wisdom to set up for the collapsed Eastern Europe something like a Marshall Plan. It was a vain hope, given that the values that had been encouraged through the 1980s recognised no imperative but profit, no morality except the market, and no arbiter except self-interest. High hope, huge optimism, as if the Shadow had been lifted, soon turned bitter.

We were walking in the Lake District that Christmas time when Romania's Ceaușescu fell. He had had a goodish press in England: after all, he was quite a nice guy really, wasn't he? Of all the Communist rulers Ceaușescu had the reputation of being the most decent, and indeed he had been received by Her Majesty and given an honorary Knighthood. He was the only Communist ruler who did not send his troops to help Russia suppress the Prague Spring in 1968. He had a good PR job, but the truth came out as quite, quite different.

We switched on the television news, happily tired after a long wet walk round the horseshoe of hills that surrounds Coledale in Cumbria. And there, on the screen, was the chaos that was unfolding by the minute, the moment when the Comrade suddenly realised that the crowd in the square were not cheering him but booing, the panic flight in the helicopter... His pilot said later that crew members were held at gunpoint. One of them had to sit in Ceauscescu's lap. Vasile Malutan, the pilot, well into the flight, told Ceaușescu that their aircraft had been spotted by radar and would probably be shot down. Ceaușescu ordered him to land immediately, and Ceaușescu and his wife Elena, and two security guards, stopped a passing car, ordered its four occupants to get out and then drove off. But on the way they were recognised, taken prisoner, and shot. On Christmas Day, the season of peace and goodwill. Last words? Some say Ceaușescu, as the guns were raised, hailed the Socialist republic and freedom, and that his wife said, 'But you are our children!' Others say she swore with naked hatred. Which myth do we want to believe and why?

Until quite recently (by my standards) Romania in its poverty did not figure much on most people's radar. Those who are over about 35 now perhaps remember those events surrounding the fall of the dictator; Enescu's music and perhaps bits of Bartok's *Romanian Dances* the musical will recall, and those of more dubious tastes will of course think of Vlad the Impaler *aka* Dracula. Mostly the country is a wide, level plain formed over millennia by the Danube floods, its dullness relieved by the ever changing light and the drama of great skies. And looking at it with the appraising eye of the smallholder I once was, I know that if farmed properly it could feed Europe.

I went many times, to Bucharest or Constanta. First impressions had not been good: immigration took hours, with every passport read from cover to cover by unsmiling functionaries whose history must have been with Ceaușescu's Securitate. (Once again, you have to use the people of the earlier apparatus, for they know where the keys are. Just change the uniforms – and in all the Eastern bloc no country had a higher proportion of its citizens in the security forces.) I think they put the rest of them – those not inspecting passports – as traffic policemen to contradict the traffic lights in the middle of five lane intersections on the great boulevards laid out when the city was planned in the nineteenth century. Predictably, chaos: it took the best part of an hour to move a mile, and that slowness tests the resources of your conversation with your driver – to whom it was normal, of course. The city stank. What made things worse was all the evidence of what a beautiful city it had been before the debilitating blight of Communism. The French had had a lot to do with its elegant style, with the Art Nouveau of some of the ironwork, and they had laid out the new capital on a scale to which Paris, huddled round its mediaeval cradle, could never aspire. Tree-lined boulevards radiate from monuments – even an Arc de Triomphe. Wide parks and lakes punctuate the buildings. But that traffic... and then you see the dreadful concrete flats shoved crudely into the elegance, almost as if in deliberate insult by the Communists. They must have had to demolish solid, good buildings to erect what even they must have realised was rubbish. Now many of those Communist era buildings bear prominent red circles that warn people that to buy a flat in one of them is very much at their own risk, for the building is so poor and the concrete so rotten that in the next earthquake, already overdue, they will – not might, will – collapse as the tremors turn the alluvial soil into a fluidised bed. But you also see the garish way the new capitalism covers Corinthian pillars and graceful cornices with 5 metre high adverts for deodorant, and, by the river, you see the awful Folly of the Palace Ozymandias Ceaușescu built for himself and his fiend-like queen, a 'People's Palace' the people paid for but from which they never received the slightest benefit: ten storeys up – and ten down, to the Bomb shelter which would protect the Leader and his entourage while the rest of Bucharest fried. It is so big they say they had to weave the carpets inside. An avenue of blank faced flats for the *nomenklatura* stands respectfully at a distance. Albert Speer, father of Totalitarian Classicism, be proud of how your style has spread across the lands of tyranny! A balcony half way up the palace's facade must have made the Comrade, when he stood there, look ridiculous: like Pope's Timon, 'a puny insect, shivering at a breeze'. But irony is not a dictator's or any ideologue's long suit, and laughter is always dangerous.

★

But among colleagues there, and among students, there was a sense of adventure, as if all of a sudden the bottled up excitement of exploring ideas and wrestling with words, the only, and deceptive, tools we have to make sense of things, was fizzing out like shaken champagne opened clumsily. But such champagne is still champagne: the excitement that buzzed through the dull grey halls and lecture rooms of the University deserved that wine and Strauss to go with it. People talked and talked, and western academics were only too happy to go and join in and wish that our own people, especially students, did not lazily and yawningly take for granted that of which these folk had been deprived for three generations. I felt ashamed more than once at my own lack of learning beside these people, in whom the polymathic fire burned bright and who could move so easily between so many languages. (I had a Romanian pupil in England, once. He was not especially bright, but was appalled at the general ignorance and linguistic incompetence he found among fellow undergraduates at one of the best universities in the world.)

Mihaela, my friend and colleague, speaks six languages fluently, besides her own: Portuguese, Italian, German, French, English, Russian. She can pun in at least three of them, and signs herself with her English nickname, Mickey. I once asked her how she had managed this linguistic *tour de force*. She looked at me very straight, almost pityingly. 'Dear, dear Charles, you have no idea. Under the Comrade it was dangerous to do much, and one could go nowhere, and there was no money, so all one could do was learn languages and travel in the library. You English have no idea how lucky you have been.' And then came a rare, paradoxical, moment of acknowledgement of some gratitude to that past. 'Before Ceauşescu all the education was in Russian culture, Russian this, Russian that, Russian language. But he turned us to the West, to where we belong, and to our parent Latin, to the Empire. It was a sort of independence. And he built an educational system that worked. Whatever his motives he gave us that.' Leading seminars with her graduate students forces me to agree, and to deplore the abandonment in the complacent West of all aesthetic, linguistic, and educational standards in the names of things quite bogus, called equality, or 'relevance'.

★

There was one of Mickey's colleagues at the University, a woman of a certain age, elegant, urbane, travelled. She knew Paris well, and London. She was charming, and clearly a good scholar. Her clothes showed the style of a good couturier. She talked of her weekend place in the country, to which one day I must surely go, she said. But after a while I began to be aware that the others treated her socially with courtesy but no warmth. I knew Mickey well enough by now to ask her quietly one evening why this was. 'Well,' she said, 'we all knew her husband was one of the Big People, and she had a very easy time of it. Always getting business trips abroad with him and coming back with new clothes and a tan. We had not got quite enough to live on. She would tell us about dinners she had had in Paris. We never knew whether we could trust her not to report anything we said to Them.' In that reply is the most terrible of all consequences of tyranny, of whatever sort: the destruction of trust, the trust without which human beings cannot in the end function as a society. I was sorry for Roxana: she had paid, perhaps undeservedly, a high price for elegance.

Ceaușescu's reign had been, indeed, a dangerous time, to put it mildly. People disappeared, often. Suspicion was everywhere. Anyone might be an informer. You trusted nobody. Mickey and her husband Cesar have a small, elegant flat, of 1930s vintage, about half a mile

from where the Palace now stands. They told me of the
morning when they woke up to hear, a street away, the
bulldozers moving in, with no warning, to demolish the
good middle class housing over nearly 200 acres to make
space for that monstrous Folly. That is why there are so
many stray dogs: for those displaced had nowhere to take
their loved pets, and just had to turn them loose, and they
have bred, as dogs will. Mihaela and Cesar told me she
once had to queue for two hours to get two aspirin for
their sick child – at a time when the Leader was plastering
the columns of his palace with gold leaf. They told me
of the systematic destruction of the middle class by the
Communists, the confiscation of land, the inefficiency
of the collective farms, the normality of torture. It is all
true. As you drive across that fertile plain, every ten miles
of so there are the buildings of a derelict collective farm.
Ceaușescu and his gang had wrecked the economy, and
sold every jot and tittle of the produce to the West to get
foreign exchange to line their own pockets. His people
were hungry, and were blithely told by his docile media
that 'research had shown' that people who were slightly
hungry worked better, and so they ought to get up from
a table still wanting more. And now the land was hardly
farmed at all. But here and there, a bright little house sat
among a few well-tended fields, and a little horse pulled
a cart with dung to the ploughland. In those spots lived
some of the lucky ones who somehow had managed to
buy back the land that had been theirs – perhaps since
the time of Michael the Brave, Prince of Wallachia 400

years before. But no middle class, so no entrepreneurial class; and the field is open for international capital, the multinationals, and the Mafia. Indeed: we ate once at a restaurant called Chez Marie – very good indeed, and very reasonably priced. But Mihaela told us that on Saturdays you did not go there: it was the Mafiosi place, which is why the food was good, and cheap...

★

I left my briefcase behind at Chez Marie. It had been a good evening to conclude yet another conference. There is always a sort of sadness in knowing we go back to airports and then to gumboots and taking the dog out on the morrow. As it was getting late, a colleague from Glasgow had attempted to sing 'Nessun Dorma' from *Turandot* – not wholly unsuccessfully, and it was true – and the diners (not just us) had clapped and smiled and called 'Bravo!' and two couples sent bottles of wine to our table. It was hardly surprising that in the summer dusk, walking and talking the long way back to the hotel, I did not notice my loss. But then: panic, for it had really important papers in it. The porter called me a taxi, and within minutes a worryingly dented Dacia turned up. The porter told him 'Chez Marie', and the Romanian equivalent of 'step on it!', and the driver, a little man with sharp black eyes and a bent cigarette at the side of his mouth, gave me a sort of odd look and gestured to the car. Did he think I had Mafia contacts? I got in beside him.

He stepped on it, O he stepped on it. We sped through traffic lights at red, overtook on the inside, were honked at at intersections, the tyres squealed on corners, and I had absolutely no idea where we were. We certainly were not going through any part of Bucharest I knew. I thought, 'Here I am, in an unmarked taxi, called by a porter whom I don't know, with no form of identification on me save a credit card, going where I do not know in the middle of the night in a city with a dickey reputation for Mafia influence and operations, and nobody knows where I am.' I had no phone. The driver was grimly silent – but I would not have understood him anyway – gripping the wheel and leaning forward as he faced down the oncoming traffic. I began to wonder, and think of the family at home... and then, we turned a corner, and then, with a screech, we stopped outside Chez Marie, still lit up, with music playing into the summer night. Yes, my briefcase was there, yes, they had been expecting me to come back as the hotel porter had rung them, and yes, they very much hoped I would come again... The driver was waiting, still grimly gripping his wheel, his engine panting. I got in, and off we went for a repeat performance of the journey out. We drew up, if that is the word, outside the hotel. He said something I did not understand, and then rubbed the thumb and fingers of his right hand together. Money, the fare, of course. But how much? I got out and signalled to the porter to come. 'How much does he want? He has been very quick indeed.' The porter told me. It would not have bought a couple of cups of coffee at home. I gave the man double – after all, I had Romanian *lei* which I did not think I would use and which were not worth exchanging back to pounds, and he had risked his own life as well as mine for me. He looked at me amazed, with those little sharp black eyes. His face cracked into a big smile showing uneven brown teeth, and said, via the Porter, 'It is too much! He is too generous like all these English! I will not take it!' In the end, he did, and we parted on excellent terms, him pumping my arm up and down as he shook my hand, and waving out of the window as he drove away. I slept well.

★

I have come with time and many visits to like this town, to like its faded grandeur, to feel the washing hung from sumptuous window mouldings somehow normal. I have come even to feel a sort of hope. I like the vitality and courtesy of its folk, I like even the cars, sometimes. (Some old Renault 12s, here called Dacia, are parked for ever in cobbled back streets with green mould on their flat tyres and a small plant growing in the corner of the windscreen.) I like the intellectual vigour and thrust I keep on encountering in Bucharest – nothing run down there! The life of the mind is something that really matters, and is given a respect that possibly, unlike Germany or France, it has never had in England. And Bucharest's lovely parks... my favourite, the Cişmigu park on Boulevard Regina Elizaveta, goes back to 1847 before any Romania existed:

Bucharest was the capital of Wallachia, argued about for centuries by Turks and Austrians and Hungarians and Transylvanians and later Russians. Much of the present park was a vineyard, planted around a spring: this had been tapped when there was a bad outbreak of bubonic plague in 1795. Prince Alexander Mourousis, the Grand Dragoman of the Ottoman Empire and Prince of Wallachia – his family was Albanian – sent his two sons to Dura's property to escape the plague in the town in that stifling summer, for the area, now so central and busy with encircling traffic, was then empty. In the 1840s the Lacul lui Dura neguțătorul (the 'Lake of Dura the merchant'), into which the spring flowed, was just a pool outside the town. People went there for wild fowl and fishing. The loudest noise would have been the quacking of mallards or the slow creak of an oxcart. In Turkish the word *Ceşme* means a public fountain, and a *cişmigiu* was the person whose job it was to build and maintain public fountains. The name stuck: the man who looked after Bucharest's fountains just happened to be living in what became the park, and poor Dura's once ownership of his vineyard was forgotten.

I first saw it in a warm May, after a night's spring rain. Mihaela had arranged for a graduate student of hers to show us something of the city. After several churches and dutiful admiration of the Cranachs in the National Gallery we ended up in the café by the water, conversation – poor girl! – becoming easier by the minute. The lake was dotted with rowing boats, children played in sand pits, black-clothed old women in white headscarves watched them. In an artificial grotto built into the side of the hill whence the spring flowed, lovers mooned, but with none of the embarrassing public intimacy that seems the modern norm in selfish England. Along neat gravel walks elegant women strolled, chatting to their friends (whom they silently and smilingly outbid in chic) beneath the pollarded plane trees, past the busts of Romania's greatest and best here modelled in bronze. Men played chess on stone tables with inlaid squares. It was tidy, beautifully kept, unlittered, no rowdiness. And then, I saw it in Autumn when the nymphs had departed and the trees' tent was broken, the lake was drained, and men were cleaning it and preparing it for skating in the hard frost that will surely come. Soft-eyed dogs made nests against the cold in the drifts of fallen leaves. A crow (of sorts) shuffled its feathers above where the card players sat a month before. I hope they leave each year the drifts of leaves for the dogs. Crows can take care of themselves.

★

Once I was invited to the conferring of honorary degrees in the University. Formally attired, we processed to our places to 'Gaudeamus igitur', which, no longer *iuvenis*, felt somehow inappropriate for me to sing. (But it is nice to include oneself in that first person plural.) The new Doctors made graceful speeches, we processed out to Brahms, and were given little glasses of sweet pseudo-champagne. Then off we went to the old University Library building, facing what had been the Royal Palace. Good mannered Classical porticos lined the square that had seen the moment when the Leader on his other, Party HQ, balcony first realised the game was up, that his people were not cheering but jeering. The Library building, which borrows a dome from the Pantheon, its decor from Versailles, and its portico from the Invalides suddenly became the last redoubt of the losers, and the tanks shelled it until the building was a ruin. So, much of it is restored: beautifully, elegantly. We were fed royally in its foyer and made to think hard in its Aula Magna. As I stood, about to speak, on the platform, I thought, as one does, 'How did I get here? This is a long way from Beach Road County Primary School... help!' But the awful moment, like the lecture, passed. At the end of the long day, we all went off for one of those long dinners that Eastern Europe does well and takes seriously. So they should. Wine flowed, whisky (for the brave) followed. The air was blessedly cool as we walked back to the hotel, talking of everything and nothing. As we passed by the Library I noticed that a building behind it, which, when I had been on earlier visits, had been left in ruins, now had a glass and steel addition, and had been seriously tidied up. That had been the torture HQ of the Securitate, and the plan had been to leave its gutless façade and eyeless windows as a memorial to those who had suffered there. But real estate is expensive stuff, and it now houses an

American management consultancy company. That says much.

★

It is a long drive to Constanta. Going by train was not recommended by colleagues who had done it, and though I vastly prefer trains to cars, they seemed to know what they were talking about. So we drove.

Getting out of Bucharest was slow, slow, slow. It was warm, sweaty weather and the Dacia was cramped. We had to keep the windows closed because of the throat-smarting, eye-stinging fumes of the slow traffic. Gradually the flashiness of new offices, showrooms, light industry with which Bucharest sprawled into the countryside gave way to more and more grass, then trees, then real fields, just then bare after harvest. I began to feel more at home. Finally, we pulled out to overtake an old wooden tumble cart, unexpectedly with old car wheels on its axle. Slowly, so as not to startle the plump but apparently bored horse that was pulling it, the car overtook it and at last, there was the way onto the dual carriageway.

We drove for three pretty featureless hours. The car windows were now thankfully open, and let in smells of hot earth, occasionally of a harvested crop, occasionally of dung spread on a little field. The tyres drummed on the straight concrete road. My earnest colleague next to me in the back seat wanted to talk about Literary Theory, but the barrage of fashionable French names – Lacan, Barthes, Bourdieu, Derrida, Saussure – reduced me to a sort of stupefied silence. Perhaps rudely, I fell asleep, that uncomforting, tetchy sleep when you are not quite dead to the world but aware of your body constrained in small space, of people occasionally saying things, of being hot and sweaty. My colleague poked me awake when we crossed the summer-shrunk Danube: 'You said you wanted to see this.' Umm. (First sensible thing she has said...) I saw how deep the sediments were, with a muddy grey, unattractive, slow river at the bottom of the – well, ravine, but a big one. One of the two great rivers of Europe. Even less attractive than it was when seen at Vienna. Look up 'Famous Danube River Poems by Famous Poets' on the Web and you get the answer, 'Sorry, no famous poems have been posted in this category.' Ella Wheeler Wilcox wrote a poem on the Blue Danube, but she was talking about the Waltz. (I have met some people who like her work. My mother used to quote her lines, 'Laugh, and the world laughs with you; weep, and you weep alone,' but, challenged, could never recall where she had read them.) I don't think that apart from Johann Strauss the Danube ever had a composer either, whereas the Moldau/Vltava had Smetana and the Rhine Schumann and Wagner. The vast plain the river has made cannot have changed that much over the centuries: it was always wide skied, with big raptors keeping a watchful eye on what might be prey as they slowly circle on the wind. An open, droughty country – scrub and savannah rather than forest would be its natural vegetation. Good land though. In my half-awake state the growl of the car's tyres became the thunder of horses coming like a tempest from the east bringing Hun, and Tatar, Cuman and Turk. For this was the frontier: over this river, which Trajan made the *limen,* Rome's writ never ran. The car's name reminds one that this was the outermost province of the Empire, and beyond lay the fabled lands that reached to China and the sunrise. Trajan's Column shows, in detail, the bloodiness with which the province was annexed. The language – with the habit, like Norwegian, of putting the definite article at the end of the word – is still basically Latin. The Dacians, through all the vicissitudes of the *Völkerwanderung,* the tussles between Byzantium, Seljuk and Ottoman, despite the Magyars and then the German speakers, kept the language of their first conquerors and proudly say, 'We are Roman.'

I stirred myself, stiff, as we came into the outskirts of Constanta. Much like anywhere else: Identikit building of negligible aesthetic appeal signalled rapid, grasping, 'development' – a word which I always distrust. By the shore, ranks of similar hotels faced the Black Sea. No matter: they provide what so many want, sun, sea, a place to pretend to the leisure and luxury of unsold time, to lay their heads and be fed, and a respite from the cares and tedium of the everyday. They could be anywhere – which is at least partly the attraction.

The University worked us hard, and there was no time for lounging on any beach. But even so, the water – it is after all the Black Sea – beckoned. I had hoped for this decades ago. Some of that water had come from the little spring at Donaueschingen and – a special place to me – the source of the Drava by Innichen high in the Dolomites. Some of it had washed the walls of Vienna and Budapest and Belgrade and all the history of *Mitteleuropa*. And just north of here the great river runs into the sea, and is commingled for ever with the mighty waters of Russia. And so, in the discretion of moonlight (for the English decorum of my outmoded generation must of course be preserved) I walked down to the beach, took off my shoes and socks and rolled my trousers up to my knees. Had it been day I might even have knotted my red spotted handkerchief at its four corners as a makeshift sun hat. After all, I had grown up near 'a famous seaside place called Blackpool /That's noted for fresh air and fun,' where such gear was in my youth to be seen every summer day. I paddled – just to be able to say that I had wet my feet in another sea. Not unpleasant; not particularly pleasant either. The rising full moon's light made a path across the water towards me, and I cast a long shadow across the beach towards the fringing pines. Loud disco music in the background accentuated the near noise of the gentle swash of the wavelets on my calves. A bigger one splashed up and soaked my trousers. Enough. Sand between my toes, on goes the footwear and off to my room to look over my lecture for the next morning. I find I do not believe a word of it.

They named the University after Ovid – Publius Ovidius Naso, or Nosey for short – the town's most famous resident who came here under compulsion when it was called Tomi. He hated the place. (So he said – but then he would, wouldn't he?) Augustus, trying to clean up Rome's Family Values in a sort of Back to Basics campaign, banished him after some scandal which may have involved his daughter. But also, reportedly, Augustus' anger could have been fuelled by this outrageous man's not only writing in the *Metamophoses* a wonderful poem that implicitly stresses the impermanence of earthly things, including self-important empires, but also lots of risqué erotic poems, and a manual of seduction in the manner of those 'How To' books like Oppian's on fishing or (indeed) Virgil's pretend agricultural manual, the *Georgics*. How to pick up girls at the Amphitheatre... how to pick up *more* girls at the Amphitheatre, the right amount of thigh pressure, how to get her friends on your side, what to do about inconvenient husbands... probably nobody will ever know the whole story. But Ovid wrote some of the finest poetry of exile here, sending it back to be copied and published in Rome, appealing to Augustus to shorten his exile from the bright life, and by his writing surely attempting to build up a groundswell of public opinion in his favour. It is hard to think of Ovid as 50 – the age he was banished – for his poetry has always given me the impression of brilliant youth. After nine years, in AD17 his banishment was indeed revoked, but he died that same year.

They put up a statue to him in the town at the back of
beyond he said he hated, where the inhabitants spoke bad
Greek and hardly any Latin. I went to see it. There in
the little square was the statue of Ovid suitably *togatus*,
musing, Great Thoughts hatching as he stands frozen
in stone with his chin pensively on his hand. A gull is
perched on his head, and squawks its annoyance when
another tries to take its place. Poor Ovid: banished from
all those sophisticated pleasures, the social buzz, of Rome
to a place where ironically people now go with delight for
their holidays and gulls bicker. But he did his whingeing
in beautiful poetry.

As Rome's grip tightened, the town grew into an
important port. In the Middle Ages the Genoese, who
had sewn up the Black Sea trade, had a major base here –
they built the lighthouse that is now one of the treasures
of the town. Its beacon would have been a welcome
guide on a thick night with an easterly wind for ships
running for the harbour, protected by its mole. Just by
the old harbour, a safe haven in Roman times, is what
is claimed to be the largest mosaic in Europe, in among
a Roman complex of workshops and warehouses. They
did their public buildings and facilities well then, and
mosaics do wear well. Now the town is full of fountains.
I asked why, and was told, 'Oh, the Mayor has a business
installing fountains...' the three dots were almost spoken,
leaving me to draw conclusions about the unsaid. People
still listen, apparently. I wonder if someone on what was

little Tomi's body of magistrates had a nice little line in contracting for mosaics?

The last afternoon, I played hookey: always in itself a pleasure which outweighs any guilt one might feel. I wandered into the old town, where once-elegant and graceful middle class houses were crumbling into a depressed disrepair. Development opportunities? – real estate, as everywhere, is a good way of laundering money. Perhaps I am just getting grumpy and suspicious as I get older. I wandered past the flamboyant nineteenth century Casino on the waterfront. A wedding was in process, and they were taking the photos – apparently the Casino is a favourite venue. A gamble on the future... And finally, I walked out on the mole to get close to the sea and the wind from the Caucasus, where I shall never go. There was a man fishing. He was old enough to have memories of before WW2 when he would have been the same age as his grandson, and before his memories of the terrible decades that separated their ages clouded his sight. I made myself understood: fishermen do. 'Catch much?' I said, or its equivalent: we had a little German in common. Not really. Not now. (What did that mean? Times were better then...? But perhaps they were?) Just then, he catches a little silver fish, drawing its weightless grace up into the heaviness of air. His grandson, leaving his rod, rushes over with an unnecessary landing net, to look. It is beautiful. With care the man unhooks it, and throws it back. In the arc of its flight, it flexes its body, echoing in little the curve of its trajectory. For a brief moment it lies on its side on the surface, perhaps stunned, and then it recovers, and darts down, down into the deep water. I am glad he threw it back. Bravely, I try to ask the man about the species of salmon that used to run up the Danube, whether he has ever seen one, but I have no net of words in which to catch my thoughts.

Time to go. 'Farewell Dinner,' then pack to pass on, as birds of academic passage do. I dropped into the Cathedral of St Peter and St Paul to pray for the peace of the world in this scarred land. (But are they not all so?) On the wall outside, challenging all with its steady Byzantine gaze, is a mosaic of Christ Pantocrator – surely even the *idea,* even if you do not believe it, is chastening to any would be Ashurbanipal, or Nero, any Hitler, or Ceauşescu, or... (fill in as desired – no shortage of modern candidates). Does it not cause cold doubt to clutch at the heart? *Major sum quam cui possit nocere fortuna* – 'I am greater than Fortune can harm' says Ovid's Niobe in *Metamorphoses* VI.194, and Marlowe's Mortimer in *Edward II*. Oh no you ain't, chum. 'Remember that thou art mortal,' said the slave in the ear of the triumphing general, standing behind him in his chariot, as his singing, drunken troops led his procession through Rome.

★

Once Mihaela and Cesar and Radu and Adina from Constanta took me to a restaurant hidden among the smart Second Empire-style buildings in Bucharest's heart. It was early summer. We passed through a narrow passage, and out into a big open courtyard. The swift-filled sky was framed by cliffs of elaborate stonework, and as the light thickened, the swifts did their daredevil, shrieking sweep and last minute bank up against the walls: exhilarating, and faster, than the murmuration of the winter starlings. A cartwheel was propped against a stone wall. There was a stable, with straw, and a manger full of hay. Ducks swam on a little pond, and in a tank trout outstared those who stared at them, mouthing silently, and perhaps rudely. Hens scuttered around in the straw. There was beer, lots of it, and country food – vegetables, the little tasty sausages called *mititei,* chunky bread. Oh, it was fake: 'old Romania', as it probably never was. (Meanly, I looked at the cartwheel, and the iron tyre showed no sign of wear.) But it was good fake, and the fake got better as the un-fake beer did its benign work. It grew dark, the stars came out, oil lanterns were lit. On a little stage, a country band struck up, full of those swooning Gypsy glissandos and accelerandos and rebatos that Enescu's *Romanian Rhapsody* so happily exploits for people in good clothes in halls miles away from any mucky farmyard or village. A few men and girls in 'national' costume began dancing the old dances, and – was she primed or not? – one of the 'Gypsy' girls came over and drew me into the circle. The step was like a Strathspey, and despite the awkwardness of English reserve I managed the set. As I thanked her for the invitation, this, er, simple country girl, who was most skilfully made up, turned away to find another to embarrass into the dance. And at the table, more congratulatory beer waited, and Cesar said, with that grin I have come to love, 'You can tell your friends you spent the night dancing with the Gypsies.' Actually, they probably were moonlighting students. But no matter; what mattered was that this myth was being created not for visitors from far, far way, for I think I was the only one there, but for Romanians themselves. It met some need to connect with a past and the ways of man and beast in the rich countryside, lost behind the gulf of the tyranny that destroyed so much of the old social structure. To be sure, there were still even then in that poor country pockets where the old ways had somehow survived, the old structures were still vital. For example, in the Maramures, which borders Ukraine and Bukovina, in the 1990s and into the 2000s men were still learning to hone the springy blade of a scythe, so that it will cut the grass for hay cleanly and sweetly. (Which is hard, as I know, for I have done it myself.) And it needs to cut easily in the toil of haymaking, and you need to be able with least effort to keep pace with the other mowers mowing in échelon – almost balletically, one pace each behind the other, so that the swing of the scythe is safe. The women and girls still learned the embroidery of the district, their village even, and used it. Many countryfolk in the main were still using horse power – as a lot were even just outside a

Bucharest noisy with car horns and below the flight paths of planes coming into the ambitious new airport. Many villages in the remoter regions had successfully, passively, glumly (which is effective) resisted the commissars and collectivisation, which everyone knew (but nobody official would admit) was no way to run farming. Further south lies the Siebenbürgen – the 'Saxon Lands,' the Land of the Seven Fortresses – on the banks of the Oli. In the twelfth century Geza II of Hungary had planted Saxons from Luxembourg, Lorraine, the Moselle valley, the Rhineland and Wallonia there to defend the south eastern border of Hungary against the ever present threat from the east: the Cumans and Tartars, and then the Turks. German is still spoken and the villages look and feel and smell and cook German. But things change so fast, even in a few short years. The young folk are leaving the old ways, and the towns where their people have been for centuries out of mind, to take the road to the town – and not to Bucharest, but to Germany. The villages are emptying, houses neat and tidy, just abandoned. Like trees deciding to walk away from their roots. Cesar, who knows the area well, said bitterly, 'And the Gypsies are moving in.' More corrosive of the old ways than any politics is the subtle subversion of economics, of consumerism, which will destroy what is left of the old culture in that beautiful land, as it will in the Maramures and the Danube delta more easily than politics ever could. (Something in me disquietingly asks, 'Does it matter? If people are happier, better fed, clothed?') So I raise my glass (again) to the little orchestra – a couple of fiddles, a hurdy gurdy – and the dancers weaving their ancient patterns, where bravura male display occludes the decorous twirling of the wide skirted girls. Myths, even constructed ones, are better than no sense of rootedness in a place and speech and music.

It was a good evening, despite bittersweet musings. We had begun with a wander past some of the older buildings, past the Bierhalle which could have been bodily picked up and transported, furnishings, *wurst* and all, from Nuremberg or Munich, past a little seventeenth century church, to the oldest church in Bucharest: Greek Orthodox. We pushed open the door, and – in what was almost an epiphany – the sonorities of Vespers turned the world inside out. People stood around, in various attitudes, moved forward to kiss the ikonostasis, and the chanting went on. As, indeed, somewhere it has done every night, to this pattern and melody, for over thirteen hundred years. Then someone opened the heavy door, and for a moment Byzantium was drowned in the roar of cars accelerating away from traffic lights. And in a few hours more I was airborne, back to the present from the dream of lost pasts that may never have been; and from the actuality of a past that is continuous to, operative in, the present. But that night was a good end. Old friendships – Horia-Roman, Radu, Mickey, Cesar, Adina – had been refreshed, new ones made. New challenges to think. Yes, on balance, a good trip. And as the plane finally lifted off to the northwest we saw the Carpathians, in their new snow, thrusting through the cloud. Below lay the villages of the ageing Siebenbürgen. What are the walled towns defending now?

I will go again, I think. But the skies are cloudier now, all over Europe, and winds blow colder than any I recall since my youth. The last time I was in Bucharest I saw street demonstrations that could have turned ugly (but did not). The police watched, quietly. An opinion poll recently showed that 60% of the people – most of them not even born in 1989! – thought things had been better under the Communists. If only they thought about the hunger, the grinding poverty, the murder camps, the ingenious and effective torture... But so everywhere, as economies slow and times get hard. I remember a conversation with a young University professor, Alyosha, in Murmansk, a town with a harbour full of rusting Russian warships in the world's biggest nuclear dustbin. (Radio Murmansk announces the day's weather and radiation forecast. Electronic bulletin boards allow the local people to do checks on the latest radiation levels as they travel to work.) Housing is terrible: the stock is old, cramped, in high demand. Food is not plentiful. There are flats they call the 'Khruschev flats' – *Khrushchyovka* – mean, prefabricated uniform units which were built all over the Soviet Union. They have a couple of rooms per family, a shared bathroom, and are built with a design life of 25 years. They are very much in demand, and regarded, said

Alyosha, as highly desirable. In 2017 there were protests when the mayor of Murmansk wanted to demolish some. Alyosha and I talked for a long time of this and that, especially of the problems of his country. And then he said, 'Many think that things were better under Stalin.' 'Do you?' I said (he was born under Brezhnev). There was a pause. 'No. But I read and they do not.'

The march of Folly goes to a good tune, and many like to keep in step with it.

★

Where *is* Szeged?' asked my neighbours, as once more I put a bag in the car, locked up the house, and took the keys over to them. I asked them, as I always do at that time of year, to water the tomatoes while I was away and to help themselves to any that came ripe, and to help themselves to the dwarf beans. 'Oh, Szeged – it's in Hungary, on the border with Serbia. Big university. Strong links with Cambridge, you know.' And then they wanted to know why I was going – 'Is it a holiday?' – 'No' –'What do you do there?' – 'Talk, give lectures, do seminars, perhaps gather material for what might be a book' – and they said they would miss me, and not to worry about anything. I am grateful.

Attila, a most peaceable and gentle man, met us off the train at the station. A façade in a sort of Austro-French style that would have done justice to an opera house fronted the grandiose approach: this had been after all the second city of the Kingdom of Hungary. It had been a long day, and, good host that he is, he made a beeline for a somewhere by the river where we could get a beer and some food. The Tisza, wide like no British river, is swelled just upstream of the town by the almost equally big Maros. The combined stream is vast, lazy, languorous, in summer a place for floating restaurants and pleasure boats playing with the current. Once it was busy with commercial traffic. There are still a lot of men who make their living from fishing the river, taking the huge catfish that are a *specialité de la région*, which can sometimes be big enough for a man to put his head in their mouths. (Why should one want to?). They are ugly brutes. Except perhaps to other catfish. Pretty well all of the beast is eaten: Attila says the only thing at which Hungarians draw the line are the gills and the stomach lining.

A boat went past: a longboat, with about twenty kneeling university students paddling. One stood at the stern beating a tom tom to keep them in time. Somewhat different to boating on Cam or Isis... It was good to be by the late summer river, which looks so benign, languorous, kind. But in winter the ice can build, and when the melt comes the floes rush down the river groaning and splintering as they ram and jam each other. If the snows melt very quickly in Ukraine, the river can rise thirty or more feet, and has done many times, spreading the rich alluvium that over millennia has helped make the Great Hungarian Plain. Then it joins the mighty Danube. (What a cliché that phrase is!)

On the embankment by the river stands a bronze sculpture, beautifully done, of mayflies. The hatch is – or was – so prolific that the locals called it the 'flower of the river Tisza' – '*Tiszavirag*'. I would love to see it, for a good hatch of these ephemerids even on the little chalk rivers of England is a wonderful sight, the surface of the water misted with the dancing white bodies that will live so short a time. One morning we went for early breakfast in a hotel that had been elegantly converted, metamorphosed, from a former courtyard house and stables. They had called it Hotel Tiszavirag... and it disconcerted me to think that a hotel should be named after a creature that is shortlived (24 hours at most), that never sleeps, has no digestive organs and so does not eat, and exists only to dance and copulate. Natural history is a wonderful thing. (A similar, wonderful, *faux pas*, in the US, when years ago a hotel chain had a TV advert with Pavarotti singing 'Nessun dorma...' – 'nobody sleeps.')

But unlike the mayflies, we had stomachs. On one ever memorable evening a small group of us – British, Norwegian, Italian, Hungarian, Kenyan – were cooked a spectacular dinner. After Kavu had said grace in Swahili, we started on the seven courses. We ambled from *pâté de foie gras* with Tokaji via wild boar and duck and beef (and matching wines) to crispy bacon with dark chocolate and finally to chestnut purée. That was an Indulgence. But that exceptional dinner apart, which would have won prizes anywhere, there was lots of memorable food: mainly fish – perch, and catfish, wonderful with paprika – and of course lots of *kaiserfleisch*. Here too they greatly regret the passing of the *Kaiserlich und Königlich* imperium, and with good reason: 100 years of peace (as the world calls peace) and growing prosperity went up in smoke in 1914.

★

One constant difficulty was that hardly anybody speaks English, none French, and few admit to German, and so buying things was awkward. Hungarian is an agglutinative language like Finnish – to which it is related – and one just does not recognise any of the roots, so guessing is impossible. One carton with a cow on it looks very like another. I bought what I thought was milk in a supermarket to put in my morning tea. It was yoghurt. Not recommended.

★

In that flat country, mile upon mile upon mile of level silt and sand, there are few places that can escape a great flood – after all, the rivers made it and can take it back. Our permanence is so temporary. In 1879 the flood washed almost the entire city of Szeged away, save for bits of the fortress, the square where in 1849 Lajos

Kossuth addressed the excited multitude from an elegant iron balcony, and the Franciscan monastery. The flood marks on the wall there are about seven feet off the floor, almost half way up the Baroque pulpit. Money flooded in (so to speak) to rebuild Szeged, from all the towns now commemorated in the new boulevards – Moscow, London, Paris, Brussels, Berlin, Vienna. The plan was grand, grandiose even, with wide boulevards reflecting the curve of the river, and elegant squares. New buildings sprang up in the latest fashions. First came the Late Imperial as envisaged by France and Austria, eclectic and witty – like the Town Hall facing on to the wonderful plane trees and gravel walks of the park, Szechenyi Ter. The patterns of glazed tiles on its roof reminded me of eastern France, its carillon of Brussels, but its variation on the Bridge of Sighs linking it to the building beside it spans no canal: keep water in its place! Then followed the extravagant, opulent, considered whimsy of the Art Nouveau, the Secession, and finally, the Jugendstil. Elegant green kiosks and phone boxes that could have been designed by Alphonse Mucha punctuate the streets. You look in the door of the Palatz Roek, and see the most gorgeous, decadent, spirals of the staircase, a swoon in bronze and gilt. The Anna Baths, in fresh pinkish stucco, hint at Turkey, and luxury, and the possibility of odalisques. Though I don't especially like any of those styles, it is a very pretty city indeed. The yellow trams crisscross the city, down the centres of the boulevards, and neatly trimmed grass fills the space between the rails.

Planes and limes and chestnuts line the bigger streets, and acacias give off their rare scent. In their boughs, at dusk in the corner of the square where we sat one evening, the crickets chirruped happily.

But, by contrast: here and there, mean, depressed, jerry-built Communist-era buildings – but not as many or as sore thumbs as in poor Bucharest – interrupt the elegant opulence with rude gestures. The buildings you put up says everything about how you think of the people who will live in them. On that showing alone, the utter moral, anti-human, bankruptcy of every Communist regime there has ever been has been apparent from their very beginnings.

Dark things stir. Signs of stress were obvious behind this smiling townscape. Few shops sold what I call frivolities – not like 'real' shops, such as ironmongers and butchers – that you need surplus income to buy. Get away from those pretty, soigné, main streets, and quite a lot of buildings are ragged, down at heel. People are hard up, disillusion with the EU is toxic and noisy. As always when confidence falters and times get harder a party that can offer scapegoats – the Roma, even (tell it not in Gath) the Jews who have returned to where before the War they had a very large community – has baleful appeal. The Hungarian Folk Museum, Szabadtéri Néprajzi Múzeum, at Szentendre, the answer to Stockholm's trail-blazing Skansen, does a wonderful job of documenting, making tactile, the life of the past – but it leaves out all mention of the great numbers of Gypsies who wandered the great plains and whose music is at the bedrock of Hungarian musical identity. The neo-Nazi far right has dug itself in well. They cleverly adopted as their badge the colours of the old Hungarian standard, the standard that Matthias Corvinus and others who wore the Crown of St Stephen – which is now present at every sitting of the Parliament – carried against the heathen of the East. Nobody could call the press free any more, or the universities, and the Prime Minister is building himself what some call a palace on the hill of Buda as if he never meant to leave.

Under the surface... I walked to the University down a tree-lined street that had once been pre-First War middle class houses of some elegance, I came to one where most of the stucco had fallen off. Revealed was quite the shoddiest bit of bricklaying I think I have ever seen – worse, far worse, than me at my youthful and incompetent worst. Mine was at least strong. This looked as if it could be blown away: like the peace, prosperity, openness of the country, fair on the outside, crumbling within.

For the troubled history of this people it presses on you – well, me – everywhere. They had a rotten twentieth century. They lost the flower of their youth, as did all Europe, in the First World War. The Heroes' Gate (Porta Heroum), the vast Jugendstil war memorial that straddles the beginning of Boldogasszony Sugárút, names the many from this place who died for the Empire, and graphically painted on the reveals of the great span are not only the angels that took them to their rest but the barbed wire on which so many charges came to grief. I found it impossible not to be moved to near tears. The trams glide underneath, momentarily shadowed by memory against the sun. Under the dreadful Versailles settlement, stupid, shortsighted and vindictive, Hungary lost a large slice of territory to Romania and Hungarians still resent it – as do the Transylvanians themselves. The dictatorial regime of Admiral Horthy the Regent cooperated with the Nazis, and Jews were deported to the camps in huge numbers – and in pre-war Budapest they were actually the majority of the citizens. On the banks of the Danube opposite Buda is one of the saddest and most sickening Holocaust memorials I have seen: dozens of bronze pairs of shoes set into the pavement. For on that spot the Arrow Cross militia ordered the Jews to take off their shoes, and then shot them at the edge of the water so that their bodies fell into the river and were carried away. Footwear was, after all, in short supply. And after the war came the Red Army, not known for civilised behaviour towards a conquered people. Then came the Uprising of 1956, crushed by the Soviet tanks in vicious street fighting in Budapest. You can still see the pockmarks of bullets on the elegant buildings – and are meant to, for they are highlighted in black so that you do not forget. Wide and spacious, Budapest's tree-lined Andrassy Utca was intended by Count Andrassy, Prime

Minister under Franz Josef after the Dual Monarchy was set up by the *Ausgleich* of 1867, to overgo the Champs Elysées. He hoped to inlay all the *sgraffito* of the grandiose buildings with gold leaf. (Only a few were so burnished.) It is a graceful prospect to delight the eye and lead it to the Heroes' Square. But the most elegant house of them all was where first the Gestapo, and then the KGB, had their torture headquarters. And now the hopes of 1989, when the world seemed young again and we unrolled the map of Europe, wiping away the stain of the Soviet empire, are looking as tired as the buildings in the side streets, where tourists do not go. The leaves fall from the lindens and the chestnuts, as they always have done, indifferent. The cold wind from the east, the first of Autumn, whirls them into little piles that clog the feet. The neighbours can be troublesome, and not just politically. Up in Ukraine a few years back someone dumped a load of cyanide in the river. It killed everything for hundreds of miles downstream, and wiped out the fishing industry for many a year. The fish are back, and the river is healthy again. Until another poison.

★

The Autumn wine festival had started, in the Cathedral Square. Our tickets suggested a series of wines we were allowed – nay, expected indeed – to go through, in order, culminating in a superb Tokaji of which it would have been churlish not to have bought a bottle. It was grand to see *le tout Szeged,* down to the smallest tots, just enjoying itself – no rowdiness, just people being happy, in the shadow of their cathedral whose big tenor bell told the quarters as they danced and drank their good wine. Lots of *czardas* and *dunka,* 'folk music', which I love – the first composer to gentrify it was I suppose Haydn, but it gets its fullest exploitation in wonderful Smetana and Kodaly and Suk and Dvorak – and of course Brahms. There was dancing: a troupe on a small stage gave a startling display, the girls whirling decorously, their skirts like bells, their legs in white woollen stockings, while the men did all the leaping and clapping and twirling consonant with aggressive male display. The watching crowd loved it. A young man in a wide-brimmed hat suddenly swept up a girl sitting quietly drinking her wine with her boyfriend and whirled her into the dance, and then whirled her back again, breathless and flushed with the insistent rhythm and the *accelerandos* and *rebatos* that must have intoxicated her grandmothers in their own youthful time. Music and dance, among the most ancient pleasures of mankind, reach to the roots of our community of being, forming us into moving patterns that just hint at the murmurations of the starlings.

And, of course, contrast: another time, a candlelit harpsichord recital in the university with Dowland and Bull and Byrd. It was in that very hall, the Auditorium Maximum, that in 1956 the students of Szeged began the protest that led to the Uprising, to the heroism of Pal

Maleter and Imre Nagy, and to the tanks in the streets literally flattening the opposition. You never get very far away from those memories. And they, and all the ghosts of the centuries of wrong, came very terribly into focus on a lovely, peaceful, sunny afternoon in the quiet of the Franciscan Monastery of Our Lady of the Snows.

When the building was new in the 13th century the Eastern March was still being converted to the Faith. The friars, with exemplary courage, were reaching out with the Gospel not only to the poor of Europe but to the heathen lands afar, even to Mongolia and China – Beijing had its own Archbishop, the Franciscan John de Marignolli, before 1300. Most of the building is late mediaeval, with the usual Baroque makeover. The walled herb garden was full of bees foraging in the healing plants, all labelled, with their properties and virtues in three languages. A place of healing, a place of peace. A place where pilgrims come, for here there is a replica of the Black Madonna of Częstochowa (Poland), and as we went in to the cool silence of the church, a girl was kneeling praying, intensely, passionately, before it. We were allowed to walk into the brothers' cloister, and up to a part of the monastery that had been turned into a museum – the church's treasures, some returned after the confiscations of the mid-twentieth century, its manuscripts, its vestments, some of the last almost as old as the oldest parts of the building. But gradually we were led to a small room where a video was playing. It was simply several old men talking, with English subtitles. These men were boys, schoolboys, who had been caught up in the persecutions of the Church by the Kadar regime after 1956. Their teacher, a friar widely loved and respected as a holy man in the town, had spoken out firmly against the cruelties and violations the police routinely perpetrated, and in the end they had arrested him in front of his pupils. As he was being taken away he gave them his last blessing, only to be struck on the face by one of the guards. The boys knew he would be taken to Budapest, and they might never see him again. Then, one by one, the police came for the boys. They were held, without any contact with their parents, until they were all in custody. These schoolboys were taken the many miles one freezing winter day to Budapest, in a locked truck with an escort of armoured cars. Arrived at that house on Andrassy Utca, they were put in solitary confinement. One by one, days later, they were taken out and interrogated, encouraged to say things incriminating of their teacher. One old man recalled how, tired, frightened, hungry, he was led to the room where he was to be interrogated, and the guard had tripped him up as he entered, had stamped with his nailed boot on his hand and told him not to be so clumsy 'next time – for there will be a next time'. There was. And then one by one they were confronted with their loved teacher, bearded, long haired, dirty, fouled. His tonsure had grown out. Finally, as he was led off to be murdered, he managed to say to them, 'Forgive them. I have done. If I do you must'. That was the last they saw. At that point the old man, an old man just like any other sitting in a room just like any other, broke down and wept.

The brochures call it 'The Town of Sunlight': 2100 sunny hours each year. Do not forget in those sunny hours how dark the darkness can be.

★

The train back to Budapest was swift, swifter far than the horses of the Magyars and the Huns who swept across this wide *Puszta* carrying all before them like the floods of the angry rivers. Cue for heroic music... to drown out the screams of memory. Reeds, browning now into Autumn, bent in the breeze in the wetter patches. The gentle undulations only stressed the flatness. Where men had ploughed the land, it showed black, peaty, then pale sand: a piebald landscape. Sunflowers at the end of their season stood in dishevelled despondent ranks, heads down, ashamed to let the sun down. I saw a field of globe artichokes, gone to their magnificent seed. Few visible antiquities in this landscape, indeed, but the memories crowd in. The land remembers. The riders from the east, a lone Englishman tramping through it and through the last of Old Europe (and writing a book about it years later), the cattle trucks carrying men, not cattle, to the slaughter. By a clump of trees, a horse – did its ancestors come from the steppes? – grazed. The telephone poles and their droops of wires flicked by, and I glimpsed a stork's nest atop a pylon, the even synclines of the wires summiting in the bristling of twigs. Some say it is a good omen if they nest with you. At Keleti railway station in Budapest – the façade of the Belle Epoque building has statues of James Watt and George Stephenson – men were playing chess on the fixed stone tables at the end of each platform. Chess trains for war, without the bloodshed.

★

Roma Dea

... Rome – the city of visible history, where the past of a whole hemisphere seems moving in funeral procession with strange ancestral images and trophies gathered from afar.

George Eliot, *Middlemarch*, Part 2, Ch. 20

At last, long, long after my sun had passed its zenith, to the Eternal City, whither, and whence, all roads have led. But the airport bus stops in front of the blowsy, overripe mass of the Palazzo della Giustizia on the Piazza Cavour, an arrival that is a poor introduction to Roma Dea for the traveller with literary or romantic associations. The postilion (or bus driver) could not really cry here, as they did of old when the diligence or the coach breasted the hills to reveal the Eternal City below, 'Ecco Roma!' How I would have loved to have been able to *walk* to Rome, along the Via Francigena, starting in Canterbury! Perhaps one day... Two friends did it in three months after he retired from the Royal Navy. (Her only regret, she said, was that she only took one bra. For you lose weight on a long walk.) As I got off the bus, Michael the actor, 'Big Apple Mike', Jenny's American brother-in-law, met me in this City to which my now lonely road had at last led me. We had not seen each other since her death. In those awkward first moments on meeting again, which all old friends who have not spoken for years will know, moments of stilted and trivial conversation, he agreed with me that the Palazzo is in the worst of heavy late nineteenth century taste, but once across the Tiber, he said comfortingly, you can turn your back on it. Surely there was more to talk about than architecture when Jenny was so present an absence?

Jenny had loved Rome, and had been there when a student, and, in due time, with her own students. It felt strange to be coming without her to a new place which she had known. For my Rome had hitherto been a Rome made by books: initially its thousand plus years of change and challenge was in my imagination but an undifferentiated moment. It lived then in a mental world made of its poetry and writing, and fiction about it – and that of a very narrow period indeed – mainly end Republic/early Imperial – in the scheme of things. A young me had coloured in my imagination with films like *Quo Vadis?* with Peter Ustinov as Nero singing while Rome burned and a most appetising Deborah Kerr tied to a stake for the beasts in the Colosseum – in fact that film was the first time I took a girl to 'the pictures', and I remember saying seriously and sententiously afterwards to her that persecution was not something we in England could be sure to avoid in our lifetimes – for we both knew of what had happened in Germany, and was happening in Russia. (My small talk, and chat up talk, was pretty poor then and has not improved much since. And I was always something of a pessimist.) Later, reading the happily gossipy Suetonius and the oblique and ironic Tacitus I filled in the outline even more with a sort of shocked, disapproving, delight in the descriptions of Tiberius' pederasty in the sea at Capri – he called the boys who swam with him his 'minnows' – or Nero's forcing women of good family at festivals to make their favours available to anyone who drifted along – or die. Walking Hadrian's Wall had stressed, as did First Form Latin text books, the military culture of Rome. The full horror, to a twentieth century liberal mind, of what happened in a Roman triumph, or in the amphitheatres around the Roman world, or of what exactly happened in the crucifixions that were handed out as a regular punishment, had not sunk in: they were simply facts in knowing which I took a sort of hot delight. But with age and more imagination that all changed. Rome's strong sunlight cast very dark shadows indeed. Yet here was – is – the epicentre of our world, the myth that fuelled the *pax Britannica* as well as the Second and Third Reichs.

★

I had seen so many photos that much was already visually familiar. Behind the hefty shoulders of the Vittorio Emanuele Monument – some say the building is like an old fashioned typewriter, others a set of false teeth – I knew that that chunky brick plainness was the Church of Santa Maria Aracoeli, a dowager next to a country hoyden in an ill-fitting dress: and that church is just where anciently the temple of Juno Moneta stood. (Whence we get the words 'money' and 'mint' – not the herb). Below, the statue of Cola di Rienzi[21] – hero of Wagner's first opera, and what a subtext that has! – pensively warns of the vanity of human wishes. The monarchy that was the fruit of the Risorgimento, celebrated in the Monument, which borrowed the clothes of Rome, as Mussolini, a dwarfish thief in giant's robes, would later do, is no more. Ancient grandeurs become the flotsam time leaves us: but they alter the way the tide runs.

And there is a lot of flotsam here. This city could – does – easily bring out the most tediously pedantic in me. The sheer density of the surviving detail of all periods, all crammed together, invites industrious seeing, collecting, listing, classifying, memorising, and, inevitably, telling. Streets, houses, palaces, monuments, placenames – all places of memory, registering in their very stone narratives, voices of the past. The first time I saw one of those iron manhole covers with SPQR on it – nobody had warned me – I did a silly (momentary, honest) doubletake about whether it *could* have survived from the republican period... Someone more geeky than I am (yet) told me that there are 13,910 monuments of the ancient city on the seven hills. (Who counted?) But, could we see it, smell it, hear it, as it actually was, that Rome which, for good or ill, has been, and is, the parent, unacknowledged or not, of so much in Europe, which we 'admire', I doubt whether we would be comfortable with it – even merely at the level of aesthetic taste, it was often a deplorable, vulgar, cityscape. A gilded Colossus of Nero, 15 metres high, nude, with him posing as the sun god Helios, stood beside the lake of his pleasure dome, the Domus Aurea, to remind all of his lasting power and glory. He would have felt at home in Las Vegas and he would have loved Trump Tower. Yet a couple of decades later Nero had been murdered, statue and monstrous house had both gone. The Flavian emperors, cynical Vespasian, honest Titus and deplorable Domitian, filled in his lake and built the monstrous and clever Colosseum for even more monstrous displays, which remain monstrous despite revisionist attempts to find an ideological justification for the slaughter of men and beasts those stones saw. The historian Tacitus, indeed, who had no problem with circuses *qua* circuses, records young Drusus, Tiberius's son, so delighting in the spectacle of human death that he put on a display of gladiatorial mayhem so profuse that even the hardened Roman populace was sickened – even though, as Tacitus coolly says, it was only 'worthless' blood that had been shed. Men with meat hooks dragged the corpses across the bloodied sand to the Porta Libitinaria. (Libitina was the ancient goddess of funerals and burials – oddly enough, often associated with Venus, a dangerous deity who is far from always the laughing, smiling, dimpled, winsome goddess of love.) The surviving decorations in the plaster of the Domus Augusti or Domus Livia on the Palatine say much about colour sense and expense – for fresco is not cheap – but are hardly restrained, chaste, monochrome Classicism in the Winckelmannian manner. Those bright frescoes from the public baths at Pompeii, which men, women and children saw, or the statues excavated from the garden of the Villa dei Papiri overwhelmed by Vesuvius, leave little to even the most ingenious sexual fantasy. As in the limerick, who does what and with which and to whom, indeed, and indeed not limited to humans. An exquisitely carved, almost life sized, marble group of a man copulating with a she-goat was a considerable attraction (in a little room to itself, to avoid frightening the horses) at a British Museum exhibition a few years ago. What puzzles me is who paid for this stuff, and why. We might have found ancient Rome hard going for what principles even we moderns have left.

I intended to do the job properly and go into the Colosseum, explore its intricate underground works, think about how the building functioned – it is a work almost of genius – but each time I tried I found I could not. I could feel the tensions rising, and a light sweat was on my palms. I could not get out of my head what had been normal in that clever place. And this was not new: when, very young, I went into the arena at Nîmes I felt the same horror without the knowledge to explain it; and much, much later, having forced myself to go in to the arena at Verona because it was where so much grand(iose) opera – which I love – had been staged, I had to turn back

as the cold stone vaults dripped animal and human fear —
and a prurient delight in seeing pain. Television and film
offer the same delight, without the smell.

★

But for a time the shadows were quiet in the sunny
excitement of being there. A minute's walk from the
Piazza Navona, where was once the Circus built by the
cruel Domitian, Elena and Franco have a flat, at rooftop
level, with a terrace. The building's foundations are
Roman, its walls mediaeval. In one direction I could see
St Peter's dome and the angel on the top of the Castel
Sant'Angelo; in the other, the dome of the Chiesa Nuova.
Just over the road in the church of Sant'Andrea delle Valle
they made a film of Puccini's *Tosca* — in the very building
where Puccini set the first act of the opera: I knew that
opera almost by heart and I could not, that first time,
go in that church without hearing Placido Domingo's
Cavaradossi in my head, and wanting to sing. I always
hope that the stars will be out when I come out... But I
have no voice, alas.

The loudest noises on Franco and Elena's terrace are the
gulls from the Tiber, who roost on the roofs and woke
me at dawn. Lemon trees bloom in pots: not quite what
Goethe dreamed of, but not bad. Seeing a gull sitting in
a lemon tree in a large terracotta pot reminds you, if you
need it, that you are not at home. Rising early, before the

streets were full, when the fruit and vegetable stalls were just being set up on the square basalt cobbles – the tourist stalls take their place later – I went down to the Cafe al Emporio, on the corner, where for almost nothing I could get an espresso, a *cornetto*, and piece meaning together out of *La Stampa* with a mishmash of deductions from what I knew of Latin and French. (We English have always had a terrible reputation as linguists: and Romans smile at how I pronounce my quite good Latin.) I went into the little Carrefour Express shop on the corner, whose walls reached back well beyond the middle ages, to get milk. The young woman minding the shop was sorting out the freezer shelves. She looked at me mystified when something made me say – my mind was again running on Puccini (*Bohème* this time) as I had just glanced across to Sant'Andrea – as her cold hands handed me my change, '*Che gelida manina…*' I did not sing it. Perhaps another time I might. Who knows what might happen?

The early morning sun sparkled on Bernini's Fountain of the Four Rivers – Nile (his head shrouded as nobody then knew where the source was), Euphrates, Ganges, and Plate (yes, Rio de la Plata), each with the appropriate emblematic animals. Franco told me that Bernini made the River who looks at the façade of Sant'Agnese in Agone shield his face as if from falling debris to comment on his rival Borromini's beating him for the commission for that building. And Borromini's reply was to put a statue of St Lucy on the façade, shielding *her* eyes from the figures on the fountain. At that early hour, the Piazza Navona was nearly deserted. The party people had gone home, and the stalls to catch the tourist, selling Pope fridge magnets, miniature Colosseums (Colossea?), Discoboloi, or Caesars, or Venuses of Cnidos (made in China) were still being cheerfully and chaffingly set up. A 'living statue' done up as the Pope was having a cigarette. The 'do your portrait in five minutes' artists were only just arriving. When tourists were fewer and richer, it was the done thing to be painted against a background of the Classical ruins to impress your dinner guest who had not travelled. One man, Giovanni Paolo Panini, (d.1765) did a very popular line indeed in his *capricci,* fantasy landscapes where he brought together most ingeniously the most famous monuments of the city. For a little extra, you could be painted into the *staffage.* There were no postcards then.

'You must see the Vatican supermarket', said Elena, 'we always shop there. It is so cheap and in Lent the fish is marvellous'. So, using a pass into Vatican City that she had borrowed from a complaisant friend ('Remember to call me Antonella'), we drive past the saluting Swiss guards into the City. At speed. For Elena takes no prisoners. The supermarket is all one expected. Red wine at 13.5% called 'Resurrezzione' is attractive; so is the chocolate and the coffee. I savour the atmosphere, people-watch as I usually do, imagining biographies. A nun catches my eye as she puts a steak in her trolley. On top of it, glancing at me, she puts a whole frozen octopus, its mouth bared and its tentacles folded symmetrically back so it looks like a cauliflower. It is Lent, after all. Our baskets full of good things to take home, we return to the car, and zoom round to the quiet behind the apse of St Peter's, where neatly clipped box hedges in the lawn are laid out in the outline of the triple tiara.

A Swiss guard appears, and looms, suspicious, as well he might. Hurriedly would-be photographer and subject scamper back to the car, and look unconcerned: we do this every day. If only. But we have got our supplies, and so back to the flat at the same breakneck speed to cook, overtaking, with much cheerful tooting of horns, Franco coming home on his moped from doing his surgery. And, full of good things and wine from the south, we sit on the terrace and talk – the best part of any meal – flows freely as the stars come out and the hookah bubbles as Elena sits on her sofa smoking it. The air is accented by the scent of her tobacco.

★

Rome is hard on the feet. I walked: and walked, and walked. I chose to do it alone. The maze of little *vicole* is easy to grasp once you remember that modern Rome is still polarized by ancient Rome. The street layout is still governed by the rebuilding by Nero after the huge fire he blamed on those pesky Christians. The Suburra is still the *louche* sort of place it was when two thousand and more years ago the Julian family refused to leave their family house there for PR reasons. And the detritus of centuries delighted me everywhere. Quite soon I got fed up with photographing odd bits of column built into a wall, or little fountains that spout drinking water at every street end, reminding of the boon the aqueducts were to the thirsty imperial city – for the Tiber was not fit to drink. Rome is full of fountains, ranging from the masterpieces of Bernini to re-used bits of modest Roman rubbish. Then, you stumble on a pretty little church nobody visits, recognisably poor cousin to the Baroque masterpieces of the Gesù or Santa Maria della Pace (fine altarpiece by Giulio Romano, who turned his capable hands to some wonderful – and, as they say, 'explicit' – pornographic frescoes in Mantua: and is also the only artist mentioned by name in all Shakespeare) or Sant'Agnese in Agone. A curving line of buildings (dwellings, workshops, an hotel) marks where the theatre of Pompey stood – golly, Pompey, Caesar's father-in-law and opponent, betrayed and beheaded by Cleopatra's brother, he built that! (Which sent my mind flying back to Elizabeth Taylor and Rex Harrison and Richard Burton in that 1963 film, and Pompey's head being drawn out of the jar in which it was pickled. No taste.) You cannot visit the theatre of Marcellus – Wren said it was his inspiration for the Sheldonian Theatre in Oxford – because people live there. They have done so for one and a half millennia. It was a fortress in the Middle Ages. (I think the Pierleoni family had it, and later the Orsini.) Augustus intended

Marcellus, his nephew, as his successor. Mark Antony was his stepfather. Virgil wrote so movingly of his death that (so it is said) Octavia his mother fainted when he read the passage in *Aeneid* VI to her (and Jean-Auguste-Dominique Ingres painted how he imagined that moment.)

I really wanted to try the acoustic in the Pantheon, surely one of the most wonderful buildings in the world,[22] but did not dare, even though it was almost empty. Its roof is a perfect hemisphere, topped by the oculus through which the rain falls on the marble pavement below as it has done since Agrippa built it. If completed, the sphere would touch the ground at the exact centre of the floor. Outside, the 'centurions' (their crests mostly the wrong way round) chatted on mobile phones. Tourists gazed with Asiatic eyes and took photos to see what it was they saw. Practised beggars circulated. I drew my intending hand out of my pocket when I saw one, well made up, go behind a corner and take out a very up-market Blackberry. (That same week a friend saw a one legged beggar in a long coat unstrap his hidden leg and walk away with his takings.) Tourists are good meat for beggars, but you never know when the need is genuine. An importunate gipsy woman tried to tell me she could not afford medicine, and showed me the soiled empty packet of what she needed. Better to be on the safe side, and give.

★

An excursion, to how one almost imagines the morning of the world. Morag knew of a garden down at Ninfa created by an Englishwoman in the Romantic English manner, and had somehow managed to get us an invitation to visit though the place was officially closed. With Elena's customary panache, we drove along the Via Appia, the first of the great highways, running from Rome to Brindisi. As the pines flicked by, I seemed to see the thinner shades cast, at fifty pace intervals, by the prisoners Crassus crucified when he put down the slave revolt of Spartacus. Some say 4000: 20 crosses every Roman mile, stretching for 200 *milia passuum*. Now, where the crosses stood, the umbrella pines line the road, bent at a steady angle by the wind off the sea: which you can smell. Those pines, or their ancestors, gave shelter from the torrid sun alike to the marching legions, each man burdened with his eighty pounds of kit, to the official in his litter, and to the country traveller. Now the car's speed makes the alternating shadows of the pines like a strobe light. Which I find disorientating, for my older eyes cannot react that quickly.

We cannot find Ninfa, and stop at a petrol station where they are not serving because they are just altering the prices: upwards. Of course. A helpful man in a van, also waiting, offers to lead us there. And so we find the Garden: it deserves a capital letter... after the stress and emotional overload of Rome, a temporary Eden, with the benison of trees and the wellbeing of water. The importunity of plants and trees grasps at the ruins of a walled village: even here, mortality and vicissitude remind, 'we have not gone away.' Flaking frescoes stained with rain glow on the apse of the roofless church. Ivy clutches broken walls, and nods triumphantly over them in great tods. Spring flowers bloom out of old earth. Once children played here and people made love beneath the absent roofs. In the river sinuous green weeds wave in the current like melusines, tempting you in. Where the old mill must have stood, in the pool, a fat fish goes about his fishy business, perhaps thinking of one of Brooke's wittier poems – who can tell what fish think of Heaven?

The first swallows are arriving... Puccini again! *La Rondine* – and Puccini's granddaughter Simonetta gave me a cold a week later when we met her while visiting the house he built at Torre del Lago with the fortune he made from *Madama Butterfly*. (I was admiring his shotguns. He was a fine shot and had a black Labrador called Scarpia.) The first swallows... I noticed a little bit of wet mud plastered on the old nest of last year which sits on the rafter of the cart shed. *Quando fiam uti chelidon?* – 'when shall I become like the swallow?' A happy man invites us to go into his walled private garden, where grapefruit and oranges and lemons are ready to the hand, like golden lamps in a green night, where we stumble on the long grass. Swans bicker on a pond that they ought to know is too small for them. *O fortunatos nimium, si bona sua norint, agricolas!* (O too happy farmers would be, if only they would know

the good things they have!) I think of Marvell's poem –
not for the first or last time – and of the *locus amoenus* of
Virgil. But realistically – I am my peasant father's son – I
pick grapefruit for breakfast, and oranges for the journey,
put them in my rucksack, and wish I dared guddle the
trout. And all the time the noise of water, and Horace,
are in my head:

> *te flagrantis atrox hora Caniculae*
> *nescit tangere, tu frigus amabile*
>   *fessis vomere tauris*
>   *praebes et pecori vago.*
> *fies nobilium tu quoque fontium,*
> *me dicente cavis impositam ilicem*
>   *saxis, unde loquaces*
>   *lymphae desiliunt tuae.*

(The dread hour of the burning Dog Star does not
know how to touch you. You offer welcome coolth to
wandering flocks, to oxen tired from the ploughs. You
shall be counted among the noble springs, for it is I who
write of you, and of the holm oak hanging over the rocky
hollow, from which your happy waters chatter down.)

A green and black snake, scales bright in the light, is
asleep in the spring sun. He (she?) hears us, and decants
into a fissure in the rocks. (Which poem am I in?) Time
stood, for a moment, still. I found myself breathing deep,
standing relaxed, tension – and that annoying need to say
anything – quite, quite gone.

Driving back, the noise of Rome, via the grandiose new city Mussolini started for the 1936 Exposition, recalled all of Juvenal's complaints about the city he knew. *Plus ça change*. But Juvenal never left Rome, despite his rudeness about it, and for all Horace's professed love of the simple, country mouse's life, his readers, and interests, were in Rome: it was/is addictive. Even so, Ninfa was so beautiful it would turn even the sternest townsman into a ninfamaniac. Juvenal, had he known it, might have changed his mind.

★

Dinner at the house of two of Elena's friends. A middle-aged French couple are staying. As the evening draws on, it turns out they are passing through Rome in order to see their son, based there, on their way back to Africa. Both are medics, both working for Médecins sans Frontières. Pierre walks with a limp: the result of having been badly beaten up some years ago in Sudan. Both have been held hostage, in fear of their lives, more than once. They are going back to where these things happened. 'People need what we can do. Things are getting worse. We may be killed.' They left the next morning. To what fate I know not.

Sometimes I wonder what use, what good, my life of scholarship has been. At least as a smallholder in my own tiny echo of Ninfa I did no harm and husbanded the land well for whoever comes after me. But I am no hero.

★

To Ostia Antica, where the cornships from Egypt, too big to get up the Tiber, came in with their cargoes to feed the multitudes in the huge city. St Paul was travelling on one of those when he was shipwrecked. A jumble of memories. A perfect day. Few people. Michael, our very own actor Roscius, struck Broadway Attitudes in the ruins of the little theatre, wearing the sort of hat John Wayne wore in *The Quiet Man*. (He looks a bit like him, and emphasises it.) I challenged him to sing, to taste the acoustic. He did: Verdi, 'La donna è mobile,' and not bad. The thermopolium, or first century equivalent of Macdonald's, is full of chattering children: perhaps things never change even if the hamburger had not been invented then. (I like *real* Hamburgers.) Lizards flicker on the warm spring tufa stones. There are inscriptions to all and sundry, the big pride of a small town, with its copy, like every town across the Empire, of the public offices of Rome. But what had a certain Gallienus done to have his name gouged almost completely out of the memorial to whatever he had done (*damnatio memoriae* means serious business)? We shall never know. But the rewriting of the past, the demolition of stories and memorials to people we don't like any more is not a new thing. Nor will we ever know what sort of relationship the Ugly Couple on the funeral monument enjoyed, or not. But they are at one in stone. I had an overwhelming sense of lives lived, of people just that moment gone off stage. Overhead the planes going into Fiumicino, the site where Claudius built his huge harbour, drone across the sky. In the intervals of quiet, the grasshoppers proclaim eternal summer.

★

I wandered far, alone, as much in time as in space. I mused on Nero, the pupil of wise Seneca the Stoic, who ruled well by his teacher's principles for a few years, and then the infection of power and flattery turned him into a tyrant. He may, like most tyrants, have believed his own myth. He ordered Seneca, his conscience, to commit suicide. (Ironically, Seneca wrote about suicide as a noble and dignified end often enough.) By the Mausoleum of Augustus (where else?) Mussolini built the sort of buildings beloved of twentieth century totalitarians everywhere, with boastful inscriptions (in decent Latin, actually) of his achievements and ambitions. Look on my works, ye mighty, and despair. Then, at the other end of town, I found below San Clemente the first century Mithraeum in what had twenty centuries ago been a private house, which had had the fifth century basilica built on top of it, and then the present baroque edifice above that. The spring that had fed the house so copiously in the sunlight of its peristyle still flows noisily, but now it is deep underground, reflecting and splintering the torchlight in the darkness. Spurred on by this trip to the Underworld, I found my way over the Monte Oppio gardens, where men and women with trowels and big hats against the sun were still rummaging in the remains of Nero's palace (the French word *fouilles* is indeed the *mot juste*), to see the lower depths of Santa Pudenziana. But the wonderful basilica of Santa Maria Maggiore... despite shortness of time, tired feet, and miles to go before I slept, it seemed churlish not to divert into this vast space, perhaps the nearest thing still standing to the old St Peter's that they demolished to make room for the present one. A nice young Iranian couple came and talked to me and asked me to tell them about the architecture, and the Classical orders. (How did they *know* how to pull my string?) They took a photograph: Me and the Mosaics. But Santa Pudenziana nearby still called: another ill-kempt little church sitting on the beginnings of Christian Rome. A beggar, covered in sores, smelly as most of our ancestors probably were, lay at the gate. He was asking for nothing. His astonishingly clear bright eyes – the eyes of Christ in the mosaics – met mine as I handed him a coin – ashamed, perhaps, I looked away, thinking of Dives and Lazarus. That is an uncomfortable story for one who has friends who are cooking dinner for him and in whose cool flat he will sleep.

Santa Pudenziana is no museum. The grubby little courtyard, well below street level, was full of children, and children's things, and nuns working with them. But I had come to see the mosaics. For the apse has a mosaic of Christ in a consul's chair, with the Apostles round him in togas with the broad senatorial stripe – unique, I think.

I knew there were levels below, down to a first century house and so I asked a passing nun (Korean, I guess) in my bad Italian, '*E possibile descendere all'* – I should have said something like '*inferiore;*' but it came out as '*inferno?*' Mildly surprised, she replied, '*Si Signor, è molto possibile,*' and then, grasping what I really meant, she continued, '*ma è molto pericoloso: è chiuso*'. So no more first century reveries... and if only one could know for sure that Hell was shut on Thursdays.

★

Not the last trip to the past... will there ever be one? I wandered over the Isola Teverina, across Fabricius' Bridge over the rapids (where the floating mills were moored), and past the church where St Bartholomew's relics are kept, to Santa Maria in Cosmedin. I was not quite sure why I was doing this, but I knew something was drawing me back to that church. I passed through the noisy Campo de' Fiori, its market a riot of flowers and vegetables, a pretty place where the colours and smells invited to ease and quiet coffee and sitting idly watching the market. But tall above the market stalls, a statue marks the exact spot where in 1600 the Inquisition burned Giordano Bruno. I feel I know him. The bronze plates on the plinth are bright with touching. An old pupil and friend of mine, Stephanie, has written good and popular novels about him. The Risorgimento – the statue is from 1889, at the height of enthusiasm for the new Italy –

claimed him as martyr for freedom of thought, which in some measure he was. Even so: press on, past the Portico of Augustus' sister Octavia (that turned later into a fish market), past the *tholos* Temple of Hercules, to where queues of schoolchildren waited to be photographed alongside the Bocca della Verità. Once, to test the truth of their evidence, litigants had to place their right hand in its mouth. I wondered if the children chattering like sparrows knew that. (Reproductions in motorway service stations in the UK only tell your weight, or something equally footling.) A small rain had begun to fall, and tyres were beginning to swish on the roads.

In Santa Maria's crypt, a perfect ancient columbarium, the niches where the urns of the dead were placed are now empty. But the place feels not so. A fourth century mosaic of Maria Theotokos stares, challenges, from the little apse. For ten minutes, or perhaps a century, I had it to myself. And then a horde of German visitors arrived, bent on improvement as only Germans can be. (Their ancestors, the Goths who came in 410BC, had less peaceable intentions.) So I left, into that gentle rain.

IV

PLOTTING A COURSE

To the Interior

You are not here to verify,
instruct yourself, or inform curiosity
or carry report.

T. S. Eliot, 'Little Gidding', Four Quartets

And so the years passed. Nothing particularly went wrong. Indeed, a lot of things went very right. But there was a sort of unease, a sense of frustration, growing in intensity as each summer yellowed on into the fall of the leaf. And the daily loneliness that all widowed people must feel grew more intense, as well as an inexplicable restlessness, like a boat quietly sleeping by a quay beginning to tug nervously at its mooring as the tide rises and the water eddies by it. It would have been easy to hug oneself into self-pity. Friends seemed ever so far away, metaphorically as well as literally. The descendants were busy with their lives and families, just as we had been at their age, and you have to accept that, for, as you travel further on the unavoidable journey, paths diverge and the common language gets weaker. That has to be faced, even if it is painful. And it is, very. There are some things you simply have no language to communicate to those who have not lived your years. So you see the young walking towards all sorts of pitfalls and problems, and there is not a thing you can do about it. Not even warn. You can't graft experience. Every generation is doomed to repeat the mistakes, in a different way and a different key, of its predecessors. That is what freedom entails.

So, what to do? Get off the unmerrygoround somehow. Holidays on your own are no fun, for the better half of happiness is sharing. Gradually the thought formed – brushed away at first, but returning stronger each time – 'Retreat: go to a monastery.' I brushed it away: after all, the last time I was on a retreat was at Whalley Abbey when I was 16, when Canon Picton, over the interminable weekend, took us through the Book of Amos, and I found the injunction to be silent so hard that I took myself off for a walk simply to talk to the trees, who did not answer back. But finally I acknowledged, in the front of my mind, not as a maverick idea, the possibility of doing it again after all these years.

So there I was, driving into the Abbey grounds, a little surprised, for I had sent off only a tentative email enquiry, to be faced with an immediate reply saying a room was booked. It was a perfect afternoon, after the morning's rain, in the autumn of my life. I parked the car, and went into the shop – I can still turn back from this unknown, something says – and asked how I might find the Guestmaster. The girl rang through, and said he would meet me in front of the church. Through the arch, then, and into the precincts. The church towered over the few people walking by the trim lawns. Absurdly – after all I was only intending to stay a few days, I was committed to nothing – I felt like the new boy at school, and had that same sudden, well remembered, grip of almost panic, a sudden churn of the stomach, at the realisation that if I went a step further the world I was used to would be different from then on. Good manners made the choice, as the prompt email had made the earlier one. For from round the corner came Brother Daniel, in the black habit of the Benedictines, dwarfed by the shelter of the west front, white hair stirred by the breeze, hand outstretched to welcome. Neither he nor anybody else asked me any questions. They just accepted my presence among them with a bow and a slight smile. Just as I was. Which was what?

The heavy door crashed behind us, like a bad change of gears, shutting out the noise of motorways and machines, and I entered into quiet: a quiet not of absence, but of purpose, that seemed to have been waiting for me. For those few days talkative, verbal (verbose?) me, was silenced. There was no need to make conversation, to make links, set the table in a roar... or chance. That is frightening.

Brother Daniel showed me up the stairs, past a big crucifix on the wall, to a pretty room, named in honour of St Hilda, Abbess of Whitby. (At that Synod, Rome won the argument.) Next to it was the Guestmaster's Scriptorium:

I never found out what he did there, but it was good to hear in that name an echo of the tireless labour of centuries of monks in making copies of those books of the past on which they and we depend as civilised beings. In my room there was a crucifix on the desk, a copy of the Rule of St Benedict, a Bible, a few devotional and historical books. But I had brought Lady Julian of Norwich with me, and my friend Eamon Duffy's gift of his book of prayers – and the laptop, for there was still some work to be done even if I was 'away'. The window looked out over a fine *Robinia* – named for Louis XIII's superintendent of the Jardin des Plantes, where his original tree, the first to come to Europe, still grows green each spring – and a wall covered in the autumn flames of pyracantha. Everywhere there was a faint smell of – is it lavender? In the corridor, paintings: a large St Scholastica, sister of St Benedict, with her dove and the Rule of her brother, and next to her another lady Saint whom I could not identify, with her hand on a skull, and opposite my door a Renaissance English noblewoman who fled abroad to escape the tide that was running and had become head of a convent in Flanders. Cardinal Allen, from my own home patch, Rossall, did the same, and founded the College at Douai. In the corridor, by extraordinary and happy chance, there was a good eighteenth century print of what had been left of Cockersands Abbey, an austere Premonstratensian house just over the estuary from Rossall, after the gangs of the two Cromwells, a grim century apart, had finished with it. I used to know that ruin well, just three walls of the chapter house, open to the sky, grass lush in its shelter save where, a foot out from the walls, the sheep and cattle had trampled a bare path as they sheltered from the westerly rain. Feed my sheep...

Quietness.

I made my way through the stone corridors to the church for Vespers, the predecessor of Cranmer's beloved Evensong. (I was welcome at the Offices, but there was no obligation to go.) I used my new pass to get through the various doors that divide the monks' part from the world outside. It is true Autumn now: the church is dim, and the dozen or so lay people in the nave need no light, for they know the office by heart's light. The only strong light is that focused on the gorgeously coloured carving of the Coronation of the Blessed Virgin high on the wall at the east. The monks chant, sometimes out of tune, their voices echoing in the lovely kind acoustic of that vast church. They go through all the psalms set for the day and the office: the whole Psalter is sung each week. Those psalms, several which go back to before the time of King David, and some of which are much later, intersect at so many points with the history of Israel, a pilgrim people that so often lost its way, just as they intersect with our own journeys, our own lost ways. They give us a language to join our voice to those ancient voices yearning for justice: 'plead my cause amongst the ungodly people.' They face up to the ultimate despair:

'My God, my God, why hast thou forsaken me?' They yearn for that joy beyond the walls of the world, 'like as the hart desireth the waterbrooks,' 'O praise the Lord, O my soul!' As my mind wanders, as it does, I remember that someone – Rowan, I think – had told me the ancient, wise, reason for chanting: the sound carries, and its measured isosyllabic statement makes sure that every word is given weight and is remembered. That was important in a time before paper and when books were rare. As they go out the twelve brothers pull their black cowls over their heads, and suddenly the centuries elide.

To supper, my first in this community. I make my way to the refectory. We eat without conversation, in formal informality. Father Abbot and Father Prior take their places on the dais, grace is said, and everyone sits. A monk begins a dramatic reading of *Revelations* 19, in thrilling instalments – and yes, I mean that! His voice echoes in the white painted stone cross-vaulted room, as Father Abbot gets up, and leads the way to the tables where a simple supper is laid out. He gestures us visitors to follow him. We eat in a communal silence accentuated by the reading. What a change! So unlike College... yet once the older Colleges had been monastic institutions and beloved Magdalene and Queens' would have known these conventions. I am glimpsing from this temporary inside what I have so often spoken about to students from the outside.

I went to walk in 'our farm,' as Brother Daniel called it, and meant it, for it is. Once it was the mainstay of the house's finances, and the Rule lays down that the brothers shall do manual work for a third of the day, besides a third in prayer and a third in study. (And these have a fine scholar's library to work in, too.) The noble woods by the river belong to the brethren as well. In an earlier time they would have been continuously managed, coppiced, the long timber grown for express purpose, and the brashings burnt in cakes for charcoal. The first mills, too, and the first weir to keep a head of water for them, must have been built then. The salmon and sea trout would have thronged the river in that earlier, less devastated, age, and doubtless they had the convenience, as they do now, of a salmon ladder to get up to the glassy smoothness of the mill pool, a smoothness that bends over the lip of the weir before falling into the foam of the unquiet rapids. In this light the fast yet forever still curve of water reflects the low sun like polished jet[23].

It is all very lovely, now. Idyllic, you might say, forgetting the origin of that word. But if you had come over the hill and looked down into this valley, or that of Rievaulx, or Fountains, or wherever, in their heyday, you would have seen the smoke from the glass making and the brewery, smelt the reek of the tannery, heard the clangour of iron on iron from the forges. For the great religious houses were major economic centres, major employers of lay labour, and great innovators – of their nature they could take the long view – in technology and industry. What they were and did lies far closer to the heart of what European history has been than many a memorable battle between largely interchangeable princes. Any number of colourful men clad in various fashions of ironmongery knocking each other off horses are far less representative of what was really going on, what really mattered, what we, late in time, have come to take for granted, than a tonsured man in a rough monk's habit patiently sharpening his quill and dipping it into ink. The quiet mycelium of scholarship works underground. In time it fruits, surprising through the familiar earth.

There is a delicious irony I can't resist including. The Cistercians – where I am was originally a Cistercian house – went into the wilderness to be ascetic and poor and contemplative. But they had a duty of scholarship, which means writing and copying. No paper then. So you write on sheepskin – parchment. One sheepskin equals one folio. Writing quite small, you need about 500 sheep to copy a Bible. But all those sheep you grow in the wilderness, give you an awful lot of wool, and meat, which, being prudent, you sell... and before you know where you are you are very rich indeed. And the monastery's community, monks, lay brothers, lay workers and their families spread themselves in charitable works and beautiful buildings and whatever, and are busy...

Even in these days measured by the ringing of the bell for the regular Offices, I find it hard to free myself of the itch to be busy, the itch to move about, to travel: it's a newish thing anyway, as even in my parents' generation, for example, most people stayed within a few miles of where they were born. Monks took a vow of *stabilitas loci* – staying in one place unless ordered elsewhere by their superior. The gardens are room enough if the mind is quiet, I think – they were so intended. Indeed, my senses are lapped by a luxury of feeling. A smell of lavender is everywhere in the hot sun. In the lavender garden are 70 varieties of the plant, all beautifully kept. The lady trimming them with a delicate pair of secateurs wears stained green gardening gloves. She says she loves doing this job for the brothers, 'who do so much for the village.' She is obviously proud of her neat lavender and tells me there are nearly 400 varieties of the plant. Nearby is the mediaeval-style 'sensory garden', laid out with the plants the old monks would have known, plants that appealed to sight and smell and touch and taste. At its centre is the stone base of an old cider press, kept moist with a trickle of water so that mosses and bryophytes can colour it with their unemphatic greens. That trickle might give you sound as well, if the birds did not turn up to sing. Round it, a camomile bench, on which perfumed cushion a lady of mediaeval romance might have sat, to think all that was in her will, or to be wooed. (As Falstaff once said, 'For though the camomile, the more it is trodden on, the faster it grows, so youth, the more it is wasted, the sooner it wears.') This is indeed a faint echo of the gardens we see painted in the margins or initial letters of manuscripts, or lauded in the springtime in courtly poetry, and it reminds too of that garden without a gate, the *hortus conclusus*, in which the Blessed Virgin sits serene and humble.

All monasteries had a physic garden, where plants of healing virtue were grown. For monks were supposed to be healers of body as well as of soul and mind. Such physic was, as we are rediscovering, often very effective. This Abbey's is now much smaller than it would have been, and certainly not on the old site, but its four quarters – gardens were often laid out as symbolic maps of Eden[24] – are divided in the old way by a pleached arbour of fig, and pear, and apple, of vine, and quince, and hop – 'hops, heresy, Bibles and beer/ All came to England all in one year' went the old rhyme about the 1530s. And medlar: that fruit the French know as *cul de chien,* and Chaucer called it 'open-arse'; his bitter Reeve likened himself to a medlar in *The Canterbury Tales*. In the borders marigolds – Mary's Gold – flare in the late sun. They are good in salads. Plants for the household too: I never knew that meadowsweet flowers yield a greeny yellow (greenery-yallery?) dye, the stems a red, and the roots a dark brown. There are plants for kitchen, and plants for poison – monkshood, which sends up its dark blue flower spikes each year in the garden at Reach, was an arrow poison, and was occasionally made into a draught that could be given to condemned prisoners. There is a notice warning people not to try the plants, and disclaiming responsibility if they do.

Families walk in the grounds in the soft afternoon as the westering sun gilds the edges of the leaves on those big trees. Many of those trees are ones the monks would never have known, for they are nineteenth century exotic plantings. The noise of water from the weir on the river, where the salmon climb the ladder in season in momentary silver arcs, is ever present. An ever rolling stream, constant only in change.

At Compline the church is quite dark, except for the light shining on the bright figures of the Coronation of the Virgin. I love this office: we used to say it in the little church in the village in Lent, I said it with my tentmate as we trekked across on the icecap in Spitsbergen, when the darkness was months away. We say it sometimes in College. It is full of memories, and it is a good end to the day, when we ask the angels to watch over us, and for a quiet night and a perfect end. And after it, at the very end of the day, we sing that lovely evening antiphon, the *Salve Regina*. At nightfall as the stars by which you could steer grew bright, it was sung at sea, once upon a time: as it was on devout Columbus' *Santa Maria* on the way to a land they thought a new Eden.

An owl hoots close outside my wide open window. And sleep – how I could sleep! – comes sweetly. I sleep rare unbroken sleep until the tenor bell heralds the new day while it is yet dark. It summons to the first of the Offices, Matins at 05:45. I let myself off that, and rise an hour later for Lauds as daylight breaks. *Iam lucis orto sidere:* 'already the star of day has risen.' *Wachet auf, ruft unse die Stimme!:* 'Awake, a voice calls to us!'

A walk in the woods, up and down the steep little hills to get the muscles going, and then reading and study. In the Physic Garden as the sun moves round I move round the seats in the arbours sculpted into the yew hedges: you could set your sundial by me. (Suddenly I understand how easy it was for Benedick in *Much Ado about Nothing*, hidden by hedges, to overhear Don Pedro and Claudio in Leonato's formal garden.) Bees enquire of the late flowers. A blackbird almost perches on my book, then realises his mistake and tells the world about it. It is Lady Julian I read, that wise anchoress of Norwich, humane, loving and lucid, who sees God as loving beyond motherhood – 'our verray mother Jesus' – and fatherhood. Just Love. And she tries, for me not unsuccessfully, to communicate that passion of Love as she journeys into that ultimate mystery and wrestles with the words to express it. The gulls cry of the not so distant sea – the sound of my childhood on the sea-sounding shore of Rossall – and quarrel over whatever gulls do quarrel about. That is part of the pattern too.

★

But. Dark shadows of the Reformation, that necessary but in the end baleful event. I could not, as an Anglican, take the sacrament at daily Mass. So, despite the genuine welcome, an uncomfortable feeling of being, so to speak, not on the inside. (Which is very much the feeling I have had in so many things all my life.) The broken Body... For I keep having the thought, which comes unbidden, that the Faith is about a relationship, not a set of arguments. It is (I think) about Jesus' question to Peter, 'Whom do you [singular] say that I am?' But as in any relationship, as soon as we put it into words and syntax we lose the heart and soul of the matter, and introduce a myriad opportunities for misunderstanding, confusion, legalism. But we can do no other, for we structure our world in words, in speech.

Perhaps silence is the right course? That is given to few. Silent praise – but that praise is not praise as we understand the term, but the expression, simply, of love. Words so often put you off. I remember one Whitsuntide, on the Backs in Cambridge, white fluff off the poplars drifting on the wind, and forming white banks, like hot snow, between the trees' boles and in the gutters. One kept tripping over various lovers – earlier selves, perhaps – and walking through Clare College gateway, my eyes dazzled by the light against which I look, I see two shapes, hand in hand. As they pass, laughing, oblivious, into the sunlight of Front Court, they stop. And face each other. He says: 'I can't stop looking at you.' No more. I had letters to deliver, and promises to keep. But it is a moment that I have never forgotten, for that is what true praise is: utter self-forgetfulness in love of all the beloved is. Put God at the centre, us looking in as we look to a lover, rather than oneself at the centre, looking out: a sort of mental Copernican revolution. And it is so hard to make happen. I don't think you can, on your own.

Off the merrygoround, going into the wilderness... this place was once a wilderness, in the strict sense, but there is another sort of wilderness inside. I have glimpsed that here. Jesus went into the wilderness, but we get it wrong when we think of 'sunbeams scorching all the day/ chilly dewdrops nightly shed.' For Galilee is a green and pleasant land. It is what we would call Countryside. Jesus went away from people, into the abundant richness of Creation, to open himself to the richness of being. (Which I think can sometimes be an agony.) This is the real refocusing, where you push aside the everyday duties and concerns and bothersome trivialities that have to be, must be, dealt with and open yourself to being quiet outside and hoping to be quiet inside. And seeing the wonderful world which you have taken for granted for so long. And you seek a relationship with the rhythm, for want of a better word, of the Universe. Adam, we are told, talked with God as a man with his friend in the cool of the evening. I think that is what we are making space for. But it is a gift, a grace, just as friendship is a mutuality. It cannot be worked at.

★

The Oblates' Room, where I could go and read when it was too dark outside, had all the daily papers, with all their silliness and scandal and news of wars and lechery: as if either were new. Monasteries are not retired from the world in any sense. And just as the Church, the chosen body – which is what the Greek/Latin *ecclesia* means – exists for those outside it, monks need to know what is going on in every awful detail so that they can 'pray the news'. That is one of their jobs, as individuals and as community: a community that supports each of its single members. I could envy that. For in my short time there I felt that support, that common mind of brotherhood. Was there any sign of what Browning so wonderfully pictured in the *Dialogue in the Spanish Cloister?* Not that I could see; but then, I was the sparrow that flew out of the dark into the lighted meadhall, and then out again into the dark. I do not know.

Brother Daniel wrote to me in answer to my letter of thanks. They would welcome me again, up to three visits in any calendar year, he said. I wondered... why not? For good?

And then... Rosanna came into my life. How we met can be of no interest to anybody but ourselves. But that chance (what is chance?) meeting altered the co-ordinates, and two roads converged from countries, cultures and times far, far apart and became as one. Hindsight, always the wise counsellor, suggests there were no other roads that could have been travelled: be that as it may. But for the rest of our journeys our paths, rough and smooth, lie together. Her Russian mother's refugee ancestry and her father's escape from Hitler's Germany on the *Kindertransport* graft *Mitteleuropa* and the windy steppes of Siberia onto my middle Englishness, a proxy memory, a stain of much darker things than England has glimpsed since the seventeenth century. (Which is not to say they cannot, will not, happen here, again. They did, do, in Ireland. And very nasty things indeed, things very – what we used to call, complacently – 'un-British,' have come out of the shadows in Britain after the Scottish referendum campaign and the Brexit vote.) I cannot ignore that grafting, unthink those thoughts, for in it I recognise that I too share the darkness: co-heir, with those like Rosanna's great grandparents, who died in the concentration camp, and in the Russian famine, or those who took them there, of infamy as well as glory. We can never untangle the dead from the living. I know that too easily I could be a willing executioner, trapped by those little (con)sequential compromises that never seem to matter. But when, *how*, do you recognise the tipping point, beyond which there is no return, no way back? When does the horrified silence, the reluctance to do anything – 'just at this moment, for now' – become complicity, irrevocable?

The way to the City, where we would be, lies through the darkness. Tolkien's Aragorn knew that.

No Islands

No man is an Iland, intire of itselfe; every man is a peece of
the Continent, a part of the maine; if a Clod bee washed away
by the Sea, Europe is the lesse, as well as if a Promontorie
were, as well as if a Manor of thy friends or of thine owne
were; any mans death diminishes me, because I am involved
in Mankinde; And therefore never send to know for whom
the bell tolls; It tolls for thee.

John Donne, 'Meditation XVII',
Devotions upon Emergent Occasions (1624)

I like islands, for I have always been a bit of a loner. I
sort of collect them now, the more sparsely populated
and remoter the better – Man, Arran, Mull, Heimaey,
Lindisfarne, Rousay, Iona, Unst. Arran's stone circles and
lonely standing stones on Machrie Moor, the chambered
and stalled cairns on Rousay, speak of ages of people like
us who lived and loved and died and left their scribbles on
the palimpsest. On Heimaey they point out the cave high
on the cliffs where 100 people hid during the Moorish
slave raid of 1627, and from the highest peak of Iceland's
new volcano you can see across to Surtsey, where never
yet men lived, a *tabula rasa*. On Lindisfarne a tombstone
reminds you of the Vikings with their battle axes and the
shore running red with blood, but most of all you also
remember Columba and Aidan and a reaching for a peace

– *shalom* – that is not of this world, but which the world needs and knows it not.

I have been to Alderney two or three times. A mild oceanic climate, defended by the Race of Alderney, goodish land, and a parish church where the last time I was there – golly, how long ago! – they still sang a Choral Evensong in the old Anglican manner. But even in the conviviality of the Divers' Arms by Braye harbour I could not help sensing that there were some things people who lived there did not want to talk about. The massive concrete of the bunkers and the gun emplacements told of another story than cheerful talk by a pub fire to the click of bar billiards. Now edged by silverweed and etched by lichen, those emplacements had been part of the Atlantic Wall of the Thousand Year Reich.

We dropped anchor in the harbour well after dark: the tide had been against us, and old *Copious* could not hurry despite us having scraped her bottom clean at low tide in Cherbourg. We turned in directly. Next morning early, I came on deck to a bright sunny morning on a new island with a fresh northerly wind pushing the waves into rocketing spray up against the massive harbour wall. Nearby, the sail training ship *Royalist* rode at her anchor, her yards lowered and her false gunports momentarily reminding of a brig of Nelson's navy. They were about already: the wind brought us whiffs of their bacon cooking. A happy morning. Mike our skipper heaved himself up the companionway onto the deck, and gestured toward the harbour wall. 'Good harbour wall in a northerly. Wonder how many Russians are in it.'

Alderney was occupied by the Germans in 1940. When their landing was imminent, six Royal Navy ships were sent to evacuate the inhabitants. A bare morning's notice, one suitcase. Leave everything else, and if you have time destroy what the enemy could use. Churchill ordered that all animals, including their pets, be killed so that 'Hitler should not have a larder.' The sunny island was garrisoned by 6,000 troops, and in 1942 two work camps and two concentration camps, Lager Sylt and Lager Nordeney, were built to house the slave labour used to build those bunkers, gun emplacements, tunnels, air-raid shelters. Lager Norderney held Russian and Polish POWs and Lager Sylt Jewish slave labourers. Control of them was transferred to the skull-badged SS in March 1943. Some say Alderney saw the greatest mass slaughter on British soil in modern times – estimates of up to 40,000 murdered have credibility. There was unspeakable cruelty to prisoners of war, especially Russian and Jewish; worked and starved literally to death, they were thrown into the new concrete of Braye Harbour wall, or just chucked over the cliffs to the sea where the gulls would gather in a screeching, quarrelling mass, as the waves battered them against the rocks, to peck out their eyes and, when the bodies sank, the big, fat, delicious crabs would move in and eat their faces and hands. There are stories of crucifixions, even on the gates of the prison camp. The German CO built a pretty retreat for himself. It is the now a desirable luxury bungalow. What ghosts does it have?

Those who came back home after the war, blameless, not in any way smirched by any hint of collaboration as people in Jersey and Guernsey could hardly avoid, found no homes. Their houses were derelict, all the wood, even front doors, burned for fuel – for the German conscripts, mere lads wrenched away from all they had ever known and held dear, felt the cold of the winter gales. The returning people found many graves. No birdsong. The place had only memories they tried to forget. And ghosts. Denial: nobody talked about it. Just as villagers and islanders, people in small communities, have to rub along with people they don't like but are stuck with, so Alderney had to rub along with a recent past for which its people have no responsibility. But the useless concrete gun emplacements of the Atlantic Wall watch, wait, remind. Do not forget: horror and tyranny are only just out of sight. But children in their angel infancy play on the beaches. Just learning to walk, toddlers strut with that strange, mechanical, stiff arm and leg gait as if they were string puppets. They laugh as the clear wavelets splash them in the warm sun. The crabs wait.

★

I like Germany. But as soon as I say that to friends in Göppingen or Stuttgart, they say, 'But we are not

"Germany"! We are quite different from the Rhinelanders, and as for those Prussians...' If I say it to my colleague in Munich, he says, 'No, you mean you like Bavaria.' And so it goes on: the patchwork history of Germany lives on in local loyalties, and to be sure, local differences – wine v. beer, one type of sausage v. another, Protestant and Catholic, endless variations of cakes, forest v. plains, the way the language is spoken. I speak it very badly, but I find I can get my mouth round its sounds and my mind round its grammar more easily that I can round the pursed lip slipperiness of French, which I speak much better. But those accents... I first spent time in Swabia when the scars of the war were still physically visible. My friends Inge and Sigrid, who were putting me up, pointed out to me the grassy curve of the road where their uncle had died in 1945 fighting the Americans. Their father, a tailor, sat in his chair, and coughed, coughed, for his health had been broken on the Russian Front. I was welcomed by the village, Ebersbach, was fed royally, and was taken to the concert for the 60th Jubilee of the local brass band, in a tent up the hill above the little town, where beer flowed and wurst sizzled, and they played loudly the 'Chorus of the Hebrew Slaves' (the programme called it the *Freiheitschor*, 'Freedom chorus') from Verdi's *Nabucco* – several times – and then lots of the oompah stuff I love, and everyone linked arms and swayed, and everyone was *Brüderlein und Schwesterlein,* and that beer... And quite soon I began to make intelligible noises, but then when I went to Munich everybody laughed at my Swabian accent, and asked me to speak English. Add to that the fact that much of what vocab I later had came from Schubert's or Mahler's songs and Wagner's operas, and you see why people called for another drink. *Ich komm so spät durch Nacht und Wind*, or *Ging heut' Morgen über's Feld* or *Guten Morgen, schöne Müllerin! Wo steckst du gleich das Köpfchen hin?*, are rather stilted conversational openings.

'Germany', in all its richness of culture, its diversity of food and farming, crops and commerce, is after all a very recent creation. Perhaps, despite Bismarck's baleful dominance, it is really a coagulation, as blood coagulates – a coagulation of different peoples and traditions seeing slightly different worlds through not quite the same language. It certainly results from a combination of the mess caused by Napoleon, misguided political choices by often inept rulers of small or not so small states, a Romantic nationalism fuelled by myths of a heroic 'German' 'mediaeval' past – the benchmark for the nineteenth century Romantics, as for Hitler, was the actually rather deplorable Heinrich the Fowler[25] – and a romantic entrapment between that imagined past and a never to be realized, endlessly deferred future. If only Talleyrand had been heeded more: *'surtout, messieurs, point de zèle.'* A little bit of Enlightenment cynicism – which once upon a time Germans did rather well – in the right place might have saved Germany, and the world, a whole load of suffering.

I taught in Munich a few times – oddly enough, to Americans spending a year at the University. I liked the place, like Gdansk painstakingly reconstructed (from photographs taken as a record by the Nazis when they knew the war was going against them) after virtual flattening of the centre by the bombing. By April 1945, 66 Allied bombing raids had destroyed most of the city's ancient centre, which had taken centuries to grow. The rest was finished off by a decade of rain and freezing winters. (Dispiritingly enough, two buildings – almost the only two – to survive untouched were the Nazi party HQ and the Gestapo HQ.) We think often enough about the people and places bombed, but what about those who *did* the bombing of Coventry, London, Munich, Hamburg, Berlin, and most outrageously, Dresden? Patrick Bishop records in his *Air Force Blue* (2017) that returning aircrew occasionally expressed shock at the destruction they were causing, having peered down at a peaceful land of fields and villages that looked like England. 'It seemed right to us at the time.' And young Germans – these airmen were nearly all little more than adolescents – must have felt the same over England, seeing Coventry burning, and France: and Guernica. Or young Germans in Goering's Luftwaffe strafing the lines of refugees on the roads in France? How did the young American pilot feel when in the last months of the war he strafed with his machine gun the road back from Plochingen to the village where my friend Inge lives when she, nine years old, was walking back from school? Why did Bomber Command, and one assumes Churchill himself, think that area bombing, a strategy which had so signally *not* worked in England, where people had stood firm, would work in Germany? And what does it do to you if you adopt the values of your enemy? J. R. R. Tolkien wrote in a letter to a friend, when the bombing campaign against Germany started in earnest, 'We are using the Ring to destroy the Ring.' 'One Ring to rule them all/ And in the Darkness bind them.'

In Dresden the firestorm that the RAF unleashed reached temperatures of 1800 degrees, fleeing people got stuck in the melted tarmac of the roads and turned into torches, and those who jumped into the river to save themselves were boiled to death. The city is now beautifully reconstructed, 'just as it was.'

Munich's centre is, well, *interesting*, with lots of little shops and stalls and no overpowering tall buildings like giant cuckoos in the nest. And there is the lovely English Garden, acre upon acre of trees and grass and running water, and people talking and walking, and dogs – always a good sign – and birds. And on warm (and not so warm days) a disconcerting number of nudists, some of whom shouldn't. Some were playing football, but not everything stops when the ball does. I stayed first in a small hotel on its edge, welcoming and friendly, with a garden where in the evening you could eat good solid sustaining food – just what you need when you are determined to walk three miles across town ('It is good for me. I am not getting enough exercise') to my next lecture. The plump, motherly, blonde waitress, who seemed to think I needed looking after and feeding up, was nearly cascading out of her *dirndl* as she leaned over me to plonk down a great plate of sauerkraut and pork and potato next to my beer. '*Genieß es, liebchen,*' 'Enjoy it, dearie,' she said, as she turned to take the next table's order. I enjoyed it all.

Happy memories. Driving back to Stuttgart one time on a bright summer day with my son we stopped for lunch at a tiny café out in the country near Ulm. We entered a room suddenly dark after the dazzling light, and silent. Awkward, I thought: they don't like us foreigners. The owner came over, face expressionless, wiping his hands on his apron, and I haltingly ordered bread and sausage. '*Woher kommen Sie?*' he asked. '*Aus England. Cambridge,*' I said, and immediately men – there were no women there – got up to shake our hands. Two glasses of the local wine appeared, on the house, those curious baked-apple-shaped goblets on their fat green stems – for this was white wine country. Then everyone else wanted to buy us a drink – *ein wenig! Ganz wenig!* – and we had to accept. Eventually, with many promises to return with *meine Frau und meine schöne Tochter* to enjoy more wine, we managed to make our excuses and leave. For we had miles to go before we slept. But as we got into the car, I said to Justin, 'I am going to have to have a sleep.' So we drove out of the village, stopped by a shady wood, and slept the sleep, if not of the just, of the just feasted. It is so easy to forget the simple friendliness most people will show if you give them the chance.

Yet these nice, friendly, generous people had had to live for 12 years with the monstrosity of Nazism, with the hounding of the Jews and Gypsies, with banners across village streets proclaiming *Judenfrei* – 'free of Jews.' Some must have been convinced by the ideology. More must have run with the crowd, done what they were told, and even enjoyed doing so, but, as always, I feel most just kept their heads down, partly in fear, partly in loyalty to their country, all in some measure tainted by omission, submission, or, more rarely I think, willed commission. But does that mean innocence? None could have been unaware of Hitler's tirades of hate, his promises of bloody revenge, the demonization of the Jews, none could have not noticed the disappearances, and the violence. And now, having to live now with the fullness of knowledge of what they only uneasily suspected then, the industrialisation of murder... 'But we really did not know, Charles,' said Inge, and I believe her. Even Sigrid, who had been old enough to join the Band of German Maidens – the girls' equivalent to the Hitler Youth – in 1938, said her main prewar memories were happy treks in the woods, games, of singing round the campfires pushing back the darkness. Some things you try not to know, perhaps. Being in the murmuration keeps the starling safe.

Can a lone starling's voice be heard against the murmuration of the crowd? How? and one man's voice against the people's...

★

Somewhere in this house there is a photo of me the last time I wore chain mail. I am wearing a knee length hauberk, and am helmeted in a fashion that was up to the minute in the Bayeux Tapestry, and I am holding a longsword. It is good for a mediaevalist, even a one as pacific as I, to experience the physical weight of the past he talks about. (And wielding a two-handed sword – if people are not too close – teaches you about some muscles you did not know you had and how vulnerable you are when both arms are raised.) I was in the museum below the rock on which the remains of Schloss Hohenstaufen brood. That castle was where the Emperors Frederick Barbarossa, Frederick II *Stupor Mundi*, and the tragic Manfred came from. Implacable opponents of the Papacy, Pope Innocent IV called them 'that brood of vipers'. (Hohenstaufen is not far in Swabia from Hohenzollern, cradle of another family that made some noise in the world. It must be something in the water.) Being in the area, with my early mediaeval interests, I could hardly not go there. Or turn up the chance to wear mail again. You move easily when you wear chain mail, but it is heavy to put on. Holding thirty pounds or so above your head like a cold floppy grey sweater strengthens your sword arm, to be sure. I looked ridiculous in it, and my face was incapable of the mean, cold, determined expression dedicated to daring duty and desperate defence which I tried to assume. In chainmail, under a helmet with a nasal, you simply must not grin back at people. It quite spoils the effect. I would have made a terrible knight or man at arms, and an even worse fighting Archbishop like Reinhold von Dassel, Barbarossa's Chancellor, or Charlemagne's legendary Archbishop Turpin of Reims. Thank Heaven I never had to be one. Sherbet and cushions and good conversation about philosophy and poetry with my Arab opposite numbers in the cool room through which the sea wind blows in Frederick II's Palermo would have been more my style.

★

So, in the end, here I am in Berlin, a stranger, yet it is so familiar. More or less consciously, I have avoided coming to it, all these years, until now. Myth and story, and now Rosanna's family history, even fear of what it will hold for me, colour the sky. But one must be systematic, factual, the best defence against too emotional a reaction. Of course one – let us stay impersonal if we can – is aware of its background, and a bit of dry history can sop up the emotions. When Prussia was a modest and not very successful state, Berlin was a backwater of a place in dull and not very productive countryside. Its ruler, the Margrave of Brandenburg – one of those Hohenzollerns – was far the weakest of the seven Electors who chose the Holy Roman Emperor – for centuries that was a Hapsburg. The real axis of a 'Germany' (that did not yet exist) was Cologne-Frankfurt-Munich-Vienna.

Brandenburg was always being overrun by assorted Swedes (in the Thirty Years' War), Imperialists, Poles, and that was after the Huns and Tartars and Magyars had got tired. You have only to look at the room in the Pergamon Museum devoted to the *Völkerwanderung*, the movements of whole peoples across Eurasia in the centuries after the Western Empire had more or less collapsed, to realize how illusory our idea of fixity and nationality is, how the tides of peoples and culture have ebbed and flowed across Europe, a flux of order and disorder, each swash making yet more changes. 'Germany' is an ethnic potpourri in the endlessly fought-over crossroads of Europe. How nonsensical to any rational person the idea of purity of 'race' is and always was!

Berlin in its heyday, in those sunset decades before 1914, many people, even Berliners, regarded as a rather new, brash and somewhat unappealing place, so new in fact that the joke was that no one was actually born there: most of its inhabitants came from somewhere else. For centuries it had been capital of Brandenburg, which grew out of the Northern March carved anciently out of the territory of the Slavic Wends. During centuries of provincial mediocrity nothing much happened to catch the attention of the world outside, or even inside. Sometimes the tiniest provincial courts can host something miraculous, as Köthen did in those years when J. S. Bach was employed there as Kapellmeister. But not Berlin. Bach gave Christian Ludwig, Margrave of Brandenburg-

Schwedt, what we now know as the six Brandenburg Concerti in 1721, and the Margrave did not even notice: probably never heard by their composer, they remained unplayed in the library for over a hundred years. Perhaps that dormant state, ruffled only by the latest invasion, is to be regretted... before Berlin became a big, rapacious, modern industrial city exerting the centripetal force of money and power. Like Balzac's Paris or Brecht's City of Mahagonny, or Dickens' London, it became a Moloch, gorging on people attracted by making a fortune, by glamour, by power, and often, like all cities, spewing out the disappointed husk. And after Bismarck it was one of great nodes of power in Europe.

Until 1945. It has risen again from that rubble, as so many lives had to. But some never did. A double line of cobbles in the pavement marks where the city was so cruelly and irrationally divided for decades. The modern city is 'bustling' – a travel agent's word – and full of building work, full of new roads and paths being laid, of new tramways perfected. The future. Everywhere you look there seems to be building. Big pink pipes abound, at ground level, then suddenly at first floor height when they have to cross a road, then back to street level. They are to take away the groundwater that keeps flooding into foundation excavations and they dump it into the nearest river, stream or pond. For the city is built on sand, lake and bog deposits, and the water is very near the surface. I can't help thinking of the metaphors of building on sand

– and of ancient things coming up and flooding your present.

But that water has uses. In the streets you keep coming across wonderfully ornate green cast iron hand pumps, like the one in the farm near my uncle's vicarage under the spout of which, occasionally, as a boy I washed. There are 2107 of them... all in running order, all delivering perfectly drinkable water. Some are well over a century old. They are independent emergency wells in case the regular water supply system collapses. When the war ended, those street pumps were crucial for 2.8 million people, and even now the city is ready for all sorts of dire scenarios: from technical faults in the water mains, to pollution (e.g. during heavy flooding), to war, even to deliberate, terrorist, poisoning. Somewhere in Berlin, the city fathers store 30 million water-purifying tablets. An efficient and prudent city.

★

We arrived at night: which is sometimes not a bad way to arrive in a new city, so you wake up fresh to new things. Our hotel was, said its brochure, 'vibrant, exciting' – they would, wouldn't they. It was in the anonymous, international style. It was full of earnest *conférenciers* trying to impress each other over breakfast and dinner. One group was from a firm which sells Werther's Originals, and we wondered what they could talk about over dinner. ('How many toffees have *you* sold this year?') The style of the place was nondescript, uniform, good – on the whole inoffensive in taste, but plastic cacti in pots on the tables were the only green. In the light well a huge, badly painted, mural of a bear faced you across the little courtyard as you came out of the lift door into the glazed corridor – Albert the Bear centuries ago gave Berlin its emblem. It had green fur, with what looked like a willy, but was just a badly painted tail. Winnie was never like this. But there was a good breakfast.

And over breakfast we planned the day. We both had copies of the tourist map, which had adverts for what you ought not to miss, what you might enjoy. A dramatic extravaganza of a rather louche if energetic and spectacular kind: is she naked or is she not? (And the huge 20ft screen outside the theatre down the road which endlessly played an HD loop of extracts from the show did not make it clear either.) (And all the other shows, things for which the Berlin of the '20s was famous, the seduction of decadence.) The brochure offered us cruises on the Spree, an undistinguished river. Or perhaps we might try 'The story of Berlin' with a picture of an unlamented Trabant in bilious green? Or a version of *The Hunchback of Notre Dame*? 'Berlin: Hauptstadt der Spione' – 'Capital of Spies' – 'a thrilling journey through the history of espionage.' (Well, there has been a lot of it here.) But then: 'A hands-on experience of history: the DDR museum'. 'The Topography of Terror' – located where stood the

Gestapo HQ, the Reich SS HQ, the Reich Security Main Office. 'The German Resistance Memorial Centre', on the site of the July 1944 plot against Hitler – and we do well to remember that there was indeed a continuing and significant, principled resistance to Nazism, not least from the Confessing Church which would have no truck with its ideology. 'Silence in the face of Evil is itself Evil; not to speak is to speak; not to act is to act,' wrote Dietrich Bonhoeffer before he was murdered. But also 'The Berlin WALL: die Mauer' – and down Friedrichstrasse, a huge lit sign screamed 'The Berlin WALL see it here', and, the blurb promised, 'Take a trip back to the divided Berlin of the 1980s. The monumental panorama presents in scale (1:1) the everyday life next to and with the Berlin Wall on a fictitious Autumn day in East and West.' Later, the Stasi Museum: all they had to do after 1945 was change the uniforms: nothing else changed. A culture based on suspicion, fear, terror, seamlessly joining the 1930s to the 1980s with a few added delights learned from Stalin's Russia. When trust – in people, institutions, law – goes, how shall the people live? Or love?

What is happening here? Are people enjoying, feeling pleasure, in what was suffered? Is all the horror of the criminal state turning into something quaint, as anodyne as playing at being Roman soldiers on an English Heritage site of a summer Sunday? You can buy Stasi caps and insignia at Checkpoint Charlie – and whole uniforms on the web. Or is it so ambiguous as not to be definable in such simple terms? 'Brave tourists are paying to spend a night in Latvia's notorious Karosta Prison which has been turned into a hotel,' reports the *Daily Mail*. Why? Built around 1900, it was used as a Nazi and Soviet military prison, in which hundreds of prisoners were killed – most of them shot. During World War II, the Nazis sentenced Latvian deserters to death at this prison. Guests can enjoy the 'full prisoner experience' in Communist-era conditions – including death threats, warning gunfire and cries of despair from fellow inmates. They have to sign a release form acknowledging that they will be treated as a prisoner, complete with verbal abuse and hard physical exercise.

Is it the depressing three generation/one century cycle again? The generation that suffered and acted, their children who knew their parents and could remember what they said, and the children's children for whom it is safely de-emotionalised and safely 'history' – and who may find a prurient glamour in it. 'Those who do not know their history are doomed to repeat its mistakes.' (Santayana, I think.)

★

We set off. The winter cold of central Europe bit less keenly than feared, but it is chilly, overcast, with a mean little wind from the South East. There is a smell of coming snow. We walk the cold grid of streets: this was once the Eastern Sector, where nothing much changed after the war except the uniforms. Dull buildings rise against a field grey sky. Here and there is a bit of Empire flamboyance that had survived the bombing of 1945, but there are many pockmarks on the stones. Never forget. If only one could... Everywhere there are Christmas trees lying for collection by the rubbish carts, with now greying needles, discarded, tired, despised, rejected, now Christmas has been forgotten. (And O *Tannenbaum* is the tune of *The Red Flag*). Frosty. A half naked crippled man, convulsively moving his limbs, is begging in the U-Bahn. The draught from the trains makes well-clad us shiver. Was he crippled? Or was he pretending (well)? 'Don't give to beggars' – but???? In his near nakedness in mid-winter he anticipated that letter smuggled out from Auschwitz I read later that morning: two layers of thin clothing, vest, cotton pants, thin striped shirt, thin striped trousers, 'enough to freeze in.' And the food: 200g of meat per week.

It is hard not to be obsessed by the past on a grey day like this. You cannot forget it anyway: once you know you cannot unknow. You cannot forget that Hitler led his country not just to defeat but – as no ruler had ever done before – to a willed annihilation, fighting on when the war was utterly lost, to Götterdämmerung in the baleful mythology he concocted for his rule out of his beloved Wagner. By the Museums there are cannon and bullet marks on the stucco, on the stone. Idly, I put my finger into where a shot had chipped the stone. The roughness of the pockmark outraged the bland smoothness of the surface. Some columns of the porticos of the Museums have been perfectly restored, some pointedly not. Berlin is the only major Western city in modern times, I think, that endured a full scale sack, the mass rape of its women, the wholesale carting off of loot. Much of the treasure of Troy Schliemann found is still in St Petersburg or Moscow: notices in the museum cases assiduously remind us of that. That treasure had seen an earlier sack. I remember hearing on the radio, with a mounting sick feeling in the pit of my stomach, extracts read from a woman's diary written as the Russians approached. They cowered in a cellar while the American bombers droned overheard and the ground shook as they shed their load. Resignedly, waiting for what they knew would come, one said, 'Better a Russki on top than a Yank overhead.' So might the Trojan Women 'in their trailing gowns' have waited for shouts in an unfamiliar Greek, the bonds, the leading captive to be slaves to their raptors' wives. Like white-armed Andromache, like Hecuba, like Cassandra.

The Trojan war, mythical or not – probably not, and probably not in fact just one – is the Ur-war at the bottom of European history, the secular Fall. Rome traced its descent and legitimacy from Troy, and the Julian house specifically from Aeneas, providentially escaping from the Sack. No country in Western Europe in the Middle Ages did not claim some connection with Troy. The Normans, thanks to the clever fiction of Dudo of St Quentin, managed to ignore their Viking piratical past and claim Trojan Antenor as their progenitor, and the British royal line claimed descent from Aeneas' great-grandson Brutus. Elizabeth I's, Henry VII's, Henry VI's family trees show a line stretching back through Arthur and Lear and Cymbeline to Brutus. People and poets even fancifully called London 'New Troy' in the fourteenth century.

Ever since I had seen the Mycenaean treasure in Athens decades ago I had wanted to see the treasure of Troy that Schliemann had excavated. Alas, much of it was taken as war booty by the Russians, and in the cases in the Pergamon Museum frequent notices apologise for the replicas on show because the real stuff is far away 'against international law.' Schliemann actually paid the Ottoman authorities a very large sum for the things he found at what he was sure was Troy, the hill of Hisarlik. (The Turkish means 'the Place of Fortresses', which might suggest folk-memory.) So I suppose Schliemann had as good a title to ownership as you will ever get in the antiques market. But the spoils of war fill our museums and galleries. As St Augustine drily observed in his *City of God*, 'what are great kingdoms but robberies?' and Chaucer's Manciple echoes him: there is no difference between the robber and the king except that one has more power and is more successful than the other.[26] The stuff from Schliemann's digging was beautiful, intricate, delicate, worked with a precision that beggars belief when artificial magnification was millennia in the future. But what sticks in my memory most is the photo of Sophia, Schliemann's beautiful second wife, wearing the golden headdress of Troy, the wide gold band across her forehead as millennia earlier it had graced the brow of a forgotten queen. What did Sophia feel, knowing that? What was she like, the woman who wore that gold when it was new?

Schliemann and his first wife Ekaterina had divorced – in the USA, because divorces were easier to come by there – and he knew he would need in his project the intimate help of someone versed in Greek culture of the times. So he advertised for a wife in the Athens newspaper. His friend, the Archbishop of Athens, suggested his relative, Sophia Engastromenos, aged just 17. As she fitted his specification, he married her almost at once (1869). Their two children were called Andromache and Agamemnon. Only reluctantly did he allow them to be baptized, and he added to the ceremony by putting a copy of the *Iliad* on their heads and reciting a hundred hexameters from it. I would love to know which.

It is curiously disturbing so powerfully to be reminded of the Sack of the City in the City that had been sacked when the world changed, again. From a *terminus post quem* to a *terminus post quem*.

★

In the Museum they have wisely put Nefertiti in a room on her own, and they don't press on you the religious revolution to monotheism she and her consort Akhnaten attempted. (Which does matter: Psalm 104 and the Pharaoh's *Hymn to the Sun* have a lot of parallels, as it happens.) She was beautiful, even allowing for the conventionalisation of the individual in royal portraits. Her face is unusually symmetrical, a harmony in mathematics. She has the slightest of wrinkles under her eyes, round her perfect mouth. She seems alive with all the elegiac beauty of older women. (Richard Strauss' Marschallin!) A woman stood nearby, gazing, weeping. I know what she was feeling, for I had found unexpected but insistent tears in my eyes when I first saw the bronze Charioteer at Delphi, and sat for half an hour just living by gazing. Aesthetic experience – of the Charioteer, of seeing a Bellini Madonna for the first time, or walking up the hot bright steps into the cool light and rhythms of San Miniato al Monte – can be cognitive, a tacit knowing that changes the coordinates of the way the world is seen from that point on in ways that evades linear, rational, explanation.[27] It just is. Someone once said to me that her life divided into pre-Dante and post-Dante. She was, as it happens, exactly *nel mezzo del cammin di nostra vita*.

Nefertiti's is thought to have been a funerary portrait. But did she really look like that? how naturalistic was Egyptian funerary portraiture of that period? You can never know, I suppose, but in the room next to Nefertiti's solitary state, the sculptures seem to be of real people.

Portraits. There is a scribe sitting with his wife, and if you walk behind them she has her right arm affectionately round his shoulders. Does one glimpse a love beyond time? Impossible to say. But the impression of people and personality is powerful. The General of Lower Egypt: a real, punchy, pugnacious person. I would not like to get across him.

★

And in another part of the forest, (or room in the museum to be more accurate)... from fallen Troy to fallen Jerusalem to fallen Berlin...

> Lo, all our pomp of yesterday
> Is one with Nineveh and Tyre!

When the conquering Nebuchadnezzar deported the Israelites to Babylon in 598BC, and they endured their captivity there, they would have seen the eighth gate of the City, the elaborate glazed brick Ishtar Gate, its huge striding lions, and its stupendous processional way. Some certainly will have gone past these actual bricks, these lions not of Judah. 'By the waters of Babylon we sat down and wept, when we remembered thee, O Jerusalem... how shall we sing the Lord's song in a strange land?' And so the Diaspora began, scattering to the four quarters of the globe the Chosen People. It is hard here not to think of other more recent gates the deported Jews passed through, with *Arbeit macht frei* written on them.

The Ishtar Gate, reconstructed in the Museum with the original bricks when German power was at its height, is next to the replica of the huge basalt finger on which is inscribed in cuneiform the Law Code of Hammurabi. That code is a thousand years older. An eye for an eye... the old unforgiving treadmill. Justice, of a sort, as the world understands justice, but no mercy.

★

The place is made of contrasts. Ruins: memorials to, and of, ruins. Aggressive modernity: tomorrow is what matters. Cut adrift from ancient sorrow! The young folk posing for selfies by the Brandenburg Gate or Checkpoint Charlie, wearing Stasi hats, are innocent and innocents: they do not yet know how, if, sorrow will claim them. We walked past the grandiloquent dullness of Berlin Cathedral, and caught the bus to the Kurfürstendamm. We got off at the ruined church they call *der hohle Zahn*, the 'hollow tooth'. That would do for later. Lunch called. We walked down Tauentzienstraße to the KaDeWe – the Kaufhaus des Westens. Nearby, in May 1912, Rupert Brooke began – or says he did – 'The Old Vicarage, Grantchester', which is one benchmark for all who practise nostalgia and dream of an England that never was. Auden and Isherwood drank there; Isherwood dreamed up Sally Bowles. (It was known colloquially as

Café Größenwahn – the Café Delusions of Grandeur.)
We took the lift up to the KDW food hall, ascending
silently past clothing and kitchen goods and furniture
and whatever else to acres of beautiful, plenteous food.
We ordered *Weissbier* and *Bratwurst mit Kartoffelsalat*: after
all, when in Rome... Afterwards, burpily happy, we went
down into the cold grey street. Outside this temple to
consumption of all kinds, in the bitter wind, gypsies in
colourful dresses begged. As their ancestors had done. 'A
picture to the place/ A quiet, pilfering, unprotected race,'
John Clare calls them. Further on, a man with a face that
brooked no questions silently held out a dingy cap. The
small rain was streaking his hair flat on his forehead. I had
no change to give him.

We walked, not talking now, to the Hollow Tooth, the
Kaiser Wilhelm Memorial Church. They built it two
years after his death in 1888. If only he had not lived
so long, if only his son had not succeeded only when
he himself was dying, Bismarck's long and rapacious
rule might have ended and the world been spared the
consequences... But might have beens are meaningless
byways. It happened. Inside the ruined tower remain
some of the costly mosaics that once proclaimed the might
of the Second Reich. Along the vault is a procession of
Hohenzollern princes, early, mediaeval, more recent.
Other mosaics show important monarchs in medieval
Germany. All are in the pomp of politic piety. The
new Emperor, dead a few years when the mosaics were

made, is a new Charlemagne, and behind him, following dutifully, with the same expression of stern resolve on his face, is his grandson, now Emperor, the useless left arm deftly hidden. The succession to the new Empire is in safe hands. Or one unsafe one.

In 1916, some German journals carried the story that on a hillock where lay the bodies of scores of young men with their lives before them, fallen in the terrible combats of Flanders field, William II had halted, and, after a moment of silent meditation, had cried out, 'Ich habe das nicht gewöllt!' – 'I have not wished that!' But it was a consequence of consequence of consequence of choice: no escape from responsibility.[28]

Inside the new church, on the south side, is a large drawing. Its fragile paper shows a charcoal sketch of the Blessed Virgin. A German soldier who knew he would soon die drew it during the terrible siege of Stalingrad. Below the vault of kings and princes, the romanticised procession of pomp and ancient circumstance, just where the light catches it, is the Cross of Nails from the roof of Coventry Cathedral, burnt out in an air raid in 1940. After the raid, the Provost of Coventry, Richard Howard, inscribed on the walls of the roofless chancel, 'Father forgive.' For we are all guilty.

★

We had decided, Rosanna and I, to walk to the Jewish Museum in silence. I feared what experience lay ahead. Under that leaden sky, with those dead trees of Christmas outside the houses, waiting for the dump truck to take them away, it was hard not to remember those other roads winding:

> ...in the listlessness of ancient war,
> Languor of broken steel,
> Clamour of confused wrong, apt
> In silence. Memory is strong
> Beyond the bone

As T.S. Eliot knew, the burden of too much knowledge is very heavy – but is human sympathy too big a burden to bear when others bore so much more, and the fear first? What I have is nothing to what they felt. There was a letter from Theresienstadt on display, and the clear cursive German hand traces the black ink across the page with cheerful news about moving in with a little boy who needs to get to sleep, as if they were simply moving house in an unmad world. Whom is the writer trying to reassure, whose fears allay?

Rosanna had relatives who died in Theresienstadt. Now they are just another few names, an entry and a date, in the archives in the Wiener Library. After D-Day, the Nazis permitted representatives from the Danish Red Cross and the International Red Cross to visit Theresienstadt in order to quieten rumours about the extermination camps. Theresienstadt was presented as a 'model camp.' It worked, the Red Cross made a favourable report, and following the visit, the Nazis decided to make a propaganda film in the camp. A Jewish prisoner, Kurt Gerron, an experienced director and actor, directed it. He had appeared with Marlene Dietrich in von Sternberg's *The Blue Angel*. The film was intended to show how well the Jews were living under the kindly protection of the Third Reich. The Jews of Theresienstadt apparently lived a relatively comfortable existence despite the hardships of the war, with a thriving cultural centre, a bandstand in the park, a café, shops and a bank. The children were told that they must call the camp SS leader 'Uncle.' When he gave them a tin of sardines – some of them would never have seen such a thing, let alone eaten the contents – on camera they were primed to chorus, 'Not sardines *again*, Uncle!' Shooting took eleven days in September 1944, as the leaves were turning gold and falling. As soon as the film was finished, the director and most of the cast were dispatched – the word dehumanises them to bits of cargo, or parcels, just things – to the gas chambers of Auschwitz, and then to the autumn bonfires of the crematorium. When the Russians arrived at the camp in May 1945, they found thousands of boxes full of ashes. They made a human chain to dump them in the river Ohře nearby. The ashes would float grey for a while on the surface, then be whirled away by the current to where the Ohře flows into the mighty Elbe, and thence to the anonymity of the sea. So many lives.

I had read H. G. Adler's account of Theresienstadt. In the
1780s the Emperor Joseph II built it on a grid pattern as a
garrison for 4000 soldiers, naming it after his mother (and
so recently co-ruler), Maria Theresa. But by 1943 45,600
people, mainly Jews, were crammed into the place, many
elderly and sick. Many sent there had no grasp, could
not grasp, what awaited them: one classy woman from
Frankfurt, getting off the packed train, asked a young
man – he was one of those who did survive – 'Young
man, please find me a nice hotel.' Even when what
was to happen *was* clear, in very midst of darkness and
degradation, they made an amazing cultural life: over
2900 lectures, and chamber music concerts, given by a
mainly highly educated body of inmates. There were
15 performances of Verdi's *Requiem*. (What must it have
been like to sing that *Dies Irae*?) Light in the darkness,
and the darkness comprehended it not. The grey-clad
guards looked on, secure in Himmler's reassurance (in a
speech to his underlings at Poznan) that they remained
decent, civilised men while processing mass murder.
'Only obeying orders.' Some went home to their families
and played Mozart. The régime turned good into bad
and bad into good: 'Evil be thou my good' says Milton's
Satan. Arriving in Auschwitz, Primo Levi tells of trying
to quiet his thirst on an icicle. A guard chopped the icicle
away. Levi asked why. 'Here there is no why,' said the
guard. Lying became necessary, a good – to survive, to
quiet one's conscience. Anyone, whether or not SS or
those Jewish functionaries who to save themselves (for a

time) co-operated in the implementing of immoral orders became pulled into complicity, a reorienting of the moral compass to nihilism. Yet when language loses connection to truth and honesty, how is human life possible? The sleep of reason begets monsters. How do you answer, as Karl Popper pointed out, the Nazi to whom you have *proved* the nonsense of his doctrine, when he says, 'I spit on your proof'?

Iris Murdoch once wrote a powerful book, *The Sovereignty of Good* (1970). If they were so sure what they were doing was 'right' – as Himmler stressed to his underlings in that speech in Poznan – why did they bother, on Hitler's orders, to make Theresienstadt look so civilised for the Red Cross? How did the SS guard stand being called 'Uncle', by smiling children? Why in 1936, before the Olympics, when Berlin was full of visitors, did they bother to clear the newsstands of Julius Streicher's rabid anti-Semitic paper, *Der Sturmer*? Why were so many of the killing processing plants located in the east, outside Germany's borders? Was it lest ordinary Germans, many with a touching if naïve faith in Hitler even to the end, should be forced to know that concentration camps, of which there were many, terrible enough in all conscience, on German soil, were only a hint of what the régime was doing? This is the terrible paradox of evil: it has no power unless it pretends to be, can masquerade as, good. It is caught it in the web of The Good, it has no language of itself. It is utterly sterile, parasitic. You cannot invent a new primary colour. The Devil appears in the likeness of an angel of light, like our heart's desire, as they used to say six hundred years ago. He has to, or he is powerless.

★

The baroque façade of the Jewish Museum hardly prepares you for the utterly disorienting deconstructivist extensions Daniel Libeskind designed. His building is a twisted zig-zag you can get to only by an underground passage from the old building: the two have no visible connection above ground. Their two worlds seem miles apart. Yet somehow one led — leads — to the other. Libeskind said he wanted his building to embody three ideas: the impossibility of understanding Berlin's history without understanding the enormous intellectual, economic and cultural contribution made by Jewish Berliners; the necessity of integrating physically and spiritually the meaning of the Holocaust into the city's consciousness and memory; thirdly, that only through acknowledging and incorporating this erasure and void of Jewish life in Berlin, might the history of Berlin and Europe have a human future. A line of voids, empty spaces that cut through the building from basement to roof, represent 'That which can never be exhibited when it comes to Jewish Berlin history: Humanity reduced to ashes.'

They welcome you to the museum most affably. The staff wear scarves which sensitively allude to Jewish prayer shawls, and they chat cheerfully as they sell you a ticket and point out the loos. For them it is just a daily job, this custodianship of the history of official murder, and I am sure they joke and flirt and get bored just like any other museum guide or attendant. And why not? Did one expect hushed voices as at a funeral? And indeed, the museum is not just about the horrors of that terrible last century, but also celebrates the huge artistic, intellectual and industrial role Jews – often German first, Jews second – played in German life.

Somewhere Walter Benjamin, that remarkable interpreter of the occluded meanings of everyday things, of commodity, remarks that objects preserve memory and remind us of what is lost. Their presence points to what is absent. It may be in his maddening and exhilarating and tiresome and unputdownable *One-Way Street* (1928), where he evokes a dense cityscape of shops, cafes, apartments, all buzzing with noisy social interactions, plastered with advertisements, signs, posters, slogans. There is no semblance of linear narrative, and he entices you in a seemingly random sequence of reminiscences, dreamlike fantasies, aphorisms, jokes, off-the-cuff remarks, serious philosophical issue, and seemingly unserious philosophical parodies, and cutting political commentaries. It's not a bad impression of what it must have been like to know the ferment of Berlin in the

Weimar period. (Benjamin killed himself on the Spanish border in 1940. He was trying to escape to the USA from the Nazis.) The material things in the museum are trivial, unimportant, mostly valueless, but are also threads in a frayed tapestry that you pull and will never know what will unravel. A letter. A cup and saucer. A little menorah, used in Theresienstadt. A neatly folded towel which a mother carefully packed into a case when her little son was going away to safety on the *Kindertransport*, so that he could wash and be clean. Never unfolded, it was all the son ever now had of his mother, the neat folds into which her hands had packed her love. A notice by a school report pointed out that 'racial theory' was part of the curriculum even in primary school, and told of a small boy, the only Jew in his class, in a small village primary school having to do the subject. Classmates looked at him sideways to see how he was taking it. There would have been sniggers. The outcast. The scapegoat.

I went into the Void. Down to the cross-perspective, disorientating underworld. Asymmetric, dark, menacingly silent, cold, door bangs to behind you: can you escape? Useless. Utterly overwhelming. You can just hear the noise of the city. Occasionally a siren of mercy faintly, going away. Libeskind said architecture should not be comfortable. This building silently screams. The void, as in the room into which Mark Studdock is put in C. S. Lewis' *That Hideous Strength,* refuses rationality. This building does to you what it should. Everything in its garden, its rooms, is out of true, out of vertical, square, uncomfortable: eyes and feet lie to each other. But it tells the truth: it must do even if not in words. 'Here there is no why.'

Walter Benjamin remarks that men returning from the First World War battlefields were not richer but poorer in communicable experience. He was right: I knew some long ago, before I was wise enough to know the right questions to ask them. But how could you communicate the experience of surviving the camps? How, even worse, could you communicate, come to terms with, running them, delivering supplies, taking away the products of slave labour, organizing transport, packing men, women and children into wagons – standing room only, move down the car please! – and hosing the fouled interiors out as they were cleared of their cargo: Jews, Gypsies, political prisoners, homosexuals, the crippled – the list goes on. How did you cope, as many must have done, with pulling the bodies out of the gas chambers, extracting the gold teeth and packing the remains in the crematorium in the most economical way, for fuel is short? How do you ever communicate that? Many who had served the Nazis served the newly democratic Bundesrepublik, for you can't run a state without using the people who know where the keys are and where the pipes run. The psychiatrists of the German Psychiatric Association in the 1930s consented to the murder of some 200,000 of their charges who were in mental hospitals. Many still practised professionally after the war. What else could they do? Nobody is clean.

★

Walter Michael Goldfeld, successful Berlin businessman, cultured, musical, well read, bought *The Times* so that he could get an idea of what was really going on behind the smoke and mirrors, the fake news, of Goebbels' propaganda machine. He could quite easily have moved with his family to the USA when the first flurries of the storm that would come were felt, for he had contacts and there was no shortage of money. But to some degree he shared, as did many decent ordinary folk, the new feeling of optimism in Germany after the stupid and vindictive humiliation of the Versailles settlement, after the economic chaos that the fools who imposed it were warned by Keynes it would cause, and after the miseries of Weimar. The economy was doing well, and there was a new pride in the *Vaterland* – for which Michael had loyally fought, in the front line, in the Great War, winning the Iron Cross. The Nazi publicity machine – the rallies, the uniforms, the singing, the torchlight processions – were all huge morale boosters. But when possible emigration to the US came up in conversation, he would say, '*Hab'ich hier Murmeln gespielt?*' ('Did I not play marbles here?'): America was not home, it had no ghosts he owned. (I know what he meant.) And his business was doing very well: to be in metals at this time, in the new German boom, was a profitable place to be, especially if like him you had real technical knowledge of metal, and his firm had an international clientele. Like so many Jews, he was German through and through, for generation upon generation. And what was he to do about his parents, also good Germans through and through? Like so many, he thought the Nazis were a passing phenomenon. The good people of Germany, the land of Goethe, Schopenhauer and Beethoven – his selection, according to his son's memoir – would surely come to their senses. Surely the episodes in 1933 were an aberration, when the SA systematically smashed the windows and looted the contents of Jewish shops while decent citizens, their neighbours probably, looked on: probably horrified, but not daring to intervene against the uniformed thugs? (Who were once helpless babies innocent of wrongdoing.)

Heinz Peter Goldfeld saw a knot of boys gathered round a poster on a wall, laughing and pointing, laughing with that exaggerated body language when boys know it isn't really funny but, well, you want to show you are one of the lads. He knew one or two of them. He pushed his way to the front. There was an awkward silence. On the wall was one of the anti-Semitic posters – 'The Jews are Germany's curse!' – that Julius Streicher's *Der Sturmer* distributed. 'What are you doing here?' 'I wanted to see what I was supposed to look like.'

November 9, 1938. It is getting dark, for the nights are long now. A young boy is running an errand, making his way to the local shops, in his own little world, thinking of nothing much, hungry for his meal (when are young boys not?). He does well at school: in fact he is a very clever child, with real academic promise, and his reports, which we have, say as much. Suddenly he hears ahead of him the noise of windows being smashed, and, as he later remembered 'shouts of jubilation,' but he cannot see what is happening. A man comes towards him quickly from the source of the noise, and grasps his shoulder, urgently, earnestly and quietly saying, 'Go home, quickly: go home another way. Do not stop, or look at *anything*, but go home. Go to your mother.' He never knew who the man was.

Even Geoffrey Dawson's *Times,* which had been pretty supportive of Hitler, wrote after that, 'No foreign propagandist bent upon blackening Germany before the world could outdo the tale of burnings and beatings, of blackguardly assaults on defenceless and innocent people, which disgraced that country yesterday.' *Kristallnacht*.

Later that month, four SS men came to the door at dawn and barged in, and arrested his father Walter Michael Goldfeld on charges relating to Acts Against the German Reich. He was taken to Sachsenhausen. Michael was lucky: his wife was able to pull strings so that after three weeks he came home. Peter wrote, 'I remember the day he came home, looking haggard and very thin, his scalp roughly shaven, with his suit (he always wore beautifully tailored suits of fine cloth, even to go to prison) all crumpled up.' 'He remembered when a group of them were ordered to strip naked and line up against a wall, in order to wash those *dreckige Juden*, and fire hoses were trained on them, concentrating the jets on their genitals. Several men screamed with pain, collapsed, and were ordered up again. Michael just gritted his teeth and tried not to react at all, though in real pain, and he actually heard one of the brutes say, "Don't bother with that one! Let's concentrate on the weaklings!" One wonders how a supposedly civilised Nation could have so many pathological sadists among them, and how it came about that that they came to be so dehumanised, so debased. The awful thing is that somewhere in the world this sort of thing is still going on.'

Peter's words are bland... Did we ever think it would not? Give a little brief authority to so many men and just watch them misuse it, become bullies. Come clean about it. Give them uniforms and let the wrong people generate an *esprit de corps,* and just watch the slide. Guantanamo Bay, Abu Ghraib were run by nations who claim the moral high ground in human rights, and readily preach to others. (But does the imperfection of the speaker invalidate the rightness of what is being spoken?) America has already had two Presidents who officially see nothing wrong with torture. I sometimes compare, with great disquiet, the screaming typography, the strategies, the tendentiousness of British tabloids now with Streicher's *Der Sturmer*. Such a comparison makes one almost long for the *Daily Express* of the time when Prince Philip could call it merely a 'bloody awful newspaper.'

The Goldfelds were lucky. They could make preparations to leave. They had friends in England, who would take in the children, and then the parents would follow. They were luckier still: Jews had to hand in all their valuables to the authorities before leaving Germany. It took a longish time to get good paste copies made of the family jewellery, but in the end they fooled the robber State, and the real things were smuggled out sewn into hems and coats and linings: dangerous, for if discovered they would have been shot. The children duly went, excited, even elated, on the *Kindertransport* to the Hook of Holland, to a crossing at night of the sea they had never seen, and then to the welcome of friends in an England that then made a sanctuary for the refugee from tyranny, the broken, the man who had fallen among thieves.

Rosanna wore her Russian grandmother's pearls and earrings when she married me. We eat off the Rosenthal china her parents managed to bring out of Germany. These are her anchors to that side of what made her. Rosanna has her grandfather's Iron Cross, which he won fighting for the Kaiser. We do not know what to do with it.

Peter had a schoolfriend, a very talented young violinist. They said farewells. Peter wrote that he asked the other boy if he would be leaving. 'Where to? We know nobody outside Germany. Where could we go?' Peter never heard from him again.

★

I stood with Peter's daughter outside the flat on the corner of Witzlebenstrasse where he had lived. Just down the road is the school he attended before he had to go to a special Jewish school. There are children's bicycles neatly parked outside. The Goldfelds had the flat on the first floor, on the corner, with a balcony. Very desirable, for it overlooked the large Lietzensee park with its trees and curving lake and rockery, kiosks and water garden. He would have played there as a boy. The emptiness of the park, that midwinter day, was full of ghosts. You could almost see the shades of long-dead governesses (English of course) and perambulators, and lapdogs on leads, and waisted dresses with bustles, and hats that demanded a whole aviary to plume them, and ladies accompanied by courteous, attentive men in *favoris* and top hats, who raised their hats with a slight inclination of the upper body as they passed a lady they knew. You can remember the summer boating on the lake, the gentlemen elegant at the sculls, and children feeding the ducks. This winter day, the ducks are quiet, not very interested in anything. Where a big plane tree, well over a century old, leans over the water, two Mandarin drakes cosy up to an indifferent dowdy duck, one on each side. They nudge her, gently. 'Look how smart I am!' If ducks had moustachios to twirl, these would be doing it. The tree, and its fellow planes, are old enough to have been trees that Peter played under, and his father. There are very few really old trees in Berlin, trees that remember the summers of old Europe before the lights went out. Most the bombing destroyed.

On the ground floor below the flat where the Gestapo banged on the door early one morning to take his father away, there is a café. There may have been one there then: we do not know. But we could not bring ourselves to go in.

Facing it, over the road is the big nineteenth century grey stone pile, No. 1 Witzlebenstrasse, which was the Reichsmilitärgericht HQ. The figure of blind Justice is sculpted in the keystone of the great doorway. It became the highest appeal court of the Wehrmacht, which condemned untold conscientious objectors to death. A metal plaque on the railings records an Austrian farmer, Franz Jägerstätter: aged 36, he was shot. He was later declared a martyr and beatified by the Roman Catholic Church. How many others? And how many poor men were trapped by the rules of the organisation they served into pronouncing such a sentence?

It was not comfortable, this pilgrimage to family places, and it got worse. In some streets you trip over the

Stolpersteine, 'trip stones', little bronze squares let into the pavement, with 'Here lived', then a name, a date of birth, a date of deportation, and a date of murder. They have them in Prague too, but too many cities do not. We walked down a quiet street of good apartment houses to where Michael's parents had lived. He had had to leave the old folk behind when he left Germany, just as Rosanna's Russian grandmother, trapped in Manchuria and then escaping to China, had had to leave her parents behind in a Russia in chaos and famine after the bloodiness of the 1917 revolution. (She never knew what happened to them.) Michael's parents had been taken to Theresienstadt – a long enough journey in all conscience for two old people, but better in some ways than another person in the street who had been taken by slow train to be murdered in Riga. Outside one apartment block, just across the road from where they had lived, were seven *Stolpersteine.* A child of 8; a man of 35; a couple of 82 and 68, taken at different times. They must have watched their neighbours disappear, never to return, looking out from the ordinariness of their curtained windows, waiting, waiting for the blows on their own door. They would have known the parents. Most moving, one couple were taken on the same day Michael's parents were: neighbours in life and death. Further down the street a big enamelled metal notice on a lamp post reminds you that little Jewish children could use no transport to school unless it was over 5km from their homes. A gratuitous meanness. And murder for no other crime, as Churchill put it, than having been born.

Is this institutionalisation, industrialisation, of mass murder, with all the efficiency and trivialisation that technology can offer, what all Europe has stood for leads up to? Knowing the horrors of the twentieth century is a bruise on our minds for ever. Massacres there have been before and will be again, but never before has it been industrialized, documented, bureaucratized, trivialised with the full sanction of the lawfully elected government of a civilised state. There is only a very brittle scab over that new horror. Morally, it must be pressed, for we are formed by the events that made these things, heirs unwillingly complicit by simply being in that new twist to original sin. A resolute look at the crimes and follies of the world is a *duty*. For society is a contract between the dead, the living and the unborn.

★

In the middle of the Bethlehemkirchplatz, in Friedrichstadt, there is a gaunt steel ghost. It stands exactly on the mosaic lines marking where the Bohemian or Bethlehem Church stood until the fire from heaven destroyed it in 1943. The thin metal lines scribe on the sky the silhouette of the lost church. King Friedrich Wilhelm I of Prussia had built it in the 1730s after welcoming Czech Protestant refugees fleeing persecution by the Catholic Hapsburgs. It reminds of the generous tolerance that pervaded the foundation of the Prussian state, and is at once a memorial to a more humane age, a reminder of a barbarous one, and a hope for a future. No European state except Russia in the eighteenth century used torture: they knew it did not work. Nor did they ever utterly defeat an enemy in their mainly short wars. They knew the enemy might be next year's ally. (We threw it all away in the folly of Romanticism and Revolutions – and they *are* connected). After all, when Carl von Clausewitz in *On War* famously says that war is an extension of diplomacy by other means, man of the Enlightenment as he was, he was thinking of war between professional soldiers, and he had no vision of what has come to be the norm, total war and Mutual Assured Destruction aka MAD.

The Holocaust Memorial: 2711 five sided – but they seem to have only four – monoliths of grey concrete hold the light in a cold grip. None is exactly rectangular, none exactly aligned, none exactly vertical, some are only ankle high, others tower over weak humans. Their tops undulate. The cobbled paths between them undulate as well. Feet lie to eyes and *vice versa*. Everything is labyrinthine, out of true, but no monster lurks at the centre. There *is* no centre. The monster, the Man-Beast, is all around. Nowhere are you out of sight, able to get away, for all those long dark alleys lead to the watchers outside. Is the man-beast everywhere?

A school trip plays hide and seek, happily, noisily, in a place that shrieks silence.

★

Scapegoats. The ancient Jews each year at the Day of Atonement ritually and symbolically loaded the people's sins, intentional and not, onto two goats, and as *Leviticus* 6 enjoins, chose by lot one to be sacrificed, a blood offering before the Holy of Holies, and the other to be driven out into the wilderness to be the companion and victim of demons like Azazel. Plato in *The Republic* says that no human society could ever tolerate a wholly just and good man: he would be cast out by those who could not stomach their unavoidable perception of their own guilt forced on them by his simple existence. He would be impaled; which was the Persian equivalent of crucifixion. And this would be seen as a laudable act of justice. Humanity – human societies – comes together, finds a reassuring identity, a terrible bonding, by unloading its hatred, fear and half-understood, half-felt, guilt onto a scapegoat, an outsider, or on one of our own whom we have cast out. The anthropologist and philosopher René Girard says we feel better about ourselves, defuse our sense of guilt or inadequacy, by excluding that which challenges us, disturbs us, the Other, whom we might secretly envy. Envy, anger, frustration – they are related – gradually build up in human societies until a tipping point is reached when order and reason cede to mob rule, violence, chaos. To quell this madness, which is an existential threat to society, an exposed or vulnerable person or group is singled out as a sink for all the bad feeling, and the bad feeling bred from the bad feeling. The scapegoat: and dehumanizing the victims – *Untermenschen* – makes the persecution more potent and less guilt-inducing, and may even suggest it has a sort of pre-ordained, cosmic inevitability. (Add Social Darwinism for a truly hellish brew.) Thus is a mechanism made not only to relieve anger and envy, but also to generate pleasurable feelings of piety and self-righteous indignation. (Himmler in Poznan?) And creating villains necessarily implies corresponding heroes: we cast ourselves as heroes, our cause as noble. The myriad starlings, each different, each one unique, individual, wheeling and gyring in their murmuration, become something joyously more than a mere aggregate, and the great swift shape of the looming Beast in the sky frightens, drives away their predators from where they will settle to roost. But woe betide the starling that breaks away, goes on its own, for surely keen-eyed kestrel and swift sparrowhawk, buzzard and harrier are waiting, and know not mercy.

★

It is not the knowledge, or what the story, or story of the past, 'means' or 'what it might tell us' that matters – if such things exist at all. It is the experience that changes, that is 'the meaning'. The story of Agamemnon's coming home, processing in pomp with his booty and war-won slaves, including mad Cassandra, through the Lion Gate of Mycenae, and Clytemnestra's axe-wielding welcome as he bathed, and the entail of vengeance – fratricide, cannibalism, murder, matricide – in which that story is located; Euripides' Hecuba's terrible revenge on Polymestor for the killing of her son; the anger-driven tragedy of the *Iliad* – these do not 'mean' anything. They provoke our imaginative memory, they became part of our mental maps, they alter the way we think for ever. The tragedy of the Jews, a crescendo from the first Captivity to the Fall of Jerusalem to the Holocaust, does not 'mean': it is. By knowing we are both complicit and victim. We carry our history like a troubling ancient wound, a scar.

But.

In this hard place it does well to recall Maximilian Kolbe, a Polish Franciscan priest, prisoner 16770. When a prisoner tried to escape, the SS guards decided that ten men should die for his 'crime'. Maximilian volunteered to take the place of one. He was starved for two weeks. Still alive, they killed him by lethal injection on August 14, 1941. Then I think of Sophie Scholl, a Munich student, beheaded by the Nazis in 1943 for distributing anti-Nazi pamphlets. So were her brother, and many others. Their pamphlets called on Germans passively to resist the Nazi government, basing the intellectual argument on both Biblical and philosophical grounds. Brother and sister were allowed no defence in court. Her last words:

How can we expect righteousness to prevail when there is hardly anyone willing to give himself up individually to a righteous cause? Such a fine, sunny day, and I have to go, but what does my death matter, if through us thousands of people are awakened and stirred to action?

A copy of her sixth pamphlet was smuggled out of Germany through Scandinavia to the UK by Helmuth James, Graf von Moltke, descendant of the Moltke who commanded the Prussian forces in both the Austro-Prussian and Franco-Prussian Wars. The Allies in mid-1943 dropped millions of copies over Germany, retitling it *The Manifesto of the Students of Munich*. Sophie's stand, and the fact that the German government has put a bust of her in the Walhalla Ludwig II built by the Danube near Regensburg in Bavaria for all those other German heroes (some of whom are hardly that), reclaims the whole idea of German cultural and moral greatness. The whole world owes so much to this untidy, inventive, annoying land and its conglomerate peoples. And I take my hat off to the exemplary moral courage with which its people and governments have faced up to the very darkest of their past.

Peter Goldfeld and his family did go back. He and his Russian refugee wife, whom he had met and fallen for in Australia where the tides of history had washed them up, went back in the 1950s to the Heartland, to the culture that had made them, to Berlin, even to Wagner's

Bayreuth[29] only some few years after the War. Later they took their daughters to know their heritage. In the 1980s the Mayor, the Regierender Bürgermeister, invited Peter to Berlin. Peter went back to the reconstructed KaDeWe, to the food hall to which as a child he had been taken for those longed-for special treats. For he loved his food. When much later, full of years and wisdom and with no rancour, as he sat in his room he asked for *Spreewälder salz-dill gurken* and salami and pumpernickel, for the tastes of his childhood. The pull of places where you played marbles is strong.

★

Opposite the hotel, nearly, was the Brecht House, the house on Chausseestraße where after the exile Bertolt Brecht and Helene Weigel lived. As I pass I glance through wide windows into a room packed with eager faces, all listening intently to an exchange between a mop-haired, smiling, middle aged man in a sweater and open shirt, who is clearly the evening's speaker, and a leather jacketed woman (of whom I only get the back view but whose set of shoulder radiates high seriousness.) The topic advertised on the poster is *Das Freie Wort. Vom öffentlichen Gebrauch der Vernunft im postfaktischen Zeitalter –* 'The Free Word: of the public use of reason in the post fact age.' 'Post-Fact': a time when the Big Lie said loudly enough often becomes Truth. We have been here before. Did not Dr Johnson say 'The unadorned truth keeps humanity from despair'?

The Mystery of Love. The Victim is not dying to propitiate an angry God but to take upon Himself, absorb like a sponge that is then thrown away, the cruelty and fallenness of humanity. Hope. The darkness cannot in the end win: it implodes into nothingness. The parasite is utterly dependent on its host. *E quindi uscimmo a riveder le stelle...* And we came out and saw again the stars. All shall be well. All manner of thing shall be well.

V

IN SOUNDINGS

The Paths of the Dead

Forth, pilgrim, forth! Forth, beste out of thy stal!
Know thy countree, look up, thank God of al;
Hold the heye wey and lat thy ghost thee lede,
And trouthe thee shal delivere, it is no drede.

Chaucer, *Balade de bon conseyl*

Clearly as if it were yesterday, I remember reading for the first time W. H Hudson's *A Shepherd's Life*, and *Afoot in England*. Richard Jefferies' *Bevis: the Story of a Boy* I loved – and wished that someone had let me make a gun *that worked* in a countryside where every day was summer. A dear, dead, friend once gave me George Borrow's *Wild Wales*. Those books spoke to, gave voice to, an already passionate love for an England beyond where the pavement ends, and a fear that it might be about to be lost. For I also read – all my generation did – Rachel Carson's *Silent Spring*, and her words, effective for a time, are needed even more now, and at home in Lancashire I had seen favourite woods in full leaf ripped up. Little ponds where I caught newts and watched the summer dragonflies pausing thoughtfully on the reeds were filled in, all so that They could build yet more lines of dull bungalows.

Once it was possible, an active pleasure indeed, for someone like Borrow or Hudson to tramp through miles of countryside, meeting interest and hospitality but not losing that aloneness that feeds thought. Many did it: many had to. Many chose to do it, in the years before the Reformation, as pilgrims. I can imagine a quieter, slower England where cattle and sheep were walked to market, grazing as they went. It is not so long ago: almost within my memory, and certainly within my grandfather's. Imagine the little cattle raised on the Hebrides being swum across to the mainland at the slack of the tide to begin their journey to the hungry Lowlands, or even further south. Imagine a Britain – a Europe – covered by a dendritic web of paths gradually and circuitously converging on the bigger and bigger branches and ultimately on the trunk route to the big cities. Imagine London's Smithfield loud with the bellowing and bleating of beasts, the streets running with the warm blood of slaughtered animals – the greatest meat market in the world, as Daniel Defoe described it in the early 1700s. Imagine Longacre being exactly that: the long acre where the animals were pent before slaughter. Imagine the Shambles of York or Manchester as the butchers' rows, alive with flies in summer, terrified bullocks snorting and rolling their big soft eyes as they smelt the blood of their companions. And more coming. In 1855 Smithfield Market had to be moved to the outskirts of London, so great was the trade, so large the numbers of stock being driven through the streets.

There was a little wizened man with a nut brown face, a greasy trilby and a battered gabardine mackintosh who hovered around the cattle sales on sale day at the Cattle Market in Bury St Edmunds. He had a hazel stick, barked, and polished where his hands had held it for years, with a nail whipped to its end. If you bought a steer, say, he would sidle up to you and touch his trilby, and say, 'Drive thi beast home for thee, bor?' He got little trade when I knew Bury, but old men I knew had had him (or men like him) drive their purchases home after market, a slow progress through the quiet lanes, with a pause now and then for the beasts to take a bite of grass, or a drink at a weed-mantled roadside pond. Impossible now.

He – I never knew his name – was the last, I suppose, of those men, the drovers, whose life was spent driving the slow flocks and herds along the drove roads. A tough, almost nomadic, life, and in hard weather they welcomed the shelter and food and drink of inns like King's House on the bleak expanse of Rannoch Moor, or the Drovers' at Inverarnan by Loch Lomond, or Tan Hill on the moors above Kirkby Stephen. (Now the last caters for the car trade, and welcomes stag and hen parties, as well as walkers on the Pennine Way.) Their tracks – well, who knows how old they are? Over the centuries, in the clay counties, some of them have cut deep into the land. Unlike the narrow packhorse roads, like those over the passes in the fells of Cumbria and Craven – Sty Head, Stake Pass, Esk Hause, Smardale – which were fine for laden horses in single file, the drove roads can be 80 or 90 feet wide, often walled in drystone for mile upon mile, able to take herds or flocks of many animals, moving slowly, munching the grass as they go. (In the softer south, they are hedged, and the hedges spread as the animals no longer graze the new growth, and sometimes close over the ancient track.) I have walked many of them in the Pennines, and have been glad of the occasional deliberate dog-leg turn in the road and its walls, which offers some shelter for animals and men in severe wind or rain or snow.

Once I walked across England, alone, by old, empty ways, packhorse way and drove way and corpse way, from sea to sea. Why? I do not now know. Sometimes a starling needs to leave the great dance of everyday, fly its own path, in order to know its place as the dance resumes (like the bravura solo of the man in the dance in Szeged square melting back into the pattern of the dance and the bell-skirted girls.) Perhaps it was connected with the watershed of our son leaving home, going off far faring in icy lands I had known and would know again (but I did not know that), where the summer sun never set. Jenny had her own way of coping with that watershed, perhaps more effective than mine. Perversely – yet not quite so, for I felt I ought to get fit for the highest hills – I chose to do the traverse east to west, into the prevailing weather rather than having it at my back. There was a lot of weather. I saw hardly anyone. I camped some nights in the shelter of ancient walls with only Rough Fell or

Swaledale sheep within earshot, sometimes finding a bed and breakfast so that I could wash. Going up the dale with the Pennine moors before me I discovered just how many different sorts of stone stiles there might be, no two alike, and none easy in the damp with a big rucksack. I crossed the Pennine watershed by Nine Standards Rigg, in a horizontal rain, sploshing my way between the sodden peat hags. A respite in a Homely House at Kirkby Stephen, and next morning, on a day that seemed too bright to last, I was off again, following the old tracks across the limestone where sheep nibbled as their smaller ancestors had done thirty centuries ago, when the men who built the square fields and the round huts had found this land good, and between their settlements had made the tracks, some walled for droving stock, by which I walked. I saw no-one. Once this airy landscape was busy with work and the noise of animals and people, and sometimes, when I have walked here in fair winter weather, I have fancied I heard their voices in the wind as it combed the brown bents of the tired grasses. I dropped into the steep Potts valley and crossed the stream by the deserted farm, falling year by year into ruin as the ivy grasped it in its soft grey fingers. The rain had made the river in spate, and all the little seasonal springs were spouting into their usually dry channels, excitedly bubbling up from the limestone. Three miles east of the M6 I smelt it on the wind. Two miles east I heard it. I dripped into Shap, where the land changes from porous limestone to hard volcanic rock, and in a wet season black mud lurks. (The range of flowers and plants changes almost as sharply as you cross the road: at the ruins of Shap Abbey you see the fault.) I squelched into Patterdale, and next day had a sunny tramp up Grisedale, knees brushing the sparkling drops off the overhanging wet grasses, over to Dunmail Raise. A fresh band of rain caught me for the crossing of the next ridge from Wythburn. At last I descended from the morass of High Tove, a hill about which it is difficult to find anything affectionate to say, into beloved, familiar Borrowdale in the sunlight of a beauteous evening, calm and free. The late rain shone prismatically on the leaves, and the beck sang a loud deep song over the stones by the village. Fat Herdwick gimmers – in their woollies they care not about rain – safely grazed on the flat in-bye land in the valley bottom.

I thought it would not last. The morrow brought cloud, and mist wreathing the tops. Another front was on its way. Never mind, press on: at Seathwaite I started the ascent to Sty Head, carefully avoiding the scars modern walkers have made of the paths so that I could follow the delectably graded paved zig-zags the old folk made for their strings of pack horses going over the pass to Wasdale and down to the port which the Romans improved at Ravenglass. How old? Who knows? These passes and paths have been used since men came to this land. The Romans made their fort on Hardknott Pass to guard their traffic to Ravenglass – perhaps one of the most draughty postings in the whole empire. A lot of the walls on the hills were put up by the austere Cistercian monks, tending the sheep that made them unaccountably and undesignedly rich; some walls, the wiggly ones, are much, much older. I took a break by the tarn at Sty Head, a place full of memories. Once, when I was an undergraduate, young and foolish (not all are), I set off across its snow-covered ice and fell in, and had sternly to be sent home, with the Dean's reproach of 'Impetuous youth!' ringing in my ears; and there was once a languorous day in dappling sunlight with the children and the first Labrador splashing in the shallows while we dozed. But no dozing today. Over the higher pass to Black Sail, down Ennerdale through the dark trees, still miraculously dry, and the rain arrives just as I settle down for the night in a caravan on a farm where the lady offers Bed and Breakfast. Good. I won that one.

But the rain really meant it. It was coming down in stair rods by morning. The lady arrived at the caravan with my breakfast on a tray covered with a plastic sheet. It was good, substantial, if somewhat cool. The weather was filthy. But I was a day behind schedule and needed to catch that train at St Bees, for work will not wait.

Had I been walking to that ancient shrine of St Bega centuries ago as a pilgrim (before the Royal Injunctions of that deplorable tyrant Henry VIII banned pilgrimage), I would have been wearing a wide brimmed felt hat, a long grey cloak, and carrying a staff. If I did that sort of thing often, I might have worn little lead badges, souvenirs of various shrines visited, much as people now stick labels on the windows of their cars saying 'Torquay', or 'We've Been To [fill in as required].' As I got wetter with the rain driving into the hood of my anorak and running down my chest, I thought of the weight the long wool cloak would gather as it soaked, the drip from the soaked felt hat, and how long they would take to dry. And how foul the ways would be in the acted-out metaphor, the penance of travel. What was I, indeed, complaining about?

St Bega was, they say, an Irish princess who to avoid enforced marriage escaped across the Irish Sea to this spot that bears her name. Carved stones in the Priory church, which was controlled by the Benedictine house of St Margaret at York, certainly show that Irish-Norse Vikings settled here in the 10th century. But it was the Normans, latecomers up here, who built the fine red building that outfaces the worst the west wind can throw at it – though the struggle shows on that soft red stone. As I came out of the shelter of the headland, the wind was fierce as it came off the sea. It was a relief to come in at last out of the storm under the deeply weathered carved archivolts of the Norman doorway into the cool quiet of the nave. I stood for a moment, and little pools of water formed round each boot. I dropped my rucksack, eased my shoulders from the pull of the straps, and looked to where the rumours of the returning sun shone through the three lancet windows in the west, here, where prayer has been valid. There was nobody there except the angels.

I stripped off, put on less damp clothes. And sat, while the storm outside buffeted the old stones, erasing grain by grain yet more of the work of men's hands.

★

Coming over from Shap, via Swindale, and dropping down into Mardale, where the reservoir now covers the old village, I had picked up the old Corpse Road. Freshets of water were running down its incised steepness, ponding behind rocks, picking at the stones. Once upon a time, when parishes were bigger, settlements smaller and houses far asunder, burial in consecrated ground often meant carrying the dead over roads like this, over miles of wilderness, up hill and down dale, to the parish church. Mardale as a chapelry of Shap had no right of burial till the 1740s . The dead of that little hamlet, strapped in their shrouds to the back of a pony, were carried miles over the hills to Shap, where they could be buried. Roads like these litter the west and north of these islands, largely forgotten. They are on Skye, and Lewis, and the Lakes, and Wales. I have followed the one near Grasmere, where there is a flat stone, the Resting Stone: here the body was put down as the bearers got their breath back for the next pull up the slope. No problem going down: this was a one way traffic. Now walkers in bright clothes eat their sandwiches on it. But those paths the dead took are there in the fat soft south too, forgotten.

There is a busy road in the village near where I live called The Causeway. People assume it is something to do with water, for this is on the edge of the Fens. Not a bit of it. Centuries ago, when the monks of Ely built their canal across the fen, the commercial centre of the village moved from the higher land to be along the fen edge, as a result of the lucrative trade that developed. It grew into a new settlement – Newnham – a mile and more from the church, and so the Corpse Way was named. Again, in the hamlet where I live, which never had a parish church, the road that runs past my back door runs for half a mile as tarmac, then, when the tarmac swerves right and becomes a long straight traverse to the bank of the Cam across the fen, only recently impassable in a wet winter, it turns into a green road to the next village. Barston Drove – the road has been called that since the thirteenth century, because of the lime trees that once fringed it – runs round the low hill where a man who worked that land before me, and got the dirt of it under his fingernails, dropped a flint scraper for me to find; where Iron Age farmers stored their corn in pits; and where someone, once, dropped a coin Mark Antony had minted in Egypt. Roman *caliga* and Saxon *scoh* slipped in greasy chalky mud in winter and in summer raised the white dust along that road. For centuries, the forebears of this hamlet were carried along it to their last rest in the democracy of the dead. We know only a tiny number of their names: along it in 1521 Water de Rech would have been carried. His family – six sons and perhaps two daughters – was wealthy enough from this good land, and the water trade, to put up one of the newly fashionable brasses to him and Alice his wife in the church. Was the Richard Water who died six years earlier, and has his own brass, his father? Hard to say: but there is still a house called Water Hall, beside Barston Drove, and I have corresponded with a Water descendant who lives in Australia. But Barston Drove, with all its coming and going, all its ghosts, is seen now only by the occasional man on a tractor, the odd rider, and the fraternity of dog walkers. For though some of the old roads sometimes sleep under modern tarmac, many are just empty, no longer leading where people want to go. Prince Charles Edward in 1745 brought his army from Scotland to Kendal by the springs of the Livennet, where now the loudest summer noise above the trickle of water is the larks, through the Lune Gorge and onto the road through Killington which the busy Romans had built to get up to their forts at Brougham and Carlisle and the Wall. The secretive hedges almost close its deep track now.

★

You could become quite geeky, as they say, about old, 'lost', roads, about tracing them on maps and on the ground, just as you can get quite excited by driving along the A5, Watling Street, where it is clearly on the Roman route to Chester, or on the exhilarating A15 north of Lincoln where it rushes along the scarp to meet the Humber. There is in the Fylde of Lancashire where I grew up a persistent legend about the Dane Pad, a road crossing the quagmire of Marton Moss and leading north to – well, where? Nobody has ever been able conclusively to show it existed or where it ran. Yet Kate's Pad north to Pilling from the ford of the Wyre was real enough, and cuttings in the peats showed the split tree trunks laid end to end. It seems to have reached a crossing point on the Ribble where a ferry ran its trade into living memory: and may well go back to the Neolithic. But nobody's boot now disturbs the quiet. And that is true about so many of the pilgrim routes that only a score or so generations back crisscrossed England, and Europe, and the Near East. To Canterbury, to Glastonbury, to Bury St Edmund's, to Walsingham, to the Holy Blood at Hailes, to the Rood of Bromholm, to Durham... all busy for centuries with palmers and pilgrims seeking the saints, and wandering wide in the world, wonders to hear. The Walsingham pilgrimage, like all of them, was prohibited by Henry VIII, despite his having gone there twice himself, walking the last mile barefoot. His commissioners pillaged the rich shrine and that improvident monarch sold everything off at knock down prices to greedy courtiers on the make: and most of them were pretty nasty folk. And the walking stopped. Or did it? The man who in the 1920s so successfully re-started the Walsingham Pilgrimage, Fr Alfred Hope Patten, recalled how as a child he had a constant dream of hearing the tread of pilgrims passing the house on the old pilgrim way where he lived.

I try to imagine, sometimes, an England – nay, a Europe – which was in a literal sense a holy land, a place where the mental and not so mental landmarks were major and minor shrines, saint's names, the names of churches dedicated to this or that saint. The parish was your social, administrative as well as spiritual unit. Very many people went on some sort of pilgrimage at some time in their lives, and on the daytime roads little bands of pilgrims would be a common sight, making their way to the next place of safe refuge before the darkness fell – which is why most pilgrimages were in summer. Almost everybody, people of all sorts and conditions, actually travelled far more and far further than we often realise. You could make a pilgrimage to the relics in the neighbouring parish church, or you could set off for months or years to one of the really big shrines abroad like Jerusalem, Rome, Cologne or Compostella. (One practical as well as devotional benefit in those long absences might be very welcome, for while you were away all lawsuits and claims against you were suspended.)

I have spent a good part of my life teaching, every year, Chaucer's *Canterbury Tales* and Langland's great pilgrimage poem, *Piers Plowman*. Much of my research has been on mediaeval travel, and pilgrim narratives about the journey to the Holy Land, and the daring journeys first the friars made to the far Far East, and then traders like Marco Polo and his uncles, seeking the riches of Cathay and Ind. Quite soon there are – well, guidebooks, and as you know I have a weakness for guidebooks. A man from Florence, Balducci Pegolotti, who worked with the Bardi, bankers and merchants with fingers in most pies including Edward II's awkardnesses with his barons, wrote a handbook to the trade of the Levant and the East about 1340. He, good company man that he was, shows no interest in the wonders other travellers described, but he does tell you which inns are reliable, how much you might pay, how long it will take you to get to the next town, and the tone of his general advice to European travellers in Asia is decidedly practical: 'Let your beard and hair grow. When you get to Tana, get a guide and interpreter, and be ready to cough up for a good one, for he will save you a lot of money. Take two menservants as well, and if you want to get a woman to take with you, that's fine. There's no obligation to do so, but if you do take a woman you'll be much more comfortable than if you don't. The road from Tana to Cathay is perfectly safe. Take linens with you, for these sell profitably at Urgenje, and there you should get silver bullion, for exchanging into paper money in Cathay. The paper money is good tender for silk and all other merchandise.' *The Rough Guide to Central Asia,* almost: and a down to earth background to the nearly contemporary accounts of the Franciscan and Dominican friars who tried to convert the Tartar khans to Christianity and to make alliance with them against a very aggressive Islam.

Precisely because they are fictional, *The Canterbury Tales*, or *Piers Plowman*, give reliable glimpses of people tramping the roads of mediaeval Europe. For to work as poems they had to create impressions an audience would recognise as like its own experience of travel. First you got yourself, like Chaucer's pilgrims, to a recognised assembly point, whence a band of pilgrims, when large enough to deter robbers, might depart. This might be an inn, like Chaucer's Tabard in Southwark, which survived until it burned down in 1676. Or it might be a monastery or abbey, perhaps itself a place of pilgrimage, like Vézélay in France – one starting point of the long Compostela pilgrimage. A leader of the caravan would be chosen, who knew the way – lots of people made pilgrimages more than once. (The surname Palmer recalls how some actually made a profession of performing many pilgrimages, as proxy for other people who could not afford the time, or were not well enough, to go.)

Knowing the way... An age before maps, before signposts... Once we were walking an old holloway in deep woods in Norfolk – as it happens, an old pilgrim route. Our feet made a gentle crunching on the frosting beechmast and the dog, tired now, panted at our heels, his breath smoking in the cold air. It was growing dusk. We came to a fork in the road: two holloways of equal size, one leading left, one right. As it happened, I knew where we were, and that we had to take the right fork which would lead us in the end out of the dark wood and into the last of the waning light. But, just for a moment, I glimpsed the fear that might grip a traveller, benighted, far from shelter, uncertain of the way, and even in daylight nothing to guide him to where he wanted to go. And places outside the city, the town, were, well, 'outside', dangerous. Mediaeval people did not have the same post-Romantic feeling about the countryside we do: the Heavenly Jerusalem was very definitely a City, not a nice country estate with open aspect, gravel soil and a haha.

Of course, on a pilgrimage you would travel with all sorts and conditions of people randomly coming together. (As, today, on a coach tour or a cruise.) Pilgrimage was the only area of mediaeval society where noble and common, male and female, rich and poor, mingled with little discrimination. In your group there might be – would be – those who were driven by extreme devotion, like Chaucer's parson, or to expiate a great sin, like Henry II of England barefoot to Canterbury after the murder of Thomas à Becket. But there would always be those simply out for a good time – to make sure, almost, that when they got Absolution at the end of their trip it was jolly well worth it. Chaucer's fictional Miller, or Reeve, for example, are hardly holy, and the Wyf of Bath, a comfortably-off widow with a small cloth business, had been to Spain, to Rome, to Cologne, to Boulogne, and no less than three times to Jerusalem, for reasons we can guess – certainly not sanctity. And, just as on Chaucer's, the groups would quarrel, tell stories, make jokes, get drunk, and run up against cheats and tricksters like his Pardoner. And when they got home again, the clichéd complaint was that they were tellers of tall tales for ever after. Indeed, though the Church supported and organised pilgrimages, and grew rich on it, and out of that wealth provided many indispensable social services, many churchmen were uneasy about what pilgrimages did to pilgrims. It's amusing to recognise the similarity with the modern taste for cruises – indeed, I have met many of Alison of Bath's descendants – and to realise that 'cruise' and 'crusade' are basically the same word – as they still are in German: *kreuzfahrt*. (And what were Crusades but armed pilgrimages?)

It was big business, too. The pilgrim sea route from Bristol to Compostela was so well established that something like a regular ferry service ran across the Bay of Biscay. Along the roads of Europe were houses ready to receive travellers. The big hospices or abbeys or monasteries lodged free all who came. It was perfectly possible for a poor man to travel right across Europe, and to the Holy Land, relying simply on the charity of the Church for food, shelter and clothing. But there were also big inns, like Southwark's Tabard, the ancestors of the later coaching or post inns, which provided dormitory sleeping accommodation, and a common table, at a simple price. (Not many had beds as big as the Great Bed from the White Hart Inn in Ware, in which an eighteenth century rumour had it that 26 butchers and their wives slept an entire night for a bet. (How do you assemble 26 butchers, let alone their wives?) There were boatmen ready to carry passengers down the Loire, or the Rhone, or the Rhine, or the Po, or the Danube – expensive, but much less effort and a lot quicker than walking.[30]

Some went over the Alps to Rome or Jerusalem, and there were hospices on the passes: like the one on the Great St Bernard. Just as in John Evelyn's day later, you could hire men to carry you on a litter over the ice. Or you could avoid the Alps, and take ship at Marseille for Leghorn/Livorno; and if you were bound via Italy for Palestine, there were the Venetians. Some people walked the whole way to Palestine, but going through the Balkans and Anatolia might take an extra six months. But you could get to Venice by early Spring, when the sailing season opened. Venice dominated European trade in the Eastern Mediterranean, and by the 1300s was ruling a lot of Greece – those ruined fortresses I saw so many years ago on that first journey make sense now, as they did not then. One of the very first Fellows of Eton College, William Wey, made that journey to Palestine in the 1440s. He, like Pegolotti a century earlier, wrote a Rough Guide for other travellers: in the Piazza San Marco were men who would hire you a bedding roll, some pots and pans, and a water cask, for your sea voyage – many skippers (most indeed) provided no drink, food, or fuel for cooking it. That package cost you sixpence, and you got two pence back when – if – you returned what you had hired on your way home. Most pilgrims bought a few hens, or a pig, for the journey, and cooked their own food. Skippers would work along the coasts, and every so often put in so that passengers could buy fresh food, or fill their water casks. It cannot have been an easy journey.[31] The little boats – often of only 20 tons – must have been noisy, overcrowded, smelly to a degree, and there were pirates and slavers in plenty in the Aegean.

Arrived in the Holy Land, Muslim once more after the interlude of the Crusader kingdoms, pilgrims had to put up with the extortions of Muslim customs officials, and the (often stone-throwing) hostility of the villages on the road from Jaffa to the Holy City. The Franciscans, and the Knights Hospitaller, ran hospices to accommodate the huge numbers who came. Without them many humble folk would simply have died.

The climax of the pilgrimage, before the equally arduous journey home, was visiting the holy places and the holy relics. Around 1400, Margery Kempe, wife of a patient merchant of King's Lynn, dictated a long autobiography – if only we had his! She started with a few easy English pilgrimages – if any pilgrimage is easy! – and then went to Poland, Germany, France, Rome and Jerusalem. She can't have been the life and soul of the party. While in Middleburg in Holland, waiting for the pilgrimage to assemble for the journey down the Rhine and across the

Alps, she told her companions off for drinking, swearing and fornicating, telling them to behave as became those who were performing a spiritual duty. She admits they took a dim view of this, and she was not popular – returning from the Holy Land, they tried to leave her behind on the beach. But it is probable that a goodly number of people were like her and did take things pretty seriously, and approached holy places, and the relics, in a state of spiritual el(ev)ation: Margery, indeed, says that she 'verily saw Our Lord in a vision' while in the Church of the Sepulchre. And people like Chaucer's Wife of Bath, or Miller, could be *both* naughty and cynical, *and* genuinely devotional, in a limited sense, at the same time. The Wife's interest in sexual politics would not have stopped her performing the right number of Ave Marias or Pater Nosters at a holy place, genuinely hoping that by so doing she would escape time in Purgatory. For people like her, just as for Margery Kempe, the shrine was a place where the holy impinged on the workaday, and the unseen was almost visible.

★

You drive to Brixworth from the south through pretty enough countryside. Not really the way to do it: it ought to be done on foot, and some people still do so arrive, walking from Northampton along the track of the old railway. From the Web, 2016: 'We will depart St Anne's church (Cattlemarket Rd) at 9am and walk up through

Kingsthorpe to the railway path and up to Brixworth. A Thanksgiving prayer and veneration of the relics of St Boniface will be at about 2pm.' For Brixworth is an ancient holy site, possibly sacred even in pre-Christian times, and it is one of the very few churches in Protestant England to have managed to hang on to its ancient relic for over a thousand years despite the Taliban- or ISIS-like destruction of the sixteenth and seventeenth century iconoclasts, and later indifference.

I like Northamptonshire. They used to call it a 'shire of spires and squires.' The former remain, stone the colour of a winter russet apple pointing heavenward. The latter have left their mark on the rolling country with coverts and spinneys for foxes and pheasants – who do not get on well – and hedges just the right height and width for horses in full gallop: fine hunting country, once upon a time, and the country of smart hunts like the Pytchley. Then Brixworth: you follow the brown road sign pointing to 'Saxon Church' through dull modern building in harsh brick which will never weather. Half a mile, and you meet the old road, squiggling its ancient way from somewhere to somewhere (and you will get there eventually) and lined by houses in the lovely but soft local stone. Another brown sign tells you there are only 300 more yards, so up the little hill, past the remains of a preaching or market cross, sharp right, and into the car park.

You don't have to be fascinated by relics to want to go to Brixworth, though relics by another name are as popular as they ever were, making a sort of connection with those we revere. J. R. R. Tolkien's disreputable MA gown made a silly price at auction; so do intrinsically worthless bits of things that belonged to film stars, the Beatles, and so on. (And they need not be bought: nearly every family has an Auntie Maisie's teapot.) Brixworth is perhaps the largest mainly Saxon building still standing in England, and those first builders did it on an ambitious scale, cannibalising thousands of Roman bricks to build their arches. The Saxon work is clumsy, massy, as if the builders knew what they had to do but had almost forgotten the skills. The travelled ones, and there were many, would have seen Roman arches and barrel vaults, beyond a doubt, but how to do it was another matter. The building was already old when the Normans came along and hacked it about – no Historic England or Ancient Buildings listing to stop them then – and they were in turn a mere old-fashioned memory when some rich benefactor stuck on a Gothic chapel, now the Lady Chapel. And through all these changes the hidden Eagle of St John, once part of a Saxon cross shaft and used as rubble in the building work, watched over where Offa of Mercia founded and endowed his rich monastery about 680. Somewhere in the stone must lie hid the creatures that symbolise the other three Evangelists.

Prosaic imperatives took me to Brixworth first. I was
organising the programme for yet another study tour
by a group of American faculty, the theme for this one
being Anglo-Saxon England and the Viking invasions.
Brixworth had to be on the itinerary, and I do my
homework. I did my reading and learned how in repair
work below a window in the Lady Chapel loose stone had
fallen out revealing in the cavity a carved stone reliquary.
It contained – contains – what is beyond reasonable doubt
the relic Offa gave the church in 680, the hyoid or throat
bone of St Boniface, Apostle of the Germans, martyred
just one hundred years earlier: before Augustine came
to Canterbury. It is when you go through the gate of
the churchyard and turn to walk up the slope to the
building, seeing it from slightly below, that you grasp
how majestic, dominant, the building is. It would have
been even more so when it was new and had its original
side chapels, *portici*, especially when most buildings you
knew, however grand, were in timber and wattle and
daub. Well, the visit with the group went well. They
looked at the Roman tiles, puzzled out the lost *portici*,
were apparently interested and attentive when I explained
to them the function and use of the ring crypt – a rare
survival, even it is in ruins – for veneration of the relic.
I was the last to leave. As I thanked the churchwarden,
who had been so helpful, he said, conspiratorially, as if
what he was proposing was something slightly rather
risqué, like a collection of naughty postcards (how that
dates me!), 'Would you like to see the relic?' 'But yes,' I

replied, but thinking at the same time of the waiting bus driver with a schedule to keep, and the need to double check I had got everyone on board before setting off. (Oh yes, it happens.) He went into a secret place – I carefully did not watch – and came back holding the reliquary. He opened it, and there, a small brown object, was the bone that had vibrated to the sound of Boniface's preaching, to his calling for an axe to lay to the trunk of Thor's sacred oak, to his last prayers as he died martyred[32].

The prosaic won. As with me, at first, it usually does. It reminded me of the sort of old poultry bone I dig up in my vegetable garden. I could not, then, connect it with eloquence. 'Thank you so much,' I said. (My mediaeval ancestors would have fallen on their knees in reverence.) I shook his hand as I left, feeling I had somehow let him down. 'Thank you again,' I said. Only hours later did the full weight begin to settle, as the centuries elided: my eyes had looked on Offa's gift of inestimable price to that place, a gift made when Cuthbert was prior of Lindisfarne, made long before Bede the Venerable wrote and Caedmon sang, before Charlemagne was born. A gift made when everything that has happened since, every little choice upon choice, accident upon accident, which closes options for any future, need not have happened that way at all. 'As Bad As A Mile,' says Larkin's poem: 'the unraised hand calm, / The apple unbitten in the palm.'

All this is mere anecdote. Brixworth is one of the in-between, 'thin', places. Let the historical mind cease from troubling, and let the pedant be at rest. Be still, and know. Here there is no need to be clever. I have been many times since, and I know many for whom this place has been a turning point. I think of one woman, struggling with great grief and loss, of no faith, proud, capable, a leader, feeling drawn one winter day to enter a place she had passed many times with indifference to so familiar a part of the scenery. As she told me, the empty place was not empty. She found herself weeping. And something was saying insistently, 'Kneel. Bow your head and accept. Humility is the only real power. When you are ready, my dear.'

A day of rain and wind, though it is July. I kneel in the silent nave, a safe ship in the storm we can hear raging without, the wind washing at the ridge of the roof like the waves against a keel. 'Peace, be still.' Near the crucifix on the nave altar, in the dull pews, Rosanna sits. A light burns in the eastern sanctuary, and against its glow the crucifix is surrounded by a mandorla of light. Old eyes do that. We leave in silence, for there is too much, and nothing, to say, and the dog needs a walk.

★

The men running the little Calmac ferry from Fionnphort to Iona must have one of the most boring jobs in one of the most beautiful places in west Scotland – though the fast currents and rips in the sound can be tricky. Ten minutes to the holy place, with a whiff of diesel and hot engine. And back again. And again. And so on. But then, Charon must also have got fed up with all those short journeys across the Styx, and been irritated by all those passengers, shades, waiting for the next ferry to another world, stretching out their hands imploringly in their desire for the other shore. 'Wait for the next boat!' he calls grumpily, as he fends them off with his oar. The ferry's trips back and forth, all day, across the little sound, end with the grinding of the ramp as it goes down onto the concrete of the slades, and we go on board. In the shallows' clear water, unconcerned, sea anemones wave their florid tentacles for passing food and urchins make their slow progress across the rocks. A canny otter is regularly seen waiting near where the fishermen sometimes gut their fish. Gulls glide by on stiff wings, watchful. In season delicate terns shriek their harsh Norse name '*kria*', flutter, and dive for little fish. The air smells salt. To port we can see the sunlight on the pretty bay where in 806 Viking raiders massacred 68 of the monks. This bright place too has seen the darkness. This has been one of the fulchra of the world. It does not forget it. Maybe it still is. Will be.

Rosanna Petra and I walked in silence from the ferry. So much had already slipped into temporary irrelevance as we had moved north through England and across the Borders from normality: first the immediate pressures of work, of managing the day to day, then the traffic and people thinned out, then came the big punctuation mark of the ferry across the sound from Mull. We left the car on the other shore: you do not have the option not to distance yourself from the busy roads of the world. If you want to, take it as symbol: surrender the need to be in charge, the need to drive yourself. Just two of us, silent, and the dog, on that road many had trodden before us, though the modern road on the island only in bits lies over the old pilgrim route from Martyrs' Bay. But even so to walk that path imposes a silence on the mind. 'Listen. Be still.' Perhaps it is because we expect it to, from what we have read. Perhaps there is another reason.

This is – always was – a place pared down to essentials. No enticing luxury here, simply light, water, soil, sun: the essentials. It draws my body as it draws my spirit. It is another of those in-between, 'thin', places – indeed, you can understand why it was of Iona that George MacLeod first used that expression for places where the grace of God is breaking through like sunlight suspected through clouds. Between the tumultuous highway of the Atlantic and the wild solidity of Mull, between then and now (for 'then' is never far away), between knowing and unknowing... The Abbey church is far unlike the Celtic monastery that was once here, which is now only imaginable in the deductions of the spade.

But some things are constants. It is late Autumn – I always seem to go to Iona in Autumn, my own included – and there must be thought for the welfare and fodder of people and beasts over the dark months. It was always thus, for the neolithic people who lived here with their smaller cattle, for the people of the Isles during those long centuries when the failure of the fishing or a murrain on the cattle or hay that went sour and mouldy meant starvation. The monks farmed this land, as people had done for millennia before they came. You can't – should not – separate the work of the body from the work of the spirit. (St Benedict says as much in his Rule.) In a field by the rough road we walked on our way back to our lodging, a man was cutting a last aftermath of hay – the equinox fell on the next day – the last chance of storing a bite for the beasts before spring, and you never know how much feed your animals will need or how long you will need to keep them in from the winter's wildness. Over the last week, every waking hour of sunshine all over the islands farmers have been cutting, turning, baling. Yesterday, when the hay had already been cut and baled, a young lad was driving his tractor back and forth, dragging a drag harrow up and down, the sheep scattering on either side of him as he drove. He was scarifying the sod to encourage the new growth next spring. He rarely slowed as he crossed the field, swept a turn, straightened out, crossed again, confidently avoiding the little rock outcrops that remind of the times before man was. A grave gaggle of greylag geese watch from a distance. Nice

of him to clear the grazing for us, for it has been a long
flight south to our wintering ground from Greenland and
Iceland. Take away the machine, and a scene, a job, as old
as man as a farmer. A man at home in his homeland.

Ranald, son of Somerled, Lord of the Isles, refounded the
community as Benedictine in the 1200s, and the church's
worked stones and arches speak of France, of Rome, and
remind of that argument lost at Whitby. Ranald's sister
Beathag founded the Augustinian nunnery down the lane,
and was its first prioress. (I stood very early one windy
Autumn morning in the ruins of the hold of the Lords on
the crannog at Finlaggan on Islay. Beathag and Ranald
must have known it. Hector the Labrador's silky black
ears were flying in the wind, bright sun was bouncing off
the steep little waves in the loch. Brother and sister would
have had dogs too. The ruined chapel, as big as a large
garage, contained two unconcerned, ruminating, sheep,
who sneered at me, as sheep do.) But in Iona a curious eye
can learn to see the memories the landscape holds, and
insistent ghosts of much of the early Christian land pluck
quietly at your mind's sleeve. Notice us, they whisper.

We picked out – we had done our homework, of course
– as we went along several clues to the later Benedictine
community's buildings – they do run roughly to a pattern,
as Roman forts do. But the twelfth century monastery
was there for exactly the reason we were there, walking
that road: because Columba, centuries earlier, and what

he did, had made this a special place. What happened here changed Europe, slowly, like leaven in the dough.

AD 563: far away in the East, in the state that still calls itself Roman, Justinian reigns as hierarch and emperor. The great church of the Holy Wisdom is rededicated after a devastating earthquake. In the west, Roman centralisation is no more. Little princedoms and kingdoms impose what order they can, sometimes attempting to keep alive a memory of the *Romanitas* that had collapsed, and the monasteries guard the rumour of scholarship. In that year Columba sailed in a leather curragh with twelve companions – the number of the Apostles – from Ulster to the little island. Martin Martin, in his *A Description of the Western Islands of Scotland* (1703) says, 'The natives have a tradition among them that one of the clergymen who accompanied Columbus [*sic*] hither, having at a good distance espied the isle, and cried joyfully to Columbus in the Irish language, "Chi mi i," *i.e.*, "I see her" – meaning thereby the country of which they had been in quest – that Columbus then answered, "It shall be from henceforth called Y."' Ì: the name it has in Gaelic to this day.

Deliberately, he chose a place whence, according to his vow, he could not see his homeland. He was a well-connected man. He knew how to persuade and influence important people – many were his relatives, for he belonged to the ruling Northern O'Neills of Ulster, and was an equal to the royalty of the people among whom he settled. Like many great saints, he was far from other-worldly: he was a canny diplomat, an important person, a tough operator, who could request from his kinsman Conall mac Congaill, King of Dál Riata, as from an equal, the site for a monastery, and get it. The monastery he founded with those twelve companions was at the physical centre of the Irish/Scots polities, for the sea has always been the great highroad, the cultural accelerator. The Gaelic kings sent their sons to Iona to be educated, and Columba and his successors arbitrated in kingly disputes. Donald Munro, Dean of the Isles, in his *Description of Western Isles of Scotland* (1549) – the earliest account of the Hebrides – says, with less than wholehearted commitment to the numbers, that 8 Norse kings, 84 Irish, and 48 Scots (including Macbeth) were buried here because their remains would be near Columba's shrine. (Having seen the graveyard, they must have been quite companionably packed.)

There is not much that now remains of Columba's original monastery: a huge *vallum*, which is probably much earlier, an Iron Age bank, that conveniently was used to enclose the holy site, the well – which may have determined why the Iron Age enclosure was there in the first place – and Tòrr an Aba, 'Hill of the Abbot', where Columba is believed to have died in 597. But there does seem to have been a community living there from c.40 BC to about 220 AD. Intriguingly, Tacitus records

(*Agricola,* 38, 3-4) that during the circumnavigation (AD 80ish?), of Britain which the Governor, his father-in-law Gnaeus Iulius Agricola, seems to have ordered, they came to a hallowed place, by a holy well, somewhere in the Hebrides. Some think it was Iona. Roman pottery has been found in this spot, but pottery is so portable that it is never conclusive. Was Iona a pre-Christian sacred site? Was that why Columba chose it? Questions crowd, and so far answers do not.

He built his cell, small and modest, so his biographer Adamnán (and a successor as Abbot) says, with his own hands. Of the drystone beehive cells of his companion monks no trace remains. But the 2017 excavations have pretty certainly identified his writing hut, his *tuguriolum* (little hut), on Tòrr an Aba, whence he could see the whole precinct, and the sea beyond. Adamnán's *Life* (697), describes Columba sitting in the hut 'built on the higher ground... made of planks,' overlooking the Sound, transcribing the Psalter. (After all, transcribing books was part of what all monks did: the *Book of Kells*, associated with Columba's own hand since 1007, was probably made here, though it is probably a couple of centuries later than the saint.) He hears a shout from across the Sound, and when his unwelcome guest finally arrives (not from Porlock), in his eagerness to kiss Columba he upsets an inkhorn – a grave enough test of composure when you made your own ink. From that hut, almost a panopticon, he could oversee the day-to-day activities of the monastery and look out at the world to which his monks would go, answering Zechariah 9:10's challenge: 'he shall speak peace unto the heathen: and his dominion shall be from sea even to sea, and from the river even to the ends of the earth.' His 'Island soldiers' – Adamnán's phrase – went out into the wild, to other desert places that became powerhouses in their turn: Lindisfarne above all. Iona changed the world, the pebble that caused the landslide.

Fallen field walls – stone is cheap here – mark where crofts once had their in-bye land. Over on the western *machair* the ridges of old lazy beds remind of the long labour of men ploughing, and of women with creels on their backs carrying up kelp from the wrack on the shore to manure the land. We sat with our backs to the scarp of blown sand at the edge of the *machair*. The dog busied himself with doggy things on the tidemark. Further out, the deep water was dark as the wind stirred it, and as it shallowed and the sun illuminated it, became translucent turquoise over the white shell sand. At the very edge of the tide it was clear as gin, as thin, slow, it reached the point of the beach incline over which it could travel no further, then drew back into itself with a sigh. Every varied pebble shone minor glory, washed, tumbled over, the pebbles beneath showing as the top ones move. Nothing is stable. Far away by the dark cliffs we could see the columns of white spray shooting up from the blowhole of the Spouting Cave as the long Atlantic swells came rolling in, and sometimes a mist of spray hung in the air, held in the updraught against the cliffs. Here is where the sea tirelessly picks at the solidity, wearing the rocks away into boulders, and then stones, and then the bright pebbles where the dog paddles. A few yards away, a couple of turnstones busily perform the name we humans give them.

This was one of the days of silence – or at least, no talking – we had promised ourselves. The noise of water on the beach, wind in the grass, a sheep faraway. On a rock, just offshore, capped with pinks and silverweed, cormorants dried their wings, and a dyspeptic looking heron (probably moulting) stood hunched up and glum. Rosanna likes herons: they remind her of her adored Russian grandmother, whose nickname, as she was long-legged, was Tsaplik – Russian for heron. A few oystercatchers flew up from the edge of the tide, piping their gale-piercing, spine-tingling call. As if to answer from the moor behind the *machair* came the bubbling cry of the curlew.

As you look over the quiet land with the wind off the sea in your hair, or as you might doze on a warm afternoon on that western *machair*, rich in flowers – yellow tormentil, the quarter-inch sapphire of speedwell, the white-rimmed gold of silverweed – it is hard to recognise that it is here, in this quiet place, that so many of the things first happened that we so easily assume were always there. Many aspects of Christian practice were still being formed when Columba built his cell. Here Christian graves are first marked with a cross. Here the sacral ordination of kings (at Columba's hand) started; here started the writing of an annual chronicle, here was written the oldest Irish book, the Cathach psalter (possibly written by Columba himself). In the 600s there survive more sacred texts and books from Iona than from any other house in Europe. And, also, it was in Iona first that laws were framed to protect non-combatants in war. Now, in an age less civilised, our rulers and governors (I refuse to call them 'leaders') happily accept – but *of course* with much expressed regret – 'collateral damage.' Violence breeds violence: nothing is settled. Gustav Holst knew that so well in his *Mars* (1914). (I remember my infant granddaughter, literally infant, hardly able to talk, hearing that piece for first time, and crying with terror.) Had Holst an intuition, in what surely is one of the most frightening pieces of music ever written, that the coming War to End all War would be a Moloch that would demand the sacrifice of countless youth, that it would lead merely to the Long Weekend before the horror resumed in 1939? There are dozens of names of youths in their teens and twenties from just this little place on the War Memorial by Martyrs' Bay, yards from where the blood of the 68 monks reddened the retiring sigh of the tide.

The monks made this, deliberately, a sacred landscape, a ritual space even though men did all the humble humdrum daily things that need doing, farming, fishing, eating, drinking, washing. Very early the monastery (and indeed the island) were physically configured to reflect Jerusalem. If you could not easily go to Jerusalem – and that long and dangerous journey *was* hard – make Jerusalem come to you, in symbol. For to be as close to God as possible, the early mediaeval monastery tried to copy the earthly Jerusalem in order to lead to the heavenly. Jerusalem's reported layout is symbolically embedded in monastic spaces. On his return from a pilgrimage to the Holy Land (*c.* 680), a certain Arculf, possibly Bishop of Périgueux, in Aquitaine, was driven by storm to Scotland, to Iona, already a political and ecclesiastical hub. He described what he had seen in Jerusalem to Adamnán (d.735), Columba's ninth successor, and Adamnán wrote a very influential 3-part book, *De Locis Sanctis*, summarising the story. In Part 1 he summarises Arculf's account of nine months in Jerusalem, beginning with a description of 'the Sepulchre of the Lord and its Church, the form of which Arculf himself depicted for me on a tablet covered with wax.' Arculf's account was the first introduction to the British Isles of the detailed dimensions, even ground plans, of the churches in Jerusalem, and it became quite usual to design new buildings in the West from accounts of the holy places. For example: the precinct of Santo Stefano in Bologna replicated the Church of the Holy Sepulchre and other sites, including the Mount of Olives and the Valley of Jehoshaphat. In building monasteries and great churches, the earthly Jerusalem became the model and the Heavenly Jerusalem of *Revelation* 21 the vision. The 'Perfect Monastery' – Iona was Scotland's first, though several Irish ones were so constructed – was a model/icon of the Heavenly Jerusalem in a ritualised landscape, trying to reconcile the topography of the Old Testament and of *Revelations,* despite the obvious contradictions in Scripture.

But materialising a vision could be demanding: clearly funds would never run to *Revelation's* list of building materials, which include jasper and gold, sapphire and chalcedony, emerald and sardonyx, chrsyolite and amethyst and pearls. But you might use similarly rich and rare stones, like porphyry, marble, and Purbeck marble, and serpentine: that is why so many cathedrals and abbeys of the High Middle Ages have boldly exotic stone in their decoration, and the colours of the gems are picked up in the suites of stained glass, lenses through which one glimpses the history of the holy, and the vision of glory.

From Martyr's Bay, a way leads up to the monastery. This pilgrim road is now largely tarmac before you lift the latch of the gate, enter, and tread the ancient stones. The first time I did it I constantly had the feeling that there were people just out of my borders of vision behind, just about to overtake. But the street was, of course, empty. I think.

Walking this road, the Street of the Dead as it is in the Gaelic, was ritually to tread a *via dolorosa*. It crossed the *vallum* into the outer precinct, passed the very early Chapel of St Oran – the first Christian to be buried on Iona – then the inner rampart into the monastery itself, wound past the Stations of the Cross (only seven then, not fourteen), to stand before the three High Crosses, *iuxta crucem lacrimans*, a Calvary, before Columba's church. Once the rich carving of those Crosses – they are the earliest known, about 720 AD – would have been brightly painted too, and you would watch the changing light falling on them, as the sun – or the moon, with its different highlighting – moved round, leading you into contemplation of the Incarnation and Passion. Not only their shapes and position echo Calvary. On St Martin's Cross, still where it has stood for 1200 years, the Virgin and Child in the central boss have beneath them King David, harping, Abraham's sacrifice of Isaac, and Daniel between two rearing lions – all of which takes you back into a typological reading of the Bible narrative which would have been second nature to a mediaeval pilgrim whose knowledge of the Bible was largely through art and symbol. You walked with the Lord to His Cross before you entered the door of the church, the gate of Heaven.

When Columba died, they buried him just behind the High Crosses. The shadow cast by the setting sun falls on the door of the simple little 9th century stone shrine chapel, inside which, in the floor, two kist burials were found, which may well once have been those of Columba and Adamnán. His tomb immediately drew many pilgrims, and the shrine became one of the richest in the north, Managing the hosts of pilgrims who came was a demanding job for the monastery – not simply feeding and housing, but controlling the flow. Long before the Gothic church, which the monks had to enlarge to do that managing, pilgrims had been bringing offerings to the shrine. The relics themselves became of extraordinary value. In 824, less than 20 years after the first devastating slaughter of the brothers, a man called Blathmac joined the community. But soon afterward their fast ships brought the Norsemen again to ravage the island. As Blathmac was celebrating Mass, they entered the church and murdered the monks. Blathmac – he was canonised later – refused to show them where lay Columba's relics, the real object of their raid. They hacked him to pieces on the altar step. But why did they want the relics? Vikings were pretty good businessmen, and pagan though they were they would have reasoned that the relics of such a saint might fetch a good price if offered to other churches. After all, records abound of the trade in relics and of monasteries raiding other monasteries for relics.

Columba's chapel, north and a bit west of the church, where that evening shadow of the Cross falls, becomes the transforming Tomb below a metaphoric Golgotha. You have to stoop, and cross a threshold, a limen, into a world where the watchword was, as Walter Hilton would put it about 1380, 'we would be at Jerusalem.' From the High Crosses you pass into the church where the rumours of Heaven feed those still wayfaring wide in the world. To which far faring, as yet, they must return. There is work to do.

★

I set off alone to walk up Dun Í – a wee hill, but the highest there is on the island, and for one who loves heights better than nothing. It was one of those days when the weather can't make up its mind: one minute it promises fair, the next, over the Sound a pale gray gauze curtain softens the outline of the far big hills of Mull and before you know where you are the rain is clattering on your hood. Never mind. Near the hill's southern foot is a collapsed drystone beehive cell, the sort of thing Columba's monks would have known, a hermitage in the little wilderness. To judge by the wet and boggy path, not many people had trodden that way recently. But I was not quite alone: a raven shadowed me, riding high on the wind and saying whatever ravens do say. A female hen harrier quartered the steep hillside with unremitting purpose. Just as it reached the shoulder of the skyline and passed from view, I saw it change attitude, and clearly stoop. A rabbit, perhaps: the place is full of them. Honour in some measure satisfied by having had, in a clearing of the rain, a 360 degree view of the islands to the east and

north and south and the restless Atlantic, I went over to
the little water filled hollow, Tobar nah Aois, the Well
of Youth – though some called it the Well of Healing
or Well of Age. I prefer the first name: and have drunk a
little of it. (I might be much worse not having done so.) I
came down and rejoined the road, near where my friend
Matthew and his Mongolian wife and family camp every
year. They take some of their water from the well, after a
bracing early morning walk up the hill. Water and wells
deserve honour.

In a field, below a little rocky bluff that sheltered them
from the windy rain that had just started, a little group
of Highland cattle was grazing. A small bull calf was
paddling in the little burn. With that slow turn that their
spread of horns makes advisable, its dam turned her head
and lowed at it, as if to say, 'you just come here and be
a good boy and stop getting your hooves wet.' A young
bull came to my call at the fence, and loved having its ears
rubbed, as Hector does, and when I stopped, nuzzled me
to have it done again.

★

Behind the Abbey church stands St Michael's chapel.
The predicted steep depression had arrived, and we were
pretty soaked. I went through the door of the humble
little building under the chevrons of the round Norman
archivolts over the massy doorway. The door clunked as I

shut it, and stilled the storm. The old walls have been re-roofed, and down the space of the single-celled building runs a long table surrounded by chairs. The pale light from the simple east window picks up the grain of the polished wood. Long stalls line the walls. I sat in silence, Hector quiet at my feet, methodically licking his wet fur. There was everything and nothing to say, and nobody and everybody to say it to. The storm outside beat on the roofs and walls, dimly heard. The wind threw handfuls of rain against the window. A wild night it would be. I thought of the Irish monk in the ninth century writing a poem in the margin of the MS (now in St Gallen) he was copying, grateful for the storm: 'Hard is this wind this night. It combs the sea white as an old man's hair. This night the fierce raiders of Lochlann do not worry me, as their ships range over the wide sea.' Yes, such a wind would certainly cool a Viking's ardour. The boats would be flexing in the swell, their seams working, and they would run under bare poles. No thought of raiding. Not now.

And thinking of that poem takes me on a reverie... how international the world of those Irish monks was, how easily they moved around, deep into Europe with their learning and holiness – and their pets. Around the same time as the brother who was grateful for the storm, over at Reichenau, another Irishman wrote one of the nicest poems I know about a cat. Pangur Bán, 'white fuller', is the cat's name:

I and Pangur Ban my cat,
'Tis a like task we are at:
Hunting mice is his delight,
Hunting words I sit all night...
 'Gainst the wall he sets his eye
Full and fierce and sharp and sly;
'Gainst the wall of knowledge I
All my little wisdom try.
When a mouse darts from its den,
O how glad is Pangur then!
O what gladness do I prove
When I solve the doubts I love! ...
(Translation by Robin Flower (1861-1946)

Perhaps Beathag and Ranald too had dogs and cats they counted as friends. I am sure Columba would have had a cat.

Out into that pouring rain. Rosanna Petra joined me from the cloister and we butted our way back through the wind to the village. We met a very large American lady in a soaked Royal Stewart plaid that flapped drips from its hem in the half-gale's gusts. She was on a day trip from Oban, and proudly said, with joy in her face, that she had come across the world to visit the land of her forefathers, that she had bought a cromach, and was wondering how she would get it on the plane to take home. She said she was in the direct line from Somerled, Lord of the Isles. A happy woman. May the Fates smile on her search.

★

When the rain cleared, and the clouds that had loured upon us were buried in the deep bosom of the ocean, we walked north in the now brilliant light into a laundered world. Bright globes of rainwater sparkled on the leaves of alchemilla. On the harled drystone walls the ivy leaved toadflax glistened and the little purple flowers nodded at the sun when the wind fondled them. We made our silent way over the thin turf of the *machair*, and over the storm beach, and down to the sand where since the last tide someone had set out a little Celtic cross in white pebbles. A late butterfly dodged past – we were just another of those big things without nectar, so ignorable – low to the ground, and settled on a bit of ragwort at the edge of the rough grass. We sat in silence on the rocks, out of the strengthening south wind, by a little beach at the very north end of the island. Hector basked on the sand at our feet, occasionally waking up to do his doggy ablutions.

Across the eastern sound lies Eilean nam Ban, the Island of the Women. Idly, being well lunched and in informative mood, and forgetting our agreed silence, I began to tell Rosanna how it got its name, how Martin Martin in 1703 writes that 'The inhabitants have a tradition that Columbus [*sic*] suffered no women to stay in the isle except the nuns; and that all the tradesmen who wrought in it were obliged to keep their wives and daughters in the opposite little isle, called on that account Women's

Isle. They say likewise that it was to keep women out of the isle that he would not suffer cows, sheep, or goats to be brought to it.' She stirred. Her silence was more chastening than eloquence. Hector yawned. That beach is a place of peace now, not for instruction. But here too there was once blood, reddening this whitest of white sand. The forgiving sea washes it away, but the place remembers the Viking raid when yet more monks were slaughtered here.

The autumn sun was at its zenith. The north-flowing tide streams from the western and eastern sides of the island here come together – rather as our two lives have done - and their waves clash, and mount up in a dance of foam and criss-crossing waves as they meet. In this bright light you can see right through their pellucid green. A minor glory, and the sun makes momentary rainbows in the little spray. Beyond lie the islands, and beyond them the uttermost parts of the earth.

In an empty landscape, you can't ignore the few people you meet even if you are having a silent day. We got into desultory but friendly conversation with a man from Tennessee's Smoky Mountains, who had been to Iona several times before on his secret search, and had now brought his Brazilian wife to share his memory. He complained that the slope of Dun Í had got steeper with twenty years of rest from his feet. He farmed fainting goats – goats bred for meat and as pets – on a considerable scale, he said. I looked blank, as well most people would. 'Y'all en't heard of faintin' goats?' And he brought out a phone and showed a You Tube video of these strange animals, who have a congenital disorder that makes them stiffen and fall over when frightened. When he continued by saying, 'I sure have got coyote problems on my ranch,' to my shame, I could scarce forbear to say that as survival techniques go fainting left something to be desired, and coyotes would find them – well, easy meat. As a business model (I did not say) it might seem questionable. But then he completed the merry menagerie by telling us he had Pyrenean Mountain dogs to guard against the coyotes. It still all seemed rather exotic. But I now find that there is quite a market in these odd animals. I am not attracted.

★

In a bright morning we walked across the springy turf of the windy *machair* with the sea sounding in our ears, then, as the path steepened, onto the rocky paths that led over the moor to the bay where, men say, Columba landed. He might well have done. My friend Matthew the Ambassador who returns to the island each year to drink deep at ancient wells – including the one on Dun Í – found here a battered plastic bottle, nearly opaque with the scuffing of the sea, and in it was a message. Decipherable was an address on Rathlin Island. Three years before, a seven year old girl had cast this message into time and space, hardly hoping for a reply. She got one: the local papers made much of it, if not of the fact that the bottle's journey had followed the same currents to the same place as the Saint, to make landfall in the same cleft in the ancient rocks as men say he had done.

As we walked, under our feet were some of the oldest rocks on this blessed earth; in our close and fleeting vision, the intricacy of lichen etching them and the chocolate wet brown where the peat had shrunk away from their outcrops in the long drought of that summer, now at last over. Where the path crossed a boggy bit on stepping stones Rosanna's eye was caught by something glittering in the water: on that bed of dark peat covered by half a clear inch of water, someone had made a little pattern with a few small, rounded beach stones, a little bunch of heather, and right in the centre a little gilt cross. Three thousand years and more ago men and women did that – in the Thames, at Flag Fen, at Starr Carr, in all sorts of watery places – formal ceremonial deposition into the elemental water of something treasured, something offered. It was a curious, oddly disturbing, moment.

Rosanna and I breasted the slope and came up to the pocket of level ground that held the lochan. A notice asks you not to swim in it as it is part of the water supply. But the busy ducks and self-important drakes with their teddy boy tails (how that dates me!) can't read. Nor can the Bewick's swans. I love their imperious noses down which they look scornfully at all the world. They have flown in for the winter from Russia: this group probably come here every year for their holiday. *Cygnus columbanus:* how serendipitously well named they are for this place! They swam; they fed, long necks reaching delicately down into the water. One stayed sentinel. Were they the Children of Llyr...? It is hard not to think of the sadness of the old, half-remembered stories I read years ago when one hears their melancholy, spine-tingling trebles and altos as they take off and wheel and land again with a great spread of black webs ploughing up the water.

The path drops gently to the opening bay, open to the southwest and its mastering winter gales. Once there was a clachan here: heaven knows how old the old walls are, for styles of building that fit the materials and the weather of the land don't change much for millennia. The old folk built a great drystone wall, now fallen, grassed-over, snaking just behind the storm beach. Their animals would have sheltered behind it from the storm wind and spray. In today's warm sun a large family party had found it an ideal place for their picnic. Grandfather, perhaps impatient (as I would be) with all this inactivity, was standing on the rocky outcrop that reached out into the sea and divides Columba's reputed landing place from the Bay of the False Man. He was trying to teach his granddaughter, with a rod somewhat too big for her, how to cast a lure into the waves. How one wants to share one's delights and pleasures! But she was not an apt pupil. We wandered on, silently, for this was another silent day, past the huge cairns on the beach that people have built over the years and decades and centuries to mark their coming to this place. We added our stones to the millions. By the rocks where the seas did not quite reach, Rosanna found little patterns, offerings (to what?) of rounded beach stones, some of the serpentine that can be found here. Who? Why? Why did one stone have 'Audrey' written on it in felt-tip? But why are we surprised? Did we not find a Celtic wheel cross, four inches diameter at most, beautifully painted on a rock at the very northernmost tip of the island, a few feet above where, in a little geo, the accumulated storm-wrenched kelp heaved and sploshed with the breathing of the tide? And did we ourselves not later make a little pattern of special stones in a cleft in the rock to mark the place where Hector, whom by then we were mourning, had been so happy, and we happy watching him?

Did the leather *curragh* really land here, with Columba and his twelve companions? Who knows. There is a long tradition among pilgrims of throwing into the water a stone that carries all of the things they no longer wish to carry, as Columba here cast away his life in Ireland, and then taking away with them a stone; a mental cornerstone for their new beginning, their return, their change of heart or *metanoia*, the word used most often in Greek when speaking of spiritual transformation. I picked up a stone veined with colours, that fitted smoothly into my palm – Rosanna could have told me it was feldspathic orthoclase – and thought of what I could wish to leave behind to be scoured and rounded by the water. Fear: of not having enough, of not being enough; of comparison, of feeling 'less than...', of wanting to be 'better than... – the ramparts of the heart we learn as children, but they are not defence, only a prison. This is indeed a place where journeys might end. And might start.

★

By the shrine of Columba, we turned to enter the church. Moss covers some of the gray stones, and ferns grow out of the cracks high above. The ceiling is rounded like the upturned hull of a ship, and in an alcove a model ship with detailed rigging and limp cloth sails reminds of the journeys of the faithful across the waters for centuries. Rosanna bent her head as we went through the Norman door into the darker light inside. I stood just inside, with Hector, looking down the nave, which, unusually, slopes down rather than rises to the altar. Far down behind the altar the light of a new day shone through the window, silhouetting Rosanna, *mea Petra*, the delight of my eyes, as she walked down the aisle. She turned right to enter the quiet space of the south chapel, where people leave prayer requests, and small rounded beach stones in patterns before the icons, and a little wooden cross is silhouetted against the small light from the window. Hector, looking after her, whined gently, ears cocked. For he loved her.

VI

CODA

Landfall

... Either you had no purpose
Or the purpose is beyond the end you figured
And is altered in fulfilment. There are other places
Which also are the world's end, some at the sea jaws,
Or over a dark lake, in a desert or a city –
But this is the nearest, in place and time,
Now and in England.

T.S. Eliot, 'Little Gidding', Four Quartets

The man who was a boy on the beach, a youth on the saltings, has now journeyed to old age, even, you might say, to being an ancestor. He has been to many places and followed many dreams, to find that that is what they were. He has become comfortable in his skin by owning his discomfort. He accepts, at last, that the way to wisdom is to know one can know nothing, only listen. And that all there is, all that matters, is not knowledge or achievement, or even understanding, but Love. And that is hard for one who has spent his life being busy.

On another shore far distant from the one where he galloped with Prince Rupert of the Rhine, and drew sword for the Pretender – he has always been, and still is, a supporter of lost causes – there is a shingle bank where he feels arrival and departure very close, almost the same thing, in this, another in-between, 'thin', place. There the sea cabbage and the marram and the sea holly hold the sand and the mobile shingle with their roots, most of the time successfully. The tides stretch out the bank along the coast right from where the ebb and flow in storm and calm pills the stones out of the chalk and rolls them round and grinds them and makes them smaller and smaller until they become ideal for making the make-believe castles of children at summer Clacton. The sea has taken countless habitations of men, and Dunwich town too, where once a bishop ruled. The drift of the coast turns the rivers southward that try to breach it, yielding only occasionally to let their water through: Alde, Blyth, Ore, Deben – Sebald country, Britten country, Crabbe country before that. Behind the bulwark the spit offers against the east winds from Denmark and Holland lie quiet reed-whispering marshes, ditches with thoughtful herons, where cows graze the summer grass, and in autumn you hear the honk of the geese as they fly in from Svalbard – these are the eastern race – for their winter holiday before the 24/7 rigours of the next breeding cycle. The old man has learned to tell (usually accurately, he thinks) from their droppings what birds have been grazing – pinkfeet, brent, greylag, or Canada. He rarely wants to shoot them now: they come from their far journey, intent on their own concerns, in their own world, on which he cannot intrude. The barrier of species: how, as he has grown older, how strong has grown the desire to transcend that boundary, like the young Wart in T.H. White's *Once and*

Future King! He would shoot, if need drove him, but there is no need at this moment. The hares of Hollesley Bay are safe too – for the moment, for life is unpredictable. The hunter's mere lust that his youth had has died.

Where the road runs out – it has been getting more and more potholed for some miles, after crossing the dry heathland – just over the bridge over the dyke, there is a place where you can leave the car. As the engine dies and you open the door, the bubbling call of a curlew lets in the wildness. The blackberries on the fence will be ripe soon. Along the path to the south, the white coastguard cottages that turn their steadfast gaze to the unquiet sea are now surplus to needs, and are let out as holiday homes. They gazed out, alert equally to distress and the menace that might come from the sea, for the long decades before electronics replaced the far sight of men. Before them, the Martello Tower did the same sort of job when Boney was expected. He never came. That too is a home now. Where at Bawdsey they invented radar to keep watch on what came from the East, and stationed missiles during the Cold War, there is now a school. Among the ridges of the shingle, its parallel curves recording the high points of ancient storms, are traces of summer barbecues, and other testimony of summer laughter and children's play.

This shifting shore too has been a landfall, a place of haven, and a place to take possession. In winter the migrants flock in from the colder Continent – the geese from the far north, the fieldfares, the Bewick's swans, and the starlings in their thousands fleeing the Russian cold. Peregrines fly in, speedy, deadly as fighter planes (if you are a pigeon). The old man's mind plays on the Anglian ships, a millennium and a half ago, closing this low coast, perhaps in thick weather, with no obvious landmarks to guide you in, few safe anchorages save in the rivers whose estuaries you could only find by looking at the colour of the water and tasting it. It could all be yesterday. He himself has closed this coast at dawn in a small boat: a long, low line of thicker darkness, and he thought then of those remote ancestors and their courage and skill. But for him the lighthouse by the old MoD nuclear testing site was a sure mark: no such help for the Beaker bringers, or the tarred dark Anglian and Saxon ships. A little along the coast they buried the descendant of those newcomers, Raedwald, rich in gold, ring-giver, he who (so Bede tells us) could not make up his mind whether to be Christian or pagan and so was both – to be on the safe side. The Anglian longships must have turned over a bar like this one and paddled through the overfalls into the river with a relief that would never leave them however often they did it. Where they had come from, there was land hunger, and there were rumours of war to the east, of marauders from far, far away who travelled fast to the beat of their horses' hoofs. They are pushing west, pushing west: better leave, for we know there is good land in Britannia and we can put the sea between us and those horsemen, who, they say, drink hot blood.

The man's grandson has the binoculars at the moment, and is looking intently inland at the reeds lining the wide drain through the marsh: he swears he has seen a kingfisher. He may well have done. But he has already entered into his own world which the old man can never know. Idly, the man watches a swan on the slow water, and Orlando Gibbons' 'The Silver Swan' comes into his mind:

> The silver swan, who living had no note,
> When death approached, unlocked her silent throat;
> Leaning her breast against the reedy shore,
> Thus sung her first and last, and sung no more:
> 'Farewell, all joys; Oh death, come close mine eyes;
> More geese than swans now live, more fools than wise.'

He remembers singing it, a long time ago. He ought to call the boy, soon, for they will be waiting at home and there are promises to keep. But just a moment more in this quietude. He turns his eyes from the lad and looks to the east. A small pleasure yacht, goosewinged in the easterly breeze as she came over the horizon, folds her wings and, taking advantage of the slack water between the ebb and the flow, turns into the river. She will use the flood to help her up to the harbour, where, once, in the twelfth century, Ralph of Coggeshall tells us, they held a merman captive. Her engine takes over and the old man catches a momentary whiff of diesel. A man in bright yellow waterproofs is at the helm, and just behind him flies the Dutch tricolor. He raises a peaceable hand to the watcher. He has come from where the Angles and Saxons found themselves looking out over the restless sea to their future.

The man looks out to sea. Out east, on the very tip of the Ness, on a sandbank at the edge of the turning tide, stands a lone blackbacked gull. As the water creeps up, he will take off. Soon, unhurried. For this is what one does, as the tide makes. There is a journey to be made.

★

There can be no common peace and prosperity without common historical ideas.

H. G. Wells, *Outline of History*

ENDNOTES

1 Yet Polybius the historian comments that 'the Roman Proconsul... having restored the holy places in the Isthmus and ornamented the temples in Olympia and Delphi, proceeded to make a tour of the cities, receiving marks of honour and proper gratitude in each. And indeed he deserved honour both public and private, for he conducted himself with self-restraint and disinterestedness, and administered his office with mildness, although he had great opportunities of enriching himself, and immense authority in Greece. And in fact in the points in which he was thought to have at all overlooked justice, he appears not to have done it for his own sake, but for that of his friends...'

2 But *someone* took him seriously: we know of two, a judge in the Court of the Areopagus, Dionysus, and a woman called Damaris. The third century historian Eusebius says Dionysus became first bishop in Athens; another account says he went to France, where he suffered martyrdom under Domitian on the Hill of the Martyrs: Montmartre. His church, St Denis, rebuilt by Abbot Suger in the 1100s, is the first to exploit the power of the Gothic to illuminate the inner darkness by mediating the white light of Heaven through stone and glass and story. It was a pious fiction that it was Dionysus who wrote a hugely influential book on the angels and the great neo-Platonic, apophatic, *Mystical Theology* which altered the mind of mediaeval Europe for generations upon generation.

3 Nauplion was an important seaport, and after the Fourth Crusade of 1204, which never got near a Saracen but stormed Constantinople instead, Baldwin of Flanders was crowned Emperor, and Nauplion was held of him and his successors in feudal tenure as part of the lordship of Argos and Nauplion, initially by the de la Roche. They sold it in 1388 to the Venetians. In 1540 the Ottomans stormed it easily. The Venetians took it back in 1685 and built what is probably their last castle, Palamidi, on the ridge above the town. But the Ottomans took it back again in 1715... Nauplion was a major Ottoman stronghold during the War of Independence, and was besieged for more than a year before being starved into surrender. Because it was so well fortified, it was the capital of the First Hellenic Republic and then of the Kingdom of Greece until 1834.

4 Bibliography on request if interested. Write for details, as old adverts used to say.

5 A weird enough idea for some people, therefore a route to all the references: Peter Wohlleben, *The Hidden Life of Trees: What they feel, how they communicate* (2015), and Simard, S.W. 'Conversations in the forest: The roots of nature's equanimity' *SGI Quarterly,* 79 (2015), 8-9; M.-A. Sellosse, F. Richard, X. He, and, S.W. Simard ('Mycorrhizal networks: les liaisons dangeureuses [sic]?', *Trends in Ecology and Evolution,* 21 (2006): 621-628.

6 But I can sneak in a note: the church made going to Lohja a necessity, for its renown preceded it. Outside, pleasant, plain enough: massive stone, not a lot to draw one in. It was built sometime in the later fifteenth century when the Church was struggling with reform

– not yet Reformation. The terrible Schism when rival Popes hurled Crusades at each other had begun to settle only in 1415. Secular and church power had no idea what to do about popular reform movements like that of Jan Huss. The Council of Florence convened in 1437 to try to settle so many matters, and ended up settling few. But deliberate stimulation of an emotional and personal devotion, by art and architecture and music and affective prayer and meditation was reaching further and further into the spiritual lives of lay people. Gregory the Great, writing to Bishop Serenus of Marseilles in 599, had stressed that pictures were the books of the unlearned, and much could be taught through them. Good advice: the glaziers of Chartres Cathedral, with a large budget, knew it; the painter of crude figures on plaster in a small Norfolk church knew it; and the community of the Church of St Lawrence in Lohja put everything they had into doing it in their church.

Nobody could claim that the paintings which cover every available surface of wall, reveal of arch and window, and ceiling are sophisticated, subtly drawn, or show any awareness of what was being done with perspective and shading in Italy or Germany. The craftsmen who painted a complete cartoon picture Bible about 1530 were probably local. But crude though the execution may be, the design scheme is as intelligent as any of the great fresco series people go to Italy to see. From the Creation to the Last Judgement, via various legends of saints and martyrs, all the story is there, and the congregation in their present moment look up and are inserting themselves into a narrative, the history of the past and the history of the future. The gap closes.

The windows – tiny, though they were enlarged a century and more ago – let in little light. But the late medieval church would have been full of candles, constantly burning before the Sacrament, before the altars, and men and women and the guilds and fraternities to which they belonged would have made sure they never went out. The soft light of beeswax, unsteady in the slightest flaw of air, would in the dimness have made the walls seem fluid, and the wall paintings must have seemed to move in that light like tattoos on skin. The Story came alive.

But this extraordinary, exuberant decoration is almost the last pause before the winds of Reformation from Germany blew the calm quite away. Fear of the graven image, insistence on the Word – a logocentric, authoritarian, culture that dismissed the centuries of oculocentricity as mere idolatry – swept so much away, and the paintings were put to sleep under coats of whitewash. In their place, as if they had never been, the preaching of the word in a tongue 'understanded of the people.' (But then, were not the pictures understanded?) But how do you translate the Bible into Finnish? The 'Lion of Judah' in a land where lions are notably rare? The Finnish phrase is 'jalo peura' which really means 'noble deer', and the dragon of *Revelation* 12 is a 'salmon snake.'

7 Though he ended up painting Expressionist canvases in Kenya, his early work was profoundly affected by his time in Berlin (where after 1894 he worked with Edvard Munch), then by the later Romanticism of Russia, and by the Symbolists.

8 *Science Fact Society* (1946)

9 Start with Brian Sykes, *The Seven Daughters of Eve* (2002), if this is new to you. Apologies if not.

10 How did Muhammad Ali – not an especially nice man – get it? And how did a second son of a middling tobacco and shipping merchant in Kavala, Macedonia, come to be where he was, and found a dynasty that lasted until King Farouk?

11 His pupils made a monument for Canova himself, based on this lovely pyramid, in the church of the Frari in Venice. I had a moment of delighted recognition when I saw it, remembering the other, but it is not as good by a long chalk.

12 Roughly, 'In the time of the Borgias and the Medici we had Raphael and Michelangelo and Leonardo. In Switzerland they had peace and prosperity, and what did you get? Cuckoo clocks.'

13 Iris Origo wrote a very fine account of him in *The Merchant of Prato*. Recommended.

14 Murray's gives due weight to the beauty of the city's setting: 'from Fiesole the view of Florence encircled by its amphitheatre of mountains is obtained; and Hallam has described the scene in language so poetical and yet so true, that we give the traveller the pleasure of comparing it with the view which he will behold' – and the Guide then quotes Hallam at length, with his vision of the seminal Platonic Academy of Ficino, Poliziano, Landino

meeting sometime in the 1470s 'in a villa overhanging the towers of Florence... Florence lay beneath them, not with all the magnificence that the later Medici have given her, but, thanks to the piety of former times, presenting almost as varied an outline to the sky. One man, the wonder of Cosmo's age, Brunelleschi, had crowned the beautiful city with the vast dome of its cathedral, a structure unthought of in Italy before and rarely since surpassed.'

15 *Theses on the philosophy of history, (1940). VII.*

16 Garden gnomes of clay apparently first appeared in Germany in the early 1800s, made at Gräfenroda in Thuringia. Sir Charles Isham imported the first ones to England in the 1840s for his rockery at Lamport Hall. One survives, heavily insured. The Web, ineffably, tells me that 'Unfortunately, the world wars wiped out most garden gnome production in Germany.'

17 Mann kept open house for British visitors, inviting them for *conversazione* at the Palazzo Manetti when there was no performance at the theatre. His generosity was famous, although his close friendship with Patch, expelled by the Tribuna della Santa Inquisizione from Rome after a homosexual scandal, somewhat 'reflected on his reputation', as discreet obituaries used to say.

18 Shortly before Zoffany painted those 'uninteresting portraits', Tobias Smollett had been travelling on the route of the Grand Tour, and wrote a series of letters to his friends at home (carefully keeping copies for eventual publication) describing his experiences. I discovered his letters decades ago, and Smollett remains a favourite

corrective to too much enthusiasm – and reading old travel books when travelling yourself is like being *in* a palimpsest: it is addictive. In writing about the Uffizi, indeed, this very room, Smollett shocked his sensitive contemporaries by his freedom from those sham ecstasies which too often dog the footsteps of the virtuosi: 'With respect to the famous Venus Pontia, commonly called *de Medicis*, which was found at Tivoli, and is kept in a separate apartment called the Tribuna, I believe I ought to be entirely silent, or at least conceal my real sentiments, which will otherwise appear equally absurd and presumptuous. It must be want of taste that prevents my feeling that enthusiastic admiration with which others are inspired at the sight of this statue, a statue which in reputation equals that of Cupid by Praxiteles... I cannot help thinking that there is no beauty in the features of Venus; and that the attitude is awkward and out of character... Without all doubt the limbs and proportions of this statue are elegantly formed, and accurately designed, according to the nicest rules of symmetry and proportion: and the back parts especially are executed so happily, as to excite the admiration of the most indifferent spectator.' [as Lord Edgecumbe and Charles Loraine Smith clearly agreed] '... Others suppose, not without reason, that this statue is a representation of the famous Phryne, the courtesan of Athens, who, at the celebration of the Eleusinian games, exhibited herself coming out of the bath, naked, to the eyes of the whole Athenian people.

I was much pleased with the dancing faun; and still better with the Lotti, or wrestlers, the attitudes of which are beautifully contrived, to show the different turns of the limbs, and the swelling of the muscles: But what pleased me best of all the statues in the Tribuna was the Arrotino, commonly called the Whetter, and generally supposed to represent a slave, who, in the act of whetting a knife, overhears the conspiracy of Catiline... Among the great number of pictures in this Tribuna, I was most charmed with the Venus by Titian, which has a sweetness of expression and tenderness of colouring not to be described...' (Letter 28, February 1765).

Well, yes.

19 King Zog was an interesting monarch, who, during one of those tedious assassination attempts on his life, pulled out his own revolver and opened fire on his assailants. Nobody was hurt.

20 While the *Aeneid* was being written, Propertius, himself a fine poet, said 'Something greater than the *Iliad* is being born.' The poem immediately became canonical for Romans, their legitimising foundation myth, that traced Augustus' line from the hero Aeneas who escaped from burning Troy bringing the symbols of that city's divine authority with him.

21 Briefly: in 1347 he led a *coup d'état*, with massive popular support, and the support of Pope Clement VI, against the misgovernment of the nobles of Rome, who left the city without attempting resistance. He governed well, as Tribune − an office the name of which recalled the great Tribunes of republican Rome. He won the admiration of Petrarch, and his object was to restore Rome to its ancient greatness as 'Head of the World' and to unify Italy − an aim shared by Dante. He governed well for some months. But the nobles mobilised against him, the Pope turned on him, and he fled.

A brief restoration of his power after some years a captive ended in his death in a small riot in the city.

22 My companionable Smollett did not think much of it. Laurence Sterne, in *A Sentimental Journey through France and Italy,* (1768) which was written in part as an answer to Smollett's book, pillories him (as Smelfungus) for his bad tempered remarks: 'The learned Smelfungus travelled from Boulogne to Paris, from Paris to Rome, and so on, but he set out with the spleen and jaundice, and every object he passed by was discoloured or distorted. He wrote an account of them, but 'twas nothing but the account of his miserable feelings...I met Smelfungus, in the grand portico of the Pantheon— he was just coming out of it. 'Tis nothing but a huge cockpit,' said he—'I wish you had said nothing worse of the Venus de Medici,' replied I—for in passing through Florence, I had heard he had fallen foul upon the goddess, and used her worse than a common strumpet, without the least provocation in nature. I popp'd upon Smelfungus again at Turin, in his return home, and a sad tale of sorrowful adventures had he to tell, 'wherein he spoke of moving accidents by flood and field, and of the cannibals which each other eat, the Anthropophagi'; he had been flayed alive, and bedevil'd, and used worse than St. Bartholomew, at every stage he had come at. 'I'll tell it,' cried Smelfungus, 'to the world.' 'You had better tell it,' said I, 'to your physician.'

23 The austere Cistercians were here first, with their habits of (despite themselves) making the wilderness they chose for its hardship, poverty and solitude bloom like a garden – and themselves rich in the process. They could not help it. You need something to

write on: parchment, from sheep skins. So you grow sheep. You need about 500 skins to make enough parchment to copy a Bible, say. So you grow lots of sheep. But that means you have a lot of wool, and meat, and you sell it. You can't help making money. And as you build your church you need timber, and lead, and glass, and pigments for paint and glass, and all have to be made on the spot. So if you had come over the hill to see one of the great houses of mediaeval Europe below you, your ears would have been hit by the noise of metal working, your eyes by the smoke from kilns, your nose (if the wind was right) would have been assaulted by the smell of the tannery a mile off. (They saved the urine of the community to help with the tanning.) On the hill side opposite, you would have heard the noise of woodmen's axes and saws echoing across the valley, and seen the blue wisps of smoke rising from the charcoal burning. And at the canonical hours the tenor bell of the church would have sounded, and work in the field would have stopped for a space while the office was said. And then all starts up again. Monasteries and abbeys in the middle ages were, in fact, major employers of lay labour, major industrial centres, and major agents of charity and social care. They still are the latter: had I turned up, destitute, on their doorstep the brothers would have fed and lodged me without charge, without question.

24 Often depicted foursquare, with a fountain or apple tree at the centre, and the four quartersdivided by the Four Rivers flowing out of Paradise – traditionally, Nile, Phison or Ganges, Euphrates, Tigris.

25 The Abbey church of Quedlinburg was endowed to pray for the soul – it needed it – of Heinrich the Fowler, land grabber, scourge of the Slavs, and later the Nazi party's non-Christian patron saint. That was not his fault. In the 1930s the abbey was deconsecrated and the nuns sent packing, and it was turned into an SS temple. They ripped out the Gothic elements – too French, perhaps – and standardized on the Romanesque, far more *echt* 'German' if you claim Charlemagne as the predecessor of the Reich. Leading Nazis, led by Himmler, processed through the little town to rebury Heinrich, his skeleton now wrapped in a swastika flag and his skull crowned with a metal wreath of laurel. There was a permanent SS honour guard until – well, what Hitler wanted to be Götterdämmerung. Unfortunately, after the war it became clear that the skeleton was not his... Himmler's obsession with the arcane and the occult and the anti-Christian led him not only to this but also to his secret (and expensive) quest to locate the Holy Grail and the fabled treasure at Montségur, and to send a flypast of planes on the 700th anniversary of the mass burning of the Cathars on 16 March 1944.

26
Right so bitwixe a titlelees tiraunt
And an outlawe or a theef erraunt,
The same I seye: ther is no difference.
To Alisaundre was toold this sentence,
That, for the tirant is of gretter myght
By force of meynee for to sleen dounright,
And brennen hous and hoom, and make al playn,
Lo, therfore is he cleped a capitayn;
And for the outlawe hath but smal meynee,

And may nat doon so greet an harm as he,
Ne brynge a contree to so greet mescheef,
Men clepen hym an outlawe or a theef.

27 As Dorothy Hale and the New Ethicists are arguing. But so did Hans Urs von Balthazar, who had a great influence on the thought of Josef Ratzinger and Rowan Williams. Aesthetic experience is itself creative; theophanies lead to a cognition, a knowing beyond sequential reason.

28 I first came across this remark not in the German papers, but in G. B. Shaw's grim little fable, *The Black Girl in Search of God* (1932). It has remained with me as the epitome of so much of what being human is about.

29 Nasty as some of Wagner's attitudes were, he is not responsible for Hitler's obsessive knowledge of the music and libretti (so odd a word to use of Wagner!) and the stagecraft or the way he hijacked them to Nazi ideology. If Hitler tried to turn world politics into opera culminating in the Death of the Gods, Wagner did not. Sometimes the music – especially in *Parsifal* – is wiser than its composer.

30 In one of his letters, Erasmus gives us one of the few mediaeval descriptions simply of a journey. He was travelling on business from Basel to Louvain in 1518 – a relatively easy trip, though not as easy, perhaps, as journeys in Italy where the network of Roman roads was still in fairly good repair. He was travelling, too, as comfortably as he could afford: poorer travellers must have had a

much worse time. He began by taking a boat down the Rhine. But he was forced from time to time to walk, to use hired horses, or ride in one of those unsprung, slow carriages which were hideously tiring and uncomfortable. After Maastricht, the horses he hired, at extortionate expense, were spavined nags that could not do more than a walk. He complains about the early starts, being roused while it was still dark by the boatmen's shouts, and having to travel without breakfast. (Actually, much as I love him, I have to admit Erasmus can be a bit of a whinger.) He was often afraid: even in the well populated country between Maastricht and Louvain robbers were a menace. He was often cold, often soaked to the skin. The food was pretty bad: he complains of inns offering only 'scrawny chickens, offal, badly cooked vegetables, sour wine.' At Aachen he was given stockfish, which he liked, but it was half-cooked, and he had indigestion for three days afterwards. (He suffered a lot from dyspepsia – he was too fond, perhaps, of the staple diet of mediaeval Europe in Lent and on fast days, which was dried or salt cod.) The noise in the inns bothered him too: in one, a random assembly of more than 60 people sat down to dinner, smelly, noisy – 'especially when wine heated them.'

31 Felix Fabri, a Dominican friar, sailed to Palestine in 1484. He hated the month's voyage. Some passengers – a few – prayed constantly; some diced; some exercised by climbing the rigging; some were merely sick. But all had the chore each day of delousing their clothes and persons, for otherwise, as Fabri says, 'you will have but unquiet slumbers.' The heat and smell below decks in the early summer must have been pretty bad, and it was worse at night: for then, he complained, the rats ran all over the sleepers, and the noise

of people who snore, or who would not stop talking, made rest impossible.

32 I cannot resist yet another excursus, and I can't see how to put it in the text. Relics may well be genuine, but... In 787 the Second Council of Nicaea stipulated that all altars should contain a relic: this remains the case in modern Catholic and Orthodox rules. The market for relics in the middle ages was buoyant: definitely a seller's market. The Fourth Crusade, when it pillaged Byzantium, sent back large numbers of relics to the West, some genuine, some not – but how do you tell the difference? In Durham Cathedral lie the head of King Oswald and the bones of St Cuthbert, certainly: but the bones of the Holy Innocent that the priests under Queen Mary put under the altar are actually those of a dog, like a greyhound. The chains I have seen myself at St Peter ad Vincula in Rome just could be those than held the saint, in prison: there is no way of telling. But sometimes the comic breaks in. Once there was much talk of a Saint Expeditus, and some appealed to him, when there was need of haste, for prompt settlement of debts and so on. But his name, and so existence, may be mere clerical error in the copying of a manuscript. But there is a story...

A packing case, it seems, containing relics of a saint from the Catacombs of Rome, was sent to a community of nuns in Paris. They had asked Rome for relics for their new church. The parcel was stamped – I love the idea of Relics By Post – 'spedito', EXPRESS, but the good nuns mistook this for the name 'Espedito' and set about propagating his cult with great energy. From these simple beginnings, they say, devotion to him spread rapidly.

The story, alas, is too good to be true. St Expeditus was patron of the town of Acireale in Sicily in 1781, long before the supposedly credulous nuns, and in Germany at the same time there were pictures depicting him as a saint to be invoked against delays. But that unenviable job – for a saint – certainly depends on the play of words on his name.

★